Third Edition

Write It.5

A Process Approach to College Essays, with Readings

Linda Strahan
Kathleen Moore

Kendall Hunt
publishing company

Kendall Hunt
publishing company

www.kendallhunt.com
Send all inquiries to:
4050 Westmark Drive
Dubuque, IA 52004-1840

Published in the United States of America

Contents

Part 3   WRITING ASSIGNMENTS   67

Preface

John Briggs
Professor of English
McSweeny Chair of Rhetoric and Teaching Excellence
Director, the University Writing Program
University of California, Riverside

What is success in higher education? It depends, more than anything, upon your academic literacy—your ability to read, write, and speak on a level appropriate to your college or university. Reading, writing, and speaking in higher education are not only skills. They depend upon your *preparation*, not only your academic background but also your *dedication* to the course that assigns this textbook. You must read more, and more widely, than you have before. You will need to participate in class. Writing must be your daily task. Repeated practice is just as important in your academic work as it is in making music or competing in an athletic event. More learning, practice, and performance—perhaps more than you can now imagine—will be necessary for you to pass and prosper in this course and succeed in your studies.

This book will help you if your preparation is persistent. You will need to learn more, including how to *perform* what you know in speaking and writing. You will need to read more, and reread. To become a better reader, you will need to speak in class, and write for your instructor and your classmates, over and over. You must learn how to practice well, and to *seek* what you need to understand.

Write It .5 is a book that will assist you in these endeavors. Without your energetic investment in studying this book, however, you will be less likely to succeed. Make this book your companion and guide. Take it with you, and it will repay your attention. Invest in it. Use it to learn how to succeed in this class and in your higher education.

Acknowledgments

This book would not have been possible without the inspiration and support of the instructors in the University Writing Program at the University of California, Riverside, and the exemplary support team at Kendall-Hunt. We want to thank all of them for their encouragement and help.

Our special thanks go to our editor, Taylor Knuckey, and our project manager, Carrie Maro, for their dedicated attention to this project. We want especially to acknowledge our colleagues who used this book and provided us with valuable feedback that we have incorporated into this new edition.

Certainly, without the tireless and inspired editorial work by our friend and colleague Benedict Jones, this book would be much diminished. He has corrected errors in the manuscript, done several proof reads, made good suggestions for content and design, added bios and student activities, and generally helped keep things clear and in order. We appreciate his invaluable help.

Becoming More Familiar with Academic Culture

In order to do well in this class and in all of your college classes, it is important that you understand a few basics that most instructors assume you already know. Read and complete the activities in Part 1 so that you have a sound awareness of some of these basics.

Here is an overview of the skills and guidelines presented in Part 1:

- how to read a course syllabus to prepare for writing assignments
- some common English idioms
- guidelines for avoiding plagiarism
- tips for using a dictionary
- using the writing process
- the interdependence of three basic skills: reading, speaking, and writing

Reading a Syllabus

A *syllabus* is a document that provides students with information regarding the plan and design of a college-level course. The instructor for each course offered in your college or university will make a syllabus available in some form, hard copy or electronic, to his or her students. It is the students' responsibility to become familiar with the syllabus and use it to guide their study and preparation for each class meeting, assignment, and exam.

In order to participate productively in a course, you will have to understand the way a syllabus is to be read. Ordinarily, a syllabus will contain detailed information about the following topics related to the course:

1. a course description—

    The course description offers an overview of the class. It explains the topics, skills, and expected learning outcomes of the course. It identifies any prerequisites for the course. Sometimes it will include some information about the format of the class meetings, discussion, workshop, lecture, or lab.

2. the texts for the course—

    The syllabus lists all the books related to the course. Some of the books will be labeled "required texts." If a book appears on the "required" list, then students are expected to purchase or have a copy of that text available to them for study throughout the quarter or semester.

    Other books on the syllabus will be listed as "optional texts." An optional book is one that the instructor feels will be a valuable resource for students taking the course, but whose information will either review material from preparatory courses or offer useful supplemental material to the present course. Students need to make their decision regarding the purchase of "optional texts" on the basis of their own familiarity with the subject of the course, or their personal interest in learning more about the subject.

3. requirements for the course—

    The requirements for a course can include the names and types of exams (quizzes/midterms/final), the amount of reading, the number of papers, the types of homework assignments, and an explanation of the other kinds of assignments students must complete in order to receive a credit-bearing grade in the course.

4. other pertinent information for the course—

    If the instructor expects students to follow other instructions, rules, or guidelines in the class, they will be addressed on the syllabus. In the syllabus, students might also find a discussion of the use of computers and cell phones or university and instructor policy regarding plagiarism. It is important that students read this information carefully because it can have an impact on successful completion of the course.

5. tentative schedule of readings and assignments for the course—

   The syllabus includes a chronological plan for the class. It lists the dates of all exams and the due dates for all papers and assignments. Most often in undergraduate classes, the syllabus contains a daily plan. It lets the students know the topic or activity for each class meeting. Readings to be covered during a class are listed for the date of the class; however, students are expected to come to class prepared; this means that any readings or assignments listed for that day are to be completed **before** attending the class.

Sample Syllabus

Study the sample syllabus below and answer the discussion questions that follow it.

BW3 Lecture: Basic Writing
Fall 2012

Basic Writing 3 is a grammar-intensive writing course designed to help students strengthen their reading, critical thinking, and writing skills. Successful completion of this class with a grade of "S" ("C" or better) will qualify you to enroll in English Writing 4, a course that fulfills the Entry Level Writing Requirement.

   Note: BW3 is designed as a multi-quarter course to help students prepare most effectively for the demands of English 4. Thus, students should expect to require two quarters or more of BW3 before earning an "S" for the class.

BSWT003 Components

1. **An online lab**—To receive a satisfactory grade for BW3L, students must pass weekly quizzes related to grammar and reading comprehension. This work is found on the BW3L Blackboard site, and the grade awarded for this 1-unit course is NOT part of this lecture course. Contact Information: Keith Vance (lashv@ucr.edu).

2. **A journal project**—To receive a satisfactory grade for the journal, students must complete entries each week. The journal has its own iLearn page, where you will find instructions. If you have questions about this component of BW3

(Continues)

or you do not see the journal in your list of classes on iLearn, contact Kim Turner (kimbert@ucr.edu).

3. **A lecture**—The lecture component is our class! Assignments and grading for this component of BW3 are described in the remainder of this syllabus.

Lecture Class Policies

Attendance and Participation

You need to be in class on time every day. You may not make up any work that you miss if you are absent or tardy unless you present a doctor's note or are required at a university event. Please avoid being late to class. It is a distraction to the entire class and may adversely affect your grade; you cannot make up work you miss when you are tardy. **Bring your books to class every day!**

Plagiarism

If you are not already familiar with the University's policies concerning academic dishonesty, get that way! Plagiarism will not be tolerated in this class. You will receive a zero for any work that contains plagiarized material, even if that material amounts to less than 1% of your paper. You simply will not pass if you use someone else's ideas or words as if they are yours or without proper citation. Moreover, I will report cases of academic misconduct to the Student Conduct Office. (See for reference: http://senate.ucr.edu/bylaws/?action=read_bylaws&code=app&section=06.03).

Required Materials

1. *Write It*, 3rd ed., by Strahan, Moore, & Heumann (*WI*) 9780757589782
2. *Understanding and Using English Grammar*, 4th ed., by Azar & Hagen (*UUEG*) 9780132333313
3. *Thousand Pieces of Gold*, by McCunn 9780807083819
4. College-level dictionary
5. Internet access

Class Etiquette

1. No cell phones or other electronic devices (including headphones).
2. Rudeness or personal attacks against members of the class will not be tolerated.
3. No sleeping.
4. If you don't follow these class rules, I will ask you to leave class for the day.

Evaluation Process: 73% needed to pass the class	
Essay 1: "In Praise of Margins"	10%
Essay 2: *Thousand Pieces of Gold*	20%
Essay 3: In-class essay	20%
Homework, class assignments, quizzes, group work, participation	20%
Final Exam	30%
See the description of General Grading Standards for Essays below	

Essays—General Policies

- **Paper format:** All essays must follow MLA formatting—that is, typed and double-spaced with one inch margins on all sides. Use Times New Roman, 12-point font. (See the resources on iLearn for help with MLA format.)

- **Workshops:** There will be draft workshops for essays 1 & 3. You are expected to bring <u>COMPLETE</u> drafts of your essays to class on the days of the workshops. In other words, rough ≠ short. Failure to bring an adequate draft will lower your essay grade by ½ letter grade; failure to come to class on the workshop day will result in the same penalty.

- **Paper Submission:** When an essay is due, you must submit a printed-out paper to me so that I can write comments and suggestions for you. All essays must also be submitted to SafeAssign on the iLearn site on the day the paper is due. I won't grade your paper until you have submitted it in both forms.

Late Work Policy

- **Late Essays:** All essays are due at the <u>beginning of class</u> on the day assigned. <u>If you are late to class, your paper is counted one day late</u>. Except in verified cases of emergency or serious illness, your final paper grade will be lowered if your paper is turned in late. Specifically, I will take off ½ letter grade (5%) for each class day that it is late. If a paper is more than 1 calendar week late, I will not accept it. You must complete all essays in order to pass the class.

- **Late Homework:** Students always want to know if I accept late homework. I know that sometimes you cannot help missing a class period or two if you are sick,

(Continues)

so I will accept late homework up to two times; after that, I will not accept it. If you are absent, it is your responsibility to complete the work that is due the day you are returning. Some homework is listed on the syllabus, but you should always double-check with a classmate.

Class & Group Participation: Guidelines for Evaluation

- **Outstanding Contributor (A):** Contributions in class and/or groups reflect exceptional preparation. Ideas offered are always substantive, and they provide one or more major insights as well as direction for the class/group. If this person were not a member of the class/group, the quality of discussion and work would be diminished markedly.

- **Good Contributor (B):** Contributions in class and/or groups reflect thorough preparation. Ideas offered are usually substantial and provide good insights. If this person were not a member of the class/group, the quality of discussion and work would be diminished.

- **Adequate Contributor (C):** Contributions in class and/or groups reflect satisfactory preparation. Ideas offered are sometimes very helpful and provide generally useful insights. If this person were not a member of the class/group, the quality of discussion and work would be diminished somewhat.

- **Non-Participant (D):** This person says little or nothing in class and/or groups. Hence, there is not an adequate basis for evaluation. If this person were not a member of the class/group, the quality of discussion and work would not be changed.

- **Unsatisfactory Contributor (F):** Contributions in class and/or groups reflect inadequate preparation. Ideas offered are seldom helpful and provide few if any insights for the class/group. If this person were not a member of the class/group, valuable airtime would be saved.

> Reading assignments MUST be done on or before the day listed below. You must bring your books to class.

Course Schedule:

Subject to Change

Week Zero			**Friday, Sept. 28** • Introduction to the course

Week One	**Monday, Oct. 1**
	• **Read:** *Write It*, pp. 1–11
	• **HW due:** Assignment #1 on iLearn (grammar diagnostic)
	• **Read:** *UUEG*, Chapter 1
	• **HW due:** *UUEG*, Chapter 1, Exercises 4, 6, 8, 10, 11
	• **Lecture:** Basic Verb Tenses
		Wednesday, Oct. 3
		• **Read:** *Write It*, pp. 18–27
		• **HW due:** Assignment #2 on iLearn (Reading comprehension questions)
		• **Read:** *UUEG*, pp. 439–441 (Basic Grammar Terminology)
		• **HW due:** *UUEG*, Chapter 1, Exercises 16, 17, 18
		• **Lecture:** Basic Essay Structure
			Friday, Oct. 5
			• **Read:** *Write It*, pp. 29–32
			• **Read:** *Write It*, pp. 51–54
			• **HW due:** *Write It*
			  1. "Vocabulary Check" pp. 55–56
			  2. "Questions to Guide Your Reading," pp. 57–58
			• **Read:** *Thousand Pieces of Gold*, Chapters 1–5
			• **Lecture:** Basic Essay Structure, continued

Week Two	**Monday, Oct. 8** • **Read:** *UUEG*, Chapter 2 • **HW due:** *UUEG*, Ch. 2, Exercises 1, 4, 10 • **HW due:** *Write It*, pp. 59–60 • **HW due:** Reading Log #1 (instructions on the iLearn site) • **Lecture:** Effective Thesis Statements	**Wednesday, Oct. 10** • **Read:** *Thousand Pieces of Gold*, Chapters 6–9 • **HW due:** *UUEG*, Chapter 2, Exercises 11, 19, 27, 38 • **Lecture:** Effective Body Paragraphs (the 4 Cs)	**Friday, Oct. 12** • **Read:** *UUEG*, Chapter 3 • **HW due:** *UUEG*, Chapter 3, Exercises 4, 7, 13, 16, 19 • **HW due:** Reading Log #2 (instructions on the iLearn site) • **Read:** *Write It*: "The Shallows" (pp. 76–79) & "Hitting Pay Dirt" (pp. 81–83) • **Lecture**: Incorporating Support

(Continues)

	Monday, Oct. 15	Wednesday, Oct. 17	Friday, Oct. 19
Week Three	• **HW due:** *UUEG*, Ch. 3, Exercises 23, 30, 31, 34 • **Read:** *Thousand Pieces of Gold*, Chapters 10–14 • **Read:** *Write It:* "The Dance within My Heart" (pp. 84–86), "Blue-Sky Research" (pp. 87–90) & "Everyday Playtime for Adults" (pp. 92–95)	• **HW due:** *Write It*, pp. 61–63 (prewriting) • **HW due:** Reading Log #3 (instructions on the iLearn site) • **In-class:** Review for Test #1	• **Test 1:** Verbs #1 (Chapters 1, 2 & 3, *UUEG*) • **Read:** *Thousand Pieces of Gold*, Chapters 15–18
	Monday, Oct. 22	**Wednesday, Oct. 24**	**Friday, Oct. 26**
Week Four	• **HW due:** *Write It*, pp. 64–68 (Outline) • **HW due:** Reading Log #4 (instructions on the iLearn site) • **Read:** Student Essays 1 & 2, pp. 430–434 (*Write It*) • **Lecture:** Assessing your work and the work of others	• **Read:** *Thousand Pieces of Gold*, Chapters 19–25 • **Read:** *UUEG*, Chapter 4 • **HW due:** *UUEG*, Ch. 4, Exercises 1, 2, 10, 11, 14, 15 • **Read:** Student Essays 3 & 4, pp. 435–439 (*Write It*) • **HW due:** Assessment questions for Student Essays 1–4 (*Write It*, pp. 430–439)	• **Due:** Completed Draft for Draft Workshop for Essay #1 (bring a typed, printed-out copy to class)
	Monday, Oct. 29	**Wednesday, Oct. 31**	**Friday, Nov. 2**
Week Five	• **HW due:** *UUEG*, Chapter 4, Exercises 18, 19, 23, 25, 26 • **HW Due:** Reading Log #5 (instructions on the iLearn site) • **Lecture:** Revision Strategies (bring your new drafts to class)	• **Read:** *Thousand Pieces of Gold*, Chapters 26–33 • **Read:** *UUEG*, Ch. 6 • **HW due:** *UUEG*, Chapter 6, Exercises 3, 4, 5, 8, 9 • **Lecture:** Subject-Verb Agreement	• **HW due:** Reading Log #6 (instructions on the iLearn site) • **HW due:** *UUEG*, Ch. 6, Exercises 11, 14, 15, 19, 26, 27 • **Essay #1:** Final Draft Due

	Monday, Nov. 5	Wednesday, Nov. 7	Friday, Nov. 9
Week Six	• **Read:** *Thousand Pieces of Gold*, Chapters 24-Epilogue • **Discussion:** *Thousand Pieces of Gold*	• **HW due:** Reading Log #7 (instructions on the iLearn site) • **HW due:** Vocabulary & Prewriting for Essay 2 • **Test 2:** Verbs #2 (Chapters 1–4 and 6, *UUEG*)	• **Quiz:** *Thousand Pieces of Gold*
Week Seven	Monday, Nov. 12 **Holiday: No Class**	Wednesday, Nov 14 • **HW Due:** Outline for Essay 2 • **Read:** *UUEG*, Ch. 7 • **HW Due:** *UUEG* Chapter 7, Exercises 21, 22, 23, 27, 29, 30 • **Lecture:** Nouns and Articles	Friday, Nov. 16 • **Read:** *Write It*, pp. 102–104
Week Eight	Monday, Nov. 19 • **Draft Workshop, Essay 2** (bring a complete, typed draft to class)	Wednesday, Nov. 21 • **Read:** *Write It* (Read any two essays from the "Extended Activities" section that look good to you from pages 125–156) • **HW Due:** The discussion questions for the two essays you chose (emailed to me)	Friday, Nov. 23 **Holiday: No Class**
Week Nine	Monday, Nov. 26 • **In-Class Essay:** Day 1 • **HW Due:** *UUEG* Chapter 7, Exercises 32, 33, 34, 37, 38, 42, 43	Wednesday, Nov. 28 • **Essay 2 Final Draft Due** • **In-Class Essay:** Day 2	Friday, Nov. 30 • **HW Due:** *UUEG* Chapter 7, Exercises 45, 50 • **In-Class Essay:** Day 3

(Continues)

Week Ten	Monday, Dec. 3 • **Test 3:** Nouns, Articles & Determiners (Ch. 7 of *UUEG*)	Wednesday, Dec. 5 • **Read:** Support Essays for the final	Friday, Dec. 7 • **In-Class:** Discussion of Final Exam
Final Exam	Monday, Dec. 10 11:30–2:30 **Location to be announced**		

Follow-Up Activity

1. According to this syllabus, what are the consequences of turning work in late? Discuss whether or not you think this policy is reasonable.

2. Identify the specific dates for the in-class essay. Why do you think the amount of time given to complete this assignment is enough or not enough? What is the percentage of your final grade for this essay?

3. Explain everything you will need to have done to prepare for class on October 10. What is different about the work you are required to submit (amount, type, etc.) on October 8 compared to October 10?

English Idioms

Idioms are expressions and phrases whose meanings are not determined by the definitions of their parts. They can be understood only by context and familiarity. When you come across a sentence where you know the meaning of each individual word but still cannot understand the meaning of the sentence, there is a good chance that you have encountered an idiom.

There are two categories of idioms. *Standard idioms*, the first kind of idioms, are those expressions that convey a meaning unrelated to the sum of their parts. To help you appreciate the way idioms function, here are some examples with their definitions of common idioms in American English:

IDIOM	DEFINITION
fall in love	care about romantically
burn the midnight oil	stay up late
make ends meet	balance income and expenditures
hold your tongue	be quiet
all set	ready to start
common ground	shared beliefs or interests
down-to-earth	showing good sense; practical
draw to a close	come to an end
every now and then	fairly often; repeatedly
face up to	bravely confront or challenge
find out	learn or discover
figure out	find an answer by thinking
follow-up	additional work or research that will make something better
frame of mind	one's mental outlook
get across	explain clearly
get at	reach an understanding of; find out the meaning
get away with	do something wrong and not get caught
get to the bottom of	find the real cause of
hit the books	study
in general	usually; very often
kill time	waste time
leave out	skip or omit
let pass	disregard or overlook
make sense	sound reasonable
on the fence	in doubt; undecided
on the contrary	exactly the opposite; rather
resign oneself	accept something that cannot be changed

Related to the standard idiom is a category of expressions know as *phrasal verbs*. Phrasal verbs are verbs whose meaning is changed by the addition of a preposition. There are two kinds of phrasal verbs: separable and inseparable. Separable phrasal verbs allow other words to come between the verb and its preposition. When you use an inseparable phrasal verb, however, the preposition must directly follow its verb. To understand the difference, look at the sentences below.

Separable Phrasal Verbs

Verb	Preposition	Sentence
ask	out	Tim asked Jennifer out on a date.
hand	in	Nan handed her homework in late.

Inseparable Phrasal Verbs

Verb	Preposition	Sentence
run	into	John ran into the wall.
look	out	Look out for the sharp edges.

To be fluent in a language, you must understand the concept of idioms and be acquainted with many common idioms. Of course, you may still in your reading find sentences whose meaning you cannot comprehend. To learn whether words and phrases are being used idiomatically, you will need to rely on the dictionary. The best resource in this case is a dictionary of American idioms, but any good standard dictionary usually lists some of the idiomatic uses of a word at the end of the entry. When you are writing, the dictionary can also help by informing you whether the phrasal verb you wish to use is separable or inseparable.

Follow-Up Activity

Use your dictionary to learn the meaning of any of the idioms below whose grammatical usage or meaning is unfamiliar to you. Explain the meaning of the expression or phrase, and use it in a sentence. Then share your sentences with a classmate by reading them aloud.

bite the bullet

Definition: _____

_____

Sentence: _____

_____

hit the sack

Definition: _____

_____

Sentence: _____

_____

come across

Definition: _____

_____

Sentence: _____

_____

get the ball rolling

Definition: _____

_____

Sentence: _____

_____

proud of

Definition: _____

_____

Sentence: _____

_____

Academic Integrity: Guidelines for Avoiding Plagiarism

You may be aware of the rule that all work you turn in for credit must be your own, but sometimes students unintentionally commit plagiarism because they are unclear about what qualifies as plagiarism or infringement of copyright laws. Review the following definitions and rules, and check to see that your own paper meets all the requirements of intellectual and academic honesty.

Copyright refers to the legal ownership of published material. Any writing—a play, an essay, a pamphlet, a website—is the intellectual property of the person who wrote it. If, in your paper, you borrow that property by quoting, summarizing, or paraphrasing, you must give credit to the original author. The *fair use* laws allow you to borrow brief passages without infringing on copyright, but you must credit the source and document it properly. Your handbook will show you the correct form to use for each and every source.

Plagiarism can occur when students make poor choices—for example, when a student turns in another student's work as his or her own. Institutions of higher learning have strict policies regarding this type of plagiarism, and the consequences for this action can be significant.

Plagiarism may also be committed by oversight; a student may have forgotten where he or she found the particular material or even that the material was not his or her own. It is important during your research that you include all the source information in your notes so that you will not accidentally commit plagiarism and be held accountable for it.

Remember to acknowledge the following:

Ideas—any idea or concept that you learned elsewhere that is not common knowledge

Words and Phrases—exact reproduction of another author's writing

Charts/Tables/Statistics/Other Visuals—other forms of work done by an author or artist

Your Own Work—work of your own, done for a different assignment or purpose

Intellectual property is the result of work done by a person with the head rather than the hands; nevertheless, the result of that work still belongs to the person who did it. If a carpenter made a chair, that chair is owned by its maker. You would consider taking that chair an act of theft. Try to think of printed material as a similar object, and show that property the same respect you would any other. By doing so, you will avoid plagiarism and copyright infringement.

Follow-Up Activity

1. Look up "plagiarism" in a dictionary and then find and read the explanation it gives. Be sure to study carefully the importance of avoiding plagiarism when you summarize or paraphrase from a book, magazine, newspaper, or article.
2. Go online to the University's website and find its official statement regarding academic honesty and the definition of plagiarism. You are responsible for knowing the rules and regulations the University has posted regarding academic honesty.

Using a Dictionary

A good dictionary is an essential tool for reading and writing that both students and professional writers find helpful. A dictionary provides much useful information beyond the simple definition of a word. The dictionary tells you alternative spellings for the word, the division of the word into syllables (which guides the use of hyphens when the word appears at the end of a line and needs to be broken in two), common pronunciation of the word, other meanings of the word, and the ways a word can be used in different parts of speech, as well as related words that are formed from the main word.

Finding Words in an English Dictionary

- Words appear in the dictionary in alphabetical order. This order is strictly letter by letter. No differentiation is made between single words, names, or multiple word phrases. If the name of a person or place begins with an abbreviation, it will be alphabetized as the letters appear in the name, not as if the abbreviation were spelled out.

    For example: "St. Louis," a city, would be alphabetized as beginning with "st," not as the unabbreviated "sa" for the word "saint."

- If an entry begins with a numeral, the term is listed as if the number were spelled out.

    For example: A listing for the 4 Seasons, a musical group, would be alphabetized under the letter "f."

- If two words with completely different definitions and uses share a single spelling (*homophones*), they are often given two separate listings. You will have to consider the context in which the word is used to discover which meaning is applicable to the sentence you are reading.

> For example: The word "bowl," a noun meaning a rounded dish, would be followed by a separate listing for the word "bowl," a verb meaning to play a game with a ball and pins.

- Some dictionaries contain foreign words and phrases that have not yet been assimilated into English but are still often used and understood by English speakers. These words will appear in the main body of the dictionary but will be distinguished by a change in type face, such as bold italics. In other dictionaries, foreign words will appear alphabetically in a separate list in the back of the dictionary. Some dictionaries will not include foreign words at all.

> For example: The French word "voilà," though commonly used by speakers of English, would still be considered a non-English word and would be given special treatment if included in the dictionary.

Word Meanings

The entry for a word that has more than one meaning, as most words do, will list the various meanings in order of usage from most common to least common. These meanings will be separated numerically.

For example: A dictionary might list the meanings for the word "globe" in the following manner:

1. a solid depiction of the planet earth
2. anything spherical

Pronunciation

Directly following each entry, marked letters and symbols appear within parentheses. The information within the parentheses offers a phonetic guide for the correct pronunciation of the word. In other words, the word is represented by a spelling that reflects how it sounds. Every dictionary contains in its introductory material a *pronunciation key* that explains the way vowels and consonants sound in English. The various kinds of lines over the letters and the other icons are called "diacritical marks." These marks are standard and have the same meanings in any dictionary. The most common of these marks are a line over the letter to show that a vowel is long ($\bar{o}$), and the schwa (ə) to indicate a neutral vowel sound made in English.

> For example: In the word "manatee," which is defined as a kind of aquatic mammal, the entry for "manatee" would be followed by the following information to guide your pronunciation: (man ə tē).

You should familiarize yourself with the marks used most frequently in English dictionaries. Use the Internet and a search engine such as Google to find one or more of these useful charts.

Syllabification

Words are divided into syllables according to certain rules. Usually, the division into syllables is phonetic and follows standard pronunciation. In that case, the word is broken after an open syllable, one with a long vowel or an unstressed vowel, or after a consonant in syllables where the vowel is short or stressed.

> For example: The word "halo" would be divided into "hā-lō," but the word "halogen" would be divided as "hal-o-gen" because in the second word the "a" is not pronounced as a long vowel.

There are instances, however, where syllable division does not correspond with the way a word is pronounced. Affixes, common syllables added to a word to alter its part of speech, are not usually divided at the end of a line of type, nor are acronyms, words formed from initials.

> For example: In the word "utilitarianism," the word would be divided as "u-til-i-tar-i-an-ism."

> For another example: The acronym "UNICEF" (the United Nations Children's Fund) cannot be divided in any way.

Word Variants

Many times in English, a word will have more than one acceptable spelling. When this is the case, the dictionary will include both spellings in a single entry. The most common spelling will be given first; however, if the two spellings are used with almost equal frequency, the dictionary will precede the second spelling with either the word "or" or "also."

> For example: The color word "gray" would appear as **gray** or **grey** to indicate that both spellings are in common usage.

Grammatical Usage

Before the definition or sets of definitions, the dictionary uses abbreviations that show the part of speech the word is used as for the following definition(s). These abbreviations are standard, and you can find them listed in the introductory material of your dictionary, your handbook, or your grammar text.

When a new definition is used as a different part of speech, a new abbreviation will appear before the number for that definition.

For example: The word "ice" has multiple meanings as various parts of speech. Though the dictionary entry would include other meanings in addition to the following, the change in part of speech would be indicated as "n. [or noun] **1.** Water in its solid form; v. [or verb] **2.** To frost a cake."

At the end of an entry, the dictionary will also give form changes in the word necessary to turn it into some other parts of speech. The new word will appear in boldface type in the conclusion of the entry and will be followed by the abbreviation for its part of speech.

For example: The word "slant" means to angle away from a particular level. To change into an adjective or an adverb, the word "slant" alters. The dictionary would show this new form at the end of the entry for "slant" as **slantwise**, adv. adj.

Additional Information

Dictionaries also contain other kinds of relevant information about a word to different extents, depending on the size and function of the particular dictionary, but all give some amount of historical information about the entry. The history of a word is called its "etymology." It can include facts about the word's origin, its language derivation, its earliest dates of usage, earlier spellings, and other relevant material. This information is presented in square brackets after the definition itself.

For example: The simple word "dog" can be traced over a thousand years back, predating Middle English. The dictionary entry indicates its history as [bef. 1050 ME doggy, OE docga].

Follow-Up Activity

Use a good English dictionary to find the answers to the following questions:

1. Where in the dictionary would you find the entry for "3-D"?
2. What diacritical marks are used to show the difference in the pronunciation of the vowel in the words "hat" and "hate"?
3. Show the way the word "antiparliamentary" is divided into syllables.
4. What is another acceptable spelling for the word "theater"?
5. Mark the pronunciation you would choose for the words "bowie knife" and "Caribbean."

Using the Writing Process

The process of trying to write down your ideas, of getting them straight in your thoughts and then clear in your writing, takes time and hard work. When you sit down to write, you may have a vague idea of what you want to say, but your ideas will not be fully developed until you try to write them down because your thoughts take a clearer shape as you put them into sentences. This is why good writers know the importance of the *writing process* and use it. **Thinking and writing work together.** Good writing is produced through persistent thinking, and good ideas are fully uncovered only through writing. If you remember this one rule, you will be able to create clear, developed, and interesting papers.

Sometimes, an idea you have sounds unconvincing when you attempt to recreate it in written form. To create the most successful essays you can, you will have to use the writing process to uncover what you want to say and then develop your thoughts so that your readers can fully understand your ideas. If you are writing an essay that responds to a reading selection, you will also have to return frequently to read parts or all of the selection; each time you do, you will understand it better and thereby respond to its ideas in a more complex and interesting way.

Steps of the Writing Process

- prewriting
- drafting
- revising
- editing

Prewriting can include a variety of activities you do with your pen in hand, or your hands on the keyboard. You may like to list or diagram your ideas and observations about the subject of your paper. Sometimes clustering ideas or freewriting about your thoughts can help you get a good beginning as you explore and develop your ideas. In this stage of the writing process, you use writing to give shape to your thoughts and uncover new ideas. You will likely begin working on a writing assignment by prewriting, but it can come in handy at any time as you work on completing your paper.

Drafting refers to those times when you try to write out large sections of your paper. You won't have a full draft until you have a complete version, including the introduction, body paragraphs, and conclusion. Sometimes drafting includes cutting and pasting from prewriting activities to fill in the introduction or a body paragraph.

Don't think of the drafting stage as a linear task in which you write out the paper from the beginning straight through to the end. You may prefer to draft easier parts of the paper first, parts where you capture your thoughts and try to give them shape. You may want to begin with a working thesis and then try to draft paragraphs that support it in order to test its validity for yourself. Because the writing process is recursive, that is, it is circular and starts over perhaps several times, you will go back to these early pieces of draft and revise them once your thesis statement and ideas are more clearly shaped.

Revising happens when you allow your thoughts to influence your draft—perhaps reshaping or adding to it so that it is clearer and more compelling. You might decide to add more appropriate evidence, or to reword the thesis statement so that it overarches the body paragraphs you have written. Or you may discover that the essay does not make sense in a section or sections because you have used supporting evidence that is weak or unrelated.

Before you finish a paper, it should go through several revisions if it is to be as successful as you can make it. You will have to allow plenty of time for revision, so begin working on all of your writing assignments as early as possible.

Don't forget to read your draft aloud, either to yourself or to a friend. This will help you find places where more revising is needed.

Editing should be saved for last because it is the stage where you check your sentences to be sure that you do not have any grammar, punctuation, or spelling errors. Don't spend time checking the spelling of your sentences or your choice of vocabulary words until you are in the last stage of the process because your draft will likely change several times before you are ready to turn it in. Wait until the paper is complete, and then read it once more to check the form of your sentences.

Remember that the stages of the writing process are *recursive*, meaning they are used over and over again to complete a writing assignment. If the process is used to its full potential, it ensures that you are always open to the discovery process and the refinement of ideas, even when a first draft has been written. Using the writing process will give you greater control over your writing because your thoughts take clearer shape as you work within its stages.

Follow-Up Activity

Working with another person in the class, describe to one another the steps each of you takes to complete writing assignments. How and when do you begin? What do you do next? What are some of the other strategies you use to complete your paper? How do they compare to the steps outlined above?

Now tell each other how the writing process you have studied here could change the way you habitually write a paper. What might you do differently? How might that change help improve the way you complete a writing assignment? Offer each other any suggestions you might have.

Reading, Writing, and Speaking in an Academic Setting

Reading, writing, and speaking form an important part of academic culture. It is only when these three elements work together that great insights can be discovered, shared, and built upon by the academic community as a whole. Our society ultimately benefits. We hope you will push yourself to work with all three of these learning strategies as you complete the assignments in this book, and in all of your course work throughout your college studies. You will see that each of the three strategies supplements and strengthens the other two. If you use all three diligently, you will see how your reading, writing, and speaking ability work together to make you a better, more successful student.

This text will guide you to use reading to develop your writing. But some of the book's activities and lessons will include opportunities not only to read, but to read *aloud* and to listen to others read aloud. Researchers and educators widely agree on the important role that reading aloud plays in your educational development, whether you are a relatively new English language learner or a native speaker of English. Perhaps you have never read aloud, or been read to, especially in a formal setting such as a classroom. But your persistence and determination will soon have you feeling comfortable reading aloud, and your literacy skills will certainly improve. Studies show that reading aloud:

- promotes literacy and language development
- builds a large vocabulary
- aids achievement in school
- develops reading comprehension skills
- develops a rich imagination
- helps associate reading and enjoyment
- improves listening and reading skills
- strengthens mental and verbal skills
- sharpens focus
- internalizes language and the meaning of words
- improves the ability to speak with clarity and precision
- improves memory of what is read
- develops awareness of English language patterns, promoting proper grammar and sentence structure
- improves writing
- helps in revising and editing

Perhaps the first important step in a class such as this one is to learn to associate reading with pleasure or fun. Especially if you have not done much reading, or if English is not your first language, you may resist opportunities to read because you associate it with unpleasantness and struggle. Read the essay below; it finds reading aloud an enjoyable activity.

Some Thoughts on the Lost Art of Reading Aloud   *Essay*

VERLYN KLINKENBORG

Sometimes the best way to understand the present is to look at it from the past. Consider audio books. An enormous number of Americans read by listening these days—listening aloud, I call it. The technology for doing so is diverse and widespread, and so are the places people listen to audio books. But from the perspective of a reader in, say, the early 19th century, about the time of Jane Austen, there is something peculiar about it, even lonely.

In those days, literate families and friends read aloud to each other as a matter of habit. Books were still relatively scarce and expensive, and the routine electronic diversions we take for granted were, of course, nonexistent. If you had grown up listening to adults reading to each other regularly, the thought of all of those solitary 21st-century individuals hearkening to earbuds and car radios would seem isolating. It would also seem as though they were being trained only to listen to books and not to read aloud from them.

It's part of a pattern. Instead of making music at home, we listen to recordings of professional musicians. When people talk about the books they've heard, they're often talking about the quality of the readers, who are usually professional. The way we listen to books has been desocialized, stripped of context, which has the solitary virtue of being extremely convenient.

But listening aloud, valuable as it is, isn't the same as reading aloud. Both require a great deal of attention. Both are good ways to learn something important about the rhythms of language. But one of the most basic tests of comprehension is to ask someone to read aloud from a book. It reveals far more than whether the reader understands the words. It reveals how far into the words—and the pattern of the words—the reader really sees.

Reading aloud recaptures the physicality of words. To read with your lungs and diaphragm, with your tongue and lips, is very different from reading with your eyes alone. The language becomes a part of the body, which is why there is always a curious tenderness, almost an erotic quality, in those 18th- and 19th-century literary scenes where a book is being read aloud in mixed company. The words are not mere words. They are the breath and mind, perhaps even the soul, of the person who is reading.

No one understood this better than Jane Austen. One of the late turning points in *Mansfield Park* comes when Henry Crawford picks up a volume of Shakespeare, "which had the air of being very recently closed," and begins to read aloud to the young Bertrams and their cousin, Fanny Price. Fanny discovers in Crawford's reading "a variety of excellence beyond what she had ever met with." And yet his ability to do every part "with equal beauty" is a clear sign to us, if not entirely to Fanny, of his superficiality.

I read aloud to my writing students, and when students read aloud to me I notice something odd. They are smart and literate, and most of them had parents who read to them as children. But when students read aloud at first, I notice that they are trying to read the meaning of the words. If the work is their own, they are usually trying to read the intention of the writer.

It's as though they're reading what the words represent rather than the words themselves. What gets lost is the inner voice of the prose, the life of the language. This is reflected in their writing, too, at first.

You can easily make the argument that reading silently is an economic artifact, a sign of a new prosperity beginning in the early 19th century and a new cheapness in books. The same argument applies to listening to books on your iPhone. But what I would suggest is that our idea of reading is incomplete, impoverished, unless we are also taking the time to read aloud.

Follow-Up Activity

Form small groups to discuss the following topics. Then, report your conclusions to the class.

1. Tell the group your most recent memory of reading aloud or being read to. What was the book? Whom did you share it with? How would you describe the experience?

2. Discuss the benefits connected to reading and listening aloud, according to Verlyn Klinkenborg, the writer of the essay. Does her essay convince you? Explain.

3. If you haven't already done so, read the essay aloud. Then, describe the difference between the two experiences—when you read it to yourself versus when you read it aloud or listened to someone read it aloud.

Writing Basics

The particular argument essay that you will study in *Write It .5* will help you gain practice in critically analyzing issues, formulating logical arguments, and persuasively expressing your opinions by using the conventional rules of written English and a conventional essay structure. The thesis-centered essay is the most commonly assigned essay format in college. Its purpose is to persuade. Its formal parts are established by convention and provide a structure for presenting an argument. These parts include an introduction that orients the readers to the essay's subject, a thesis statement that presents the argument, body paragraphs that develop and support the argument, and a conclusion that closes the essay. Study Part 2 carefully because it gives you an overview of the process of essay writing and other helpful information to help you succeed in this course and in other college courses that include writing. Spend some time with these pages before moving to Part 3, where you will be asked to put them into practice. As you engage with the writing assignments in Part 3 and use the stages of the writing process to develop an essay within a particular writing context, you will want to turn back to Part 2 for guidance.

Part 2 gives you a set of strategies for critical reading, thinking, and writing, strategies that take you through the writing process as you build your response to a writing topic. As you work through the units in Part 3, turn back to these basic strategies because they will help you complete those assignments. Here is a list of the basic strategies you will learn in Part 2:

- techniques for doing a thoughtful reading of an essay
- a diagram of an academic essay's structure
- strategies for developing your ideas on a subject
- guidelines for responding to a writing topic
- suggestions for writing the introduction and a well-developed thesis statement
- a basic structure for writing supporting paragraphs
- a rubric for evaluating student essays

Steps for a Thoughtful Reading of an Essay

In our everyday lives, we read on a daily basis. We live in a literate society, so we read things like signs, emails, and menus without much effort and without thinking about them very much. In an academic setting, however, reading becomes an activity that requires effort and thought.

In order to respond appropriately to a reading selection, you will have to spend some time rereading, identifying, and analyzing the reading selection's argument and supporting evidence. Here are some guidelines to help you develop sound strategies for understanding what you read. You will need to analyze any reading selection before you can discuss its argument and respond with an argument of your own.

When you follow the steps below, your reading will become focused and productive.

1. **Read the title of the reading selection.**

   The title will tell you something about the main topic of the reading. It may also tell you something about the writer's opinion on the topic. Think about what you already know about the topic and what else you want to know before you will be ready to write an essay that presents your informed opinion about it.

2. **Learn about the author.**

   If the reading selection contains information about the writer, take note of how the writer's life or work might connect with the topic of the reading. The writer's experience with the topic might indicate his or her reliability or knowledge regarding the topic of the selection.

3. **Read through the selection once quickly.**

   This first time you read the selection, read it right through so that you get a general impression of what it is about and what the writer's attitude is toward the topic. Notice the things—people, places, experiences, concepts, for example—that the writer brings up to develop and support his or her opinion about the topic.

4. **Read again to identify the thesis.**

   Read the selection a second time, but more slowly and carefully, and with a pen or highlighter in your hand. Find the thesis and underline it. Remember, the thesis states the author's overall opinion on the topic of the reading. Often, the thesis is contained in a single sentence, but, in some cases, it takes several sentences to make the main argument of the reading selection clear. There are times, too, when the author does not state his or her thesis explicitly, but, if you read the selection carefully, you should be able to state it and then write it in the margin. The thesis is often found in the last line of the introduction, but it can also come in the middle or even the end of an essay. To help, ask yourself, "What does this author seem to want readers to think about his or her topic?"

5. **Read slowly and methodically through the rest of the material.**

    Now find and underline the evidence that the writer uses to support his or her thesis. Look carefully at each body paragraph one at a time. Often, each paragraph develops a single idea that the writer brings up because it supports his or her thesis. Look in each body paragraph for a *topic sentence*—a sentence that both presents an idea and tells how it gives support to the reading's overall opinion. As you read and study the selection, be sure to write down any thoughts you have about the writer's opinion and supporting evidence. It is your job to evaluate this evidence for its logic and validity, so be sure to make notes in the margins as you read. Mark the points that you found interesting or convincing and a few words explaining your thoughts. Note, too, any weaknesses you found. When you look back at the notes you made in the selection's margins, you should have a general idea of how convincing you found the reading and what you found to be its strengths and weaknesses.

6. **Read again for review.**

    Once you have thought through the reading selection, read it once more, looking for places where you don't quite understand what is being said. Underline any terms that you aren't familiar with, and look them up in a dictionary. Mark any places in the reading that don't fit with your understanding of the reading as a whole. Decide whether this is something the author should have revised, or whether it is something that you need to read again because you don't understand it. You may find that you need to go back to Step 4 and begin working through the reading again. Once you are certain that you understand the entire selection, you are prepared to discuss, summarize, and/or respond to the reading with your own essay.

Now use the six steps for a thoughtful reading of an essay to uncover the argument and supporting evidence of the following essay.

Sibling Rivalry   *Essay*

KELSEY O'NEILL

> *Kelsey O'Neill is a college student majoring in business. She was a high school honors student and gave the graduation speech for her senior class. The following essay is based on that speech.*

Whether your generation grew up watching *The Simpsons* (when Lisa was the perfect child and Bart was the troublemaker) or the *The Brady Bunch* (when Cindy would always get her way and Peter would

(continues)

be blamed for mischief), you are aware of favoritism. This feeling is evident when you reflect on who in your family got the prime seat on the couch, who got the best room in the house, and who would get ice cream for dessert even though they didn't finish all their dinner.

No parent will admit to it. However, studies show that 70% of mothers and fathers exhibit a preference for a single child. Fathers gravitate toward their youngest daughter, while mothers connect with their oldest son. Parents are also inclined to prefer the oldest child. In the business sense, older children are seen as "sunk costs" and a product further down the assembly line—with more time, resources, and effort invested into their development. We inevitably walk down the store aisles and come across birthday cards to give to our brother that advertise the idea that "mom liked me better" or "I'm the favorite." If this idea of favoritism weren't true, then Hallmark wouldn't have developed an entire product line on that exact premise. Even though we won't get a direct answer if we ask our parents who they like better, siblings know, and parents know, who the "golden child" is. However, even with parental favoritism and the inevitable rivalry that results, siblings have proven to be valuable to one another in teaching a multitude of life lessons.

In every language, in every country across the world, families have siblings that pester each other every minute of every day. That is just the nature of the relationship. We would be foolish to think that brothers and sisters will get along 100%, all the time, with no quarrels. In fact, sibling rivalry has been a part of some of our oldest texts. One of the first stories in the Bible talks of a rivalry between two brothers, Cain and Abel. Cain is the older sibling who repeatedly asks his parents, "Am I my brother's keeper?" Unfortunately, since nothing is done about this rivalry, the story ends with the tragic death of Abel, who is killed by his brother out of aggravation. But some siblings absolutely get along better than others, even when they compete. Take, for example, President George W. Bush and Governor Jeb Bush, who have been trying to outdo each other since they were old enough to talk. Jeb was supposed to be the more studious of the two, the one who was expected to bring the family business to success. Both sons have undoubtedly been trying to win the attention and admiration of their famous parents, much like the Kennedy family with Joe Jr. and John F. Kennedy. Even as recently as this summer, the royal wedding would not have been complete without subtle sister comparisons, when Kate Middleton, the bride, was a bit upstaged by her younger sister Pippa because the cameras and media couldn't stop photographing her and talking about her. And within the royal family, there have been clear tensions. For instance, Prince William and Prince Harry are both royal by blood, but Prince William gets to become king simply because he is the eldest. Similarly, Michael Jackson and Janet Jackson were both famous. However, Michael was more famous and rose to superstardom.

Taking a closer look at the actual structure of sibling relationships, we can draw a few conclusions. The closer in age, the closer the relationship; however, if the siblings are the same gender, there is more conflict. In general, girls are the authorities in the domestic setting. Sisters have proven to have the closest relationships, whereas brothers have the most rivalry. For brothers, it is more natural even from the beginning to compare their accomplishments, such as who walked first or spoke first. Carrying on into their adult life, they compare things like who is the better athlete, who went to the better college, or who has the best job. Siblings are a dress rehearsal for our lives; they are there for the entire ride.

But there are also instances where siblings worked together and benefitted from each other. For example, Wilbur and Orville Wright created an airplane—the first machine of its kind that was able to fly a human being. Venus and Serena Williams are tennis superstars who had to practice long hours together to achieve the status they have today. The Olsen twins were together in TV shows when they were younger, and more recently, they have established a business franchise and are known as billion dollar teens. They are ranked #48 on the list of 100 highest paid celebrities, and they landed on the list of richest people under age 40, according to *Fortune Magazine* ("40 Under 40"). Now try telling me that those sisters don't work well together. When siblings can put aside the constant bickering they endured when they were younger, they can influence society and make great contributions. Brothers and sisters actually spend more time together than they do with their parents.

Because parents leave our lives too early and spouses come too late, social skills are gained from our brothers and sisters more than anyone else in life. People may be surprised to know that 65% of teens reported feeling close to a sibling. In another study with the elderly, exactly 65% also said they felt "close" or "extremely close" to their siblings (Cicirelli 46). This proves once again the timeless bond that siblings create from a young age.

If rivalry is handled well, it doesn't have to be a problem, and can teach children valuable life lessons. Sharing, cooperating, and compromising are all gained from this experience. Is sibling rivalry really so bad? Think about it. In our society, it could be an advantage. We compete for school, recognition, jobs, awards, friendship, and relationships.

(continues)

Younger siblings learn more charismatic skills and charm in order to get what they want. This is known as the "low power strategy" since the youngest child is the most vulnerable and needs the most care. This is the way for them to get attention and resources in a large family. One study at the University of Southern California found that children who were born second were friendlier, more playful, and more sociable as judged by their elementary school teachers. Conversely, older siblings learn empathy and patience from caring for and nurturing a younger sibling. Shockingly, a study declared that siblings have a greater influence on how we develop as a person than parents do. In fact, Jeffrey Kluger, the author of *The Sibling Effect* and senior writer for *Time Magazine*, associates the influence of parents as providing a broad stroke of values and morals. He compares it to the likes of a hospital, with the parents as doctors doing Grand Rounds and checking briefly on all their patients, while the nurses work 24/7 on the ward, similar to the influence of the siblings. In other words, siblings do exert a great effect on the person we become.

Parents must understand the cause of sibling rivalry in order to minimize its potentially negative effects. Older children begin to feel threatened by a new baby, since the introduction of him or her will deflect all the parent's love, acknowledgment, and attention from the older sibling. If the parents portray their newborn as beneficial to the other siblings, comparing the older siblings to a teacher for the newborn and giving them praise for helping their younger sibling learn to crawl, play, or cooperate, siblings are sure to grow up with a strong and healthy relationship.

The lasting effects of having a sibling have proven throughout history to advance social skills in preparation for the "real world." Exposure to this hearty competition allows for the maintenance of friendships, expression of feelings, management of conflict, and negotiation of solutions in early stages that will continue for a lifetime. As parents age and young siblings enter adulthood, they must interact and rely on each other once more, assuming the similar positions they carried in their earlier years. As Jane Leder says, "Our siblings push buttons that cast us in roles we felt sure we had let go of long ago—the baby, the peacekeeper, the caretaker, the avoider. . . . It doesn't seem to matter how much time has elapsed or how far we've traveled."

Works Cited

Cicirelli, Victor G. *Sibling Relationships Across the Life Span*. New York: Plenum Press, 1995. Print.

"40 Under 40." *CNNMoney*. Cable News Network, 17 Oct. 2012. Web. 30 May 2012. <http://money.cnn.com/gallery/magazines/fortune/2012/10/11/40-Under-40.fortune/index.html>.

Kluger, Jeffrey. "Playing Favorites." *Time Magazine* 03 Oct. 2011: 44–50. Print.

Leder, Jane Mersky. Web. 30 May 2012. <http://www.searchquotes.com/quotes/author/Jane_Mersky_Leder/>.

Writing Topic

According to Kelsey O'Neill, how does sibling rivalry effectively prepare children for adult life? Do you think her positive assessment of the effects of sibling rivalry is accurate? You can support your answer by using personal examples, your own observations, and evidence from this essay as well as other readings and materials.

Follow-Up Activity

For Discussion

1. Share with the class what you identified as the thesis of this reading selection. Then read aloud the paragraph that contains it.

   Tell everyone one comment you wrote in the reading's margin and explain what in the reading led to your comment.

   Identify at least two pieces of supporting evidence for the thesis of this reading. How strong are they as support? Did they help convince you that this writer's argument makes sense? Explain.

2. Prepare and present to the class a story about one time when you and a brother or sister interacted in a way that was memorable. If you don't have a sibling, tell a story about a memory you have related to being an only child. Be sure that your presentation includes an explanation of why you chose the story you told. In other words, tell the class what was important about the experience.

3. Use the six steps for a thoughtful reading that you learned above to analyze "Sibling Rivalry." Then make a list of the reading's strengths and weaknesses. Share your lists with the class and discuss the group's overall evaluation of "Sibling Rivalry."

Strategies to Help You Analyze a Reading Selection and Develop Your Ideas for Writing a Response

Students often say that they know *how* to write an essay—that is, they know they need to write an introduction, a thesis, the body of the essay, and a conclusion—but they don't know what to write *about*—that is, they think they have no ideas to put into the essay. In fact, students have many ideas about the topic; they just need a few techniques for accessing and clarifying their ideas.

Questioning

You will have already taken the first step toward writing your essay when you did a careful reading of the reading selection and the writing topic. Looking back at your annotations is a good way to remind yourself about things in the essay you thought were important. Now you need to enter the *question phase* of your prewriting. At this point, you can ask yourself several kinds of questions:

- Questions about the highlighting:
  - Why did I highlight/underline this part of the essay?
  - How is this information important to the author's point?
  - What is the relationship between this information and the question I am being asked to write about?

- Questions about your comprehension of the reading, such as:
  - What things in this essay do not make sense to me?
  - Where do I think the author should have explained further?
  - How do the examples in the essay relate to the author's point?

- Questions about the author's ideas, such as:
  - What are some of the things that the author says that I am happy to hear someone say?
  - What things that the author says seem true to me?
  - What things that the author says seem wrong to me?
  - What thing that the author says is most important to me?
  - What idea in this essay is completely new to me?

These strategies will prompt you to analyze the ideas in a reading and form your own viewpoint. Try them out now on the essay "Sibling Rivalry" above. The answers to these questions will help you understand your own thoughts about the topic of the reading and help you see how you want to respond to the writing topic.

In addition to using questions like the ones listed above to analyze, there are several other kinds of prewriting strategies you can use. Here are two of them. Use them to decide how you would respond to the writing topic that follows "Sibling Rivalry."

Freewriting

A further step in the prewriting process that you may want to take is *freewriting*. After having answered for yourself a number of the questions about the reading and question, you still may be having trouble expanding on your initial reaction to the author's position on the topic. Pick one or more of your answers to the questions you have already answered, and just begin to write about them. While you are doing this writing, do not stop or censor yourself; just let the words come. Do this for about five or ten minutes without thinking about spelling, grammar, word choice, or even the sense of what you are saying. When you have completed this activity, you will want to take a break.

After your brief break, come back and read what you have written. Most of what you now have down on paper will not end up in your essay, but, as you read through your freewriting, you will find one or more sentences or ideas that seem interesting, important, or even compelling to you. Highlight these points and ideas.

Listing

Next, you may decide to make a list of the points that you highlighted in your freewriting. *Listing* is another technique for finding the ideas you want to write about. Be sure to list all the items from your freewriting that you thought were interesting. As you make this list, other ideas may come to you. Put them on your list as well.

Study your list. Connect with some kind of mark all the ideas that seem related to each other. When you are done, one related group of ideas will probably be longer than the others. This group should provide insight into a topic for your paper.

Follow-Up Activity

Questions for Discussion

1. Use questioning, freewriting, and listing to analyze "Sibling Rivalry" and develop some ideas of your own about the subject of sibling relationships.

2. You have used several prewriting strategies to understand "Sibling Rivalry," and you have developed some of your own ideas about sibling relationships. Now that you have followed these steps, make a list of ideas that you could use if you were to write an essay responding to the writing topic that follows "Sibling Rivalry."

3. Share with the class your list of things you could talk about in your essay, and invite classmates to give you feedback.

Prewriting strategies such as annotation, freewriting, and listing are important steps in the writing process because they lead you to form an argument of your own. Without going through this stage in the writing process, you may respond to a writing topic using only summary and paraphrase. In other words, you may only be able to repeat the ideas of the reading selection's writer rather than develop your own ideas. The ability to summarize or paraphrase another's ideas will be important when you are asked to demonstrate that you understand what you have read. But when you are asked to write an argument, mere summary or paraphrase will not be enough. You will have to bring your own voice and ideas to develop an argument of your own.

Study carefully the following pages on summary, paraphrase, and analysis. Practice these techniques so that you can distinguish each from the others and can use them with confidence when reading and responding to the reading selections in Part 3.

Summary and Paraphrase

A **summary** presents a short version of another writer's ideas. Its purpose is to convey a sense of the main points of the other writer's argument. A summary might condense a few paragraphs into one or two sentences, or several pages into one or two paragraphs.

When you summarize:

1. use *only* your own words and cite the source

   Example:

   Original

   > "London, one of the world's greatest cities, is the center of the thriving English mystery world. Beginning with Charles Dickens and Wilkie Collins, who lived and worked in London, and including Edgar Allan Poe, who attended school there, nearly every mystery writer worth his or her salt has set at least one tale against a London backdrop. Even so American a writer as Robert Parker, in his *The Judas Goat*, took Spenser across the Atlantic to pursue his quarry in London. Because of the richness of its mystery associations, modern London is a mystery reader's mecca, filled with the real sights and sounds that give the stories their authentic atmosphere."
   >
   > Barbara Hendershott, *Mystery Reader's Walking Guide: London*

   Acceptable Summary

   > Because London is the perfect setting for many well-known mystery novels, people who enjoy reading mysteries will find it an exciting and interesting city to visit (Hendershott 13).

   Unacceptable Summary or Plagiarism

   > London is the center of the English mystery world and therefore it is a mecca for all mystery readers (Hendershott 13).

   Use your own words: Notice that in the unacceptable summary, none of the words and phrases that are copied from the original are in quotation marks, but they should be because they are lifted directly from the original source. When summarizing, avoid lifting language from the original.

2. do not give background information

Example:

Original

> "Work through each exercise carefully and methodically, and the result will be an insightful and well-written essay."
>
> Linda Strahan and Kathleen Moore, *Write It Review*

Acceptable Summary

> According to Strahan and Moore, doing the exercises helps students write good essays (32).

3. do not give details

Example:

Original

> "It does not signify that man is a sparse, inhuman thing at his center. He is all right. It only says what we've always known and never had enough time to worry about, that we haven't yet learned to stay human when assembled in masses."
>
> Lewis Thomas, "The Iks"

Acceptable Summary

> Individuals, though basically good, behave badly in groups (Thomas 33).

4. do not give examples

Example:

Original

> "The time has come for a respect, a reverence, not just for all human beings, but for all life forms—as we would have respect for a masterpiece of sculpture or an exquisitely tooled machine."
>
> Carl Sagan, *The Cosmic Connection*

Acceptable Summary

> Sagan believes that, today, all life should be valued (33).

Follow-Up Activity

Look at the following passage. Read it carefully, and then write your summary of it on the lines below.

Original

"Sykes explains to me that a bit of DNA called mtDNA is key to his investigations. A circular band of genes residing separately from twenty-three chromosomes of the double helix, mtDNA is passed down solely through the maternal line. Sykes used mtDNA to discover something astounding."

David Ewing Duncan, "DNA as Destiny", p. 216

Summary

Duncan demonstrates

_____

_____

_____

_____

A **paraphrase** puts someone else's ideas into your own words. Writers use paraphrase when another writer's ideas are important to help support or explain a concept or argument, but the exact words of the other writer need simplification for the audience or are not particularly noteworthy. A **paraphrase** is a restatement of something you have read.

When you paraphrase:

1. you cite the source

   Example:

   Original

   "Work through each exercise carefully and methodically, and the result will be an insightful and well-written essay."

   Linda Strahan and Kathleen Moore, *Write It Review*

Paraphrase

> Do all the prewriting activities to the best of your abilities, and your final essay will be thoughtful and have good sentences and paragraphs (Strahan and Moore 32).

2. you choose your own words and sentence structure

Example:

Original

> "It does not signify that man is a sparse, inhuman thing at his center. He is all right. It only says what we've always known and never had enough time to worry about, that we haven't yet learned to stay human when assembled in masses."
>
> Lewis Thomas, "The Iks"

Paraphrase

> It doesn't mean that people are unfeeling and heartless. They are basically fine. It just reminds us of something that we so far ignored. When people are in groups, they do things they wouldn't do on their own (Thomas 33).

3. you do not change the length of the material being paraphrased

Example:

Original

> "The time has come for a respect, a reverence, not just for all human beings, but for all life forms—as we would have respect for a masterpiece of sculpture or an exquisitely tooled machine."
>
> Carl Sagan, *The Cosmic Connection*

Paraphrase

> Now is the time for us to begin to show appreciation for all living things. We should admire them the same way we would a work of art or value them just as we do technologies (Sagan 33).

4. you are truthful to the meaning of the original

Example:

Original

> "People who have developed a firm faith, grounded in understanding and rooted in daily practice, are in general, much better at coping with adversity than those who have not."
>
> Dalai Lama, "The Role of Religion in Modern Society"

Paraphrase

> Those who have religious beliefs that they practice every day can handle life's challenges and setbacks better than those who have no faith (Dalai Lama 113).

Follow-Up Activity

Look at the following passage. Read it carefully, and then paraphrase it on the lines below. Share and compare your version of the passage with that of a classmate. The two versions should say the same thing, but they will not be identical in word choices or sentence structure.

Original
"Sykes explains to me that a bit of DNA called mtDNA is key to his investigations. A circular band of genes residing separately from twenty-three chromosomes of the double helix, mtDNA is passed down solely through the maternal line. Sykes used mtDNA to discover something astounding."

David Ewing Duncan, "DNA as Destiny", p. 216

Paraphrase

_____

_____

_____

_____

_____

Analysis

Once you have worked with a reading to the point where you understand *what* the author is saying and can represent the author's ideas by explaining them in a short summary or by paraphrasing them in your own words, you are ready to look more closely at *how* the author presents his or her ideas to the reader. This stage of the reading process is called **analysis**. To analyze a text, you must break it down into its parts and see how these parts fit together. When you understand the way the parts relate to each other and to the author's argument as a whole, you are able to *interpret* the text and will have an in-depth understanding of what you have read.

Here are some characteristics of the writing you will want to examine to gain this deep understanding of the text. You will want to ask yourself questions about the following areas:

Attitude

- How does the author feel about the subject?
- Are the author's feelings personal or objective?

Voice

- What role (friend? teacher? judge?) is the author taking in terms of the relationship to his or her audience?
- Does the author seem to expect the audience to agree or to disagree with his or her argument, and how does the author modify the presentation of the argument to adapt to the readers' position?

Development

- What kinds of evidence (facts? examples? definitions?) does the author use to support his or her argument?
- How is the type of evidence relevant to the argument?

Purpose

- If the essay appears to be an objective presentation of findings, why does the author think it is important to share the findings?
- If the author appears to be arguing his or her opinion, what change would he or she like to have take place?

Follow-Up Activity

1. Write definitions for summary, paraphrase, and analysis. Read your definitions to a classmate and revise them so that they are clear and complete.

2. Review what you have learned so far in Part 2. Make notes about the main ideas and explain all key terms. Then, tell why you think they are important to successful writing. Share your notes with the class.

So far in Part 2, you have practiced some strategies for careful reading and have learned some ways to develop your ideas when you are asked to respond to a writing topic. Now you will learn how to present your ideas in a way that will help readers to understand your argument and follow your logic so that they will be convinced by what you write.

Study the diagram of an academic essay found on the next page. Notice that each part has a specific job to do in an essay.

A Suggested Structure for an Essay
That Responds to Another Writer's Essay

The structure of a thesis-centered essay is established by convention. That is, the thesis essay format has an introduction that contains the thesis statement, followed by body paragraphs that support it, and ending with a conclusion that gives closure to the essay.

An Introduction That Contains

-an introductory sentence that gives the reading selection's title, author, and subject
-a summary of the reading selection that includes an answer to the writing topic question
-your **THESIS STATEMENT**

Body Paragraphs That Include

-a topic sentence that gives the paragraph's central point, one that supports the thesis
- sentences that tell more about the topic
-evidence that supports the topic sentence
-a discussion of how and why the evidence ties to the thesis

A Conclusion That

-in a few sentences, reinforces your thesis and gives a sense of closure to your essay

Follow-Up Activity

Questions for Discussion

1. Tell, in your own words, what things are usually included in an introduction.

2. From studying the above diagram, what do you see as the goal of the body of an essay?

3. What are some of the ways a concluding paragraph can differ from other paragraphs in an essay?

Read the following selection and notice the bracketed annotations. These annotations identify Allan Von Niks's thesis statement, and they track a few of the elements that he includes in his body paragraphs to support his thesis. Pay careful attention to the connections between the diagram above and the annotations in Von Niks's essay, including his use of examples and other evidence to support his argument.

Use the six steps you learned for a thoughtful reading, and add your annotations to those already given.

Television: The Great Unifier

ALLAN VON NIKS

American critics love to blame technology for all of our social, economic, and familial problems; the technology that is the favorite scapegoat today is television. If you believe these critics, television is responsible for every American problem from illiteracy to juvenile delinquency, from our national economic decline to voter apathy, from obesity to violence. According to these television pundits, TV is like a national drug, a narcotic, a vast mindless wasteland, an evil disease infecting Americans. For example, Walter Shapiro, media critic for *Time* magazine, criticizes "the insidious ways in which prime-time TV distorts America's sense of itself" (95). Michael Ventura goes even further in his attack, arguing that TV is at the heart of what he sees as an escapist American people's growing alienation from reality: "Media is not experience. In its most common form, media substitutes a fantasy of experience . . . for the living fact. But in our culture, the absorption of media has become a substitute for experience" (186).

(Continues)

Pundits such as Shapiro and Ventura, in addition to absurdly over-stating their case, fail to realize that they are blaming the messenger for the sins of the message writers. What I mean by this is that television is only a tool like any other tool. It is not an evil force any more than fire, the wheel, or the lever. Tools are good or bad depending on how we make use of them. The question with TV is whether or not we are using this powerful tool positively and productively. While many critics want us to believe that we are a society of TV junkies, needing our daily fix of a destructive drug, we are in fact using television in a largely positive way in our society. While much of what is on TV is obviously either empty-headed or pure rubbish, what the critics ignore is that TV, with all of its faults, serves an essential function for our culturally and ethnically diverse society; television is the great unifier. **(THESIS STATEMENT)**

America is a unique spot with unique needs; our revolutionary experi-ment in diversity demands some sort of balancing force of unification. **(TOPIC SENTENCE)** We, as a nation, are made up of people who have come here speaking different languages, thinking different thoughts, holding different beliefs, and possessing different cultural values. **[MORE ABOUT THE TOPIC]** In America's early history, the majority of immigrants, excluding African slaves, came from Europe. Today, most of our new immigrants come from Asia and Latin America. **[EVIDENCE THAT SUPPORTS THE TOPIC]** With this change, America's diversity is now growing at a greater pace than ever before. **[MORE ABOUT THE TOPIC]** Few other countries have ever attempted this experiment in national diversity, and none of those that made the attempt have succeeded. How then can we keep so many different people from so many different cultures together as one harmonious people? How can we prevent racial violence and social anarchy from occurring as the natural results of our ethnic, cultural, and religious diversity? The answer to these questions may just lie with television. **[PARAGRAPH AS A WHOLE GIVES BACKGROUND INFORMATION THAT EXPLAINS MORE ABOUT AMERICA'S DIVERSITY]**

The primary way that TV unifies us is by acting as the first teacher and social unifier for almost all American children and new immigrants. **[TOPIC SENTENCE]** Because of our extreme cultural diversity, we can-not expect the US to stay united without the cohesive force of a common language, namely English. **[MORE ABOUT THE TOPIC]** TV teaches English to non-native speakers in a fairly easy, painless, and inexpensive way, thereby beginning their process of "Americanization." TV also teaches the essential liberal difference that allows for peaceful coexistence in our nation. A good example of a TV program that teaches this essential value is *Sesame Street*, a staple in the life of the typical preschool age child. **[EVIDENCE THAT SUPPORTS THE TOPIC]** *Sesame Street*'s primary didactic lesson to children is to accept difference and cooperate with others. In *Sesame Street*'s ideal world, Africans, Asians, Latinos, Caucasians, Birds, Monsters, and even Grouches all tolerate, respect, and even like each other. This kind of positive social message is not only found in a quality show like *Sesame Street*; even the average sitcom or TV talk show, such as *Home Improvement* or *Oprah*, tries to teach moral lessons essential to maintaining a harmonious multicultural society. **[EXPLANATION OF HOW THE EVIDENCE SUPPORTS THE THESIS STATEMENT]**

TV not only teaches essential skills and values needed to unite our society, but it also provides our society with common stories and myths. TV truly has become the common moral "book" of our time, replacing the Bible, which served this purpose earlier in our history. I don't mean to say that it is better or more moral than the Bible; I simply mean that more people watch TV today than read the Bible. Today, the stories that we all know and can discuss come not from the Bible—they come from television. If you were to ask strangers on the street about Jonah or King David, they would probably think you were insane or some kind of religious fanatic. But if you were to ask strangers what they thought of the Super Bowl, what happened on the last episode of *Friends*, who killed JonBenét Ramsey, whether O. J. Simpson was innocent or guilty, or whether they preferred *The Brady Bunch* or *I Love Lucy*, then you might just start up a conversation. All cultures need common stories to bind their people into a nation; our common stories now come from TV.

So the next time you hear some critic blaming television for all of America's problems, remember all of the positive things that TV does for us. Television may have its flaws, but it still remains an essential unifying force, and perhaps the essential unifying force, for American society.

Work Cited

Shapiro, Walter. "Video: What a Waste of (Prime) Time." *Time* 14 May 1990: 95- . Print.

Ventura, Michael. "Report from El Dorado." *The Graywolf Annual Five: Multi-Cultural Literacy*. Ed. Rick Simonson and Scott Walker. St. Paul, MN: Graywolf, 1988. 173–88. Print.

Writing Topic

According to Von Niks, in what ways does television unify American society? Do you think he is correct? Relying on your own experience, observations, or readings, support your view.

Follow-Up Activity

1. Why does Von Niks call television a tool? Explain why he labels TV in this way.

2. How does television encourage person-to-person interaction in our society, according to Von Niks? Give any examples you can think of from your own experience that demonstrate television's role in shaping the way we talk to each other.

3. Explain how Von Niks uses a well-known television show to demonstrate TV's ability to unite very different groups of people. Choose a TV show that you and your peers watch. Do you think it functions in the way that Von Niks claims *Sesame Street* or *Oprah* functions? Explain.

4. Why does Von Niks claim that, in some important ways, TV has replaced the Bible? Why does he claim that "all cultures need common stories to bind their people into a nation"?

5. Prepare and then give a three-minute presentation to the class or a partner on the future use of television, *if you were put in charge.*

Writing an Introduction to an Argument Essay

The introduction is often the hardest part of an essay to draft, but if you carefully consider the requirements of an introduction in an argument essay, especially in response to the writing topic, an introduction can also help you focus the rest of your essay.

The paper's opening creates a first impression for the readers. In addition to answering the question, it needs to do three things:

• capture readers' attention

• set the context for the paper's argument

• present the thesis statement of the essay

The first two of these things can be done in the context of answering the question, but the thesis, which is customarily but not always the last sentence of the introduction, has to follow the *directed summary* organically. That is, it must be an extension of the argument already presented. It must be the direct response of your own to that argument and show that you fully understand the author's argument. By including the thesis statement at the end of the introduction, you will ensure that readers understand the paper's purpose from the outset.

When you write your introduction, follow these steps:

• Introduce the reading selection by giving its title and the name of its author.

• Include a directed summary of the reading selection (see the next section).

• Present the thesis statement.

Be careful to avoid these missteps:

• a flat, uninteresting explanation of your plan for the essay (e.g., *"This essay will discuss. . . ."*)

• the use of a cliché to open or close the introduction (e.g., *"It is true that love is blind."*)

• the use of meaningless platitudes (e.g., *"Tomorrow will be a brighter day."*)

• the use of sweeping or overly broad statements (e.g., *"Since the beginning of time, people have wanted peace."*)

Guidelines for Writing a Directed Summary

Often when students are asked to answer a question about something they have read, their answer will require a brief summary of a particular part of the reading's argument. This kind of question, known as an interrogative sentence, is easy to identify because it will usually begin with one of the interrogative pronouns, *who, which, whom, whose,* or *what,* or another question word, such as *how, where, when,* or *why.* Students' first prewriting task is to identify the particular question or questions being asked and to isolate within the text all the material that answers that particular question or questions. While using *Write It .5*, you might find it helpful to circle all of the question words in the writing topic, and then go back to the reading selection and highlight sentences that respond directly to the question or questions being asked.

For example, imagine that you have just read the story "Goldilocks and the Three Bears" and have been asked the question "*Why* does Goldilocks go into the cabin in the woods and use things that belong to the bears?" You would have to go back to the story to find out *why* she sits on the bears' furniture, eats their food, and sleeps in their beds. It would not be enough to isolate her actions and tell *what* she has done because the question does not ask *what*; it asks *why*. You would need to explain the reasons for her actions in order to answer the question *why*. The story describes Goldilocks's physical state before each action; she is *tired, hungry,* and *sleepy*. In order to write a *directed summary* that responds to a specific question, it is necessary to answer the proper question. In your summary of "Goldilocks," you would write primarily about her physical state of being because her fatigue, hunger, and sleepiness cause her to use the bears' chairs, eat their food, and sleep in their beds.

Once you have read the writing topic, underlined the question word or words, and examined the reading selection to locate the answer to the specific question or questions, draft your answer using certain guidelines:

1. In or near the opening sentence, include the title of the essay in quotation marks.
2. Early in your summary paragraph, identify the author of the essay. The first time the author is mentioned, use his or her full name. In subsequent referrals to the author, use only the last name.

You should also avoid including any of the following in a *directed summary*:

1. minor details or points that are irrelevant to the question
2. your own opinion or ideas
3. examples of your own, and unless particularly helpful, those of the author

Advice on Writing a Thesis Statement

The thesis statement is an important part of an argument essay because it gives the writer's point of view or opinion on the subject of an essay. The paragraphs that follow the thesis statement serve to develop and support the thesis statement's point of view, so the thesis statement also unifies the essay. Any writer usually does extensive thinking and prewriting before he or she is ready to draft a thesis statement.

When writing in response to a particular writing assignment, you must be careful to follow the requirements of the assignment. All of the opening essays in the chapter of Part 2 of this book are followed by a writing assignment, called a "writing topic." These writing topics have a similar structure. You will see that each of them has, in some form, three parts. The first part asks you to summarize the reading selection's point of view on an aspect covered in the reading; the second part asks, usually using different terms, whether you agree with that point of view; and the third part asks you to support your point of view, that is, whether you agree or not, with specific evidence. To respond successfully to any of these writing topics, you will have to determine:

- the subject of the reading selection that is the focus of the writing topic
- the point of view on that subject taken by the author of the reading selection
- your point of view on that subject

Before you begin to construct your thesis, answer the following questions:

- What is the subject asked about in the writing topic?
- What is the opinion of the reading selection's writer about the subject?
- What is my opinion about the subject, and does it agree or disagree with the reading selection writer's opinion?

The writing topics in Part 3 are challenging because they ask you to deal with several elements in order to write a strong essay that responds to all of the parts of these writing topics. The thesis statements you write as you respond to these various writing topics will be complex but very important because they will have two jobs: one, to satisfy the requirements of the writing topics, and two, to unify your essays using statements that give your overarching point of view or opinion about particular subjects. Here are some guidelines:

- Sometimes students feel a bit overwhelmed by the challenge of writing a strong thesis statement, and they are led to write a thesis statement that merely says "I agree with her views," or "I disagree with him." This will not be enough for a strong thesis. A thesis statement will have to respond fully to the second part of the writing topic. In other words, it will have to state the reading selection writer's opinion about a specific subject, state whether you agree with that opinion, and present a clear opinion of your own on the subject.

- Remember that, even when you want to agree with the reading selection author's opinion, it is best to state your opinion *in your own words*. You can write a thesis statement that responds to the writing topic but avoids simply saying that you agree or disagree if you let your point of view suggest, by the way you phrase it, whether or not you agree with the selection's author.

- Here are some sample sentence patterns that show you how to write a thesis statement that makes your position clear but avoids using the words "agree" or "disagree."

Sample Patterns Signaling Agreement:

- As author X correctly states,. . . .
- It is true that. . . .
- I'm convinced that. . . .
- Like author X, I think. . . .
- X's message is important because. . . .
- X's argument that . . . is true/correct.
- My point of view on subject Y, like author X's, is. . . .

Sample Patterns Signaling Disagreement:

- Unlike author X, who claims . . . , I think. . . ."
- Although author X argues that . . . , actually. . . ."
- Author X's opinion is . . . , but actually. . . ."
- My point of view on subject Y is instead. . . ."
- Author X says that . . . , but I think. . . ."

Follow-Up Activity

Draft an introductory paragraph that responds to one of the writing topics for the two essays that you read earlier in Part 2, "Sibling Rivalry" or "Television: The Great Unifier." To do this, follow these steps:

1. Look back at the work you have already done in earlier pages to analyze the essay and develop your ideas about its subject.

2. Study the writing topic and underline the question words.

3. Look for the answer to the first part of the writing topic, the question that asks for a summary of the author's opinion on a specific subject.

4. Draft your summary of that opinion.

5. Decide what your opinion on the subject is, and determine whether it agrees with the reading selection author's opinion.

6. Draft your thesis statement using the guidelines just above this follow-up activity.

7. Now put it all together to create an introductory paragraph: Introduce the title and author of the reading selection; follow that opening with the summary you wrote in response to the first part of the writing topic; and, finally, present your thesis statement.

8. Exchange your paragraph with a classmate. Read each other's paragraphs and discuss the strengths and weaknesses of each. If there is time, rewrite your paragraph so that it is stronger.

Developing Body Paragraphs for an Essay That Presents a Thesis

Body paragraphs make up the largest part of an essay. The job of each body paragraph is to develop one point that supports the thesis statement. Taken together, these points constitute the argument of the essay. Writing a good body paragraph can be easy once you understand the criteria that the body paragraph must fulfill. Here are the three most important criteria for paragraphs in an argumentative essay:

1. an appropriate or suitable topic
2. evidence (fact, example, and/or idea)
3. a link to the thesis

Appropriate or Suitable Topic

First, write a topic sentence that states the point you wish to make in this paragraph. The point must be on topic; that is, it must introduce an argument that is relevant to the claim you make in your thesis.

Evidence

The major part of the paragraph will be devoted to evidence. Most often in your essays, that evidence will be an example, but specific facts, quotations, and ideas can also help support the topic sentence of your paragraph. You must be careful to choose a clear example, one that clearly demonstrates the point of the paragraph. Then you must explain the example with details.

Link to the Thesis

After you have given all the evidence and supplied all the details that support the topic sentence of the paragraph, you must show the way this evidence links back to the thesis of your essay. It is not enough to just provide an example. You have to tell the reader the reason this particular example connects to the main argument of your essay.

Here is an example:
Thesis:

Speaking a language at home that differs from standard spoken English can be a valuable resource for members of a family.

Appropriate Topic:

Write a sentence stating the point you wish to make in this paragraph:

The feeling of intimacy given by the use of a "family" language can be a source of comfort in times of stress.

Evidence:

Write an example that provides support for the point being made in the paragraph:

> Last year my grandmother back in Vietnam was very ill. The doctors said she needed an operation, so she went to the hospital. There was nothing my family could do to help her from so far away. We just had to wait to hear news. My mother told me to go to school. It would be a while until the phone call came telling us whether my grandmother was alive or not. My friends and teachers at school gave me their well wishes all day, but their voices were like sandpaper rubbing my heart. When I got home, there was still no word from overseas. My mother spoke to me in the dialect of her village, grandmother's home, telling me not to worry. The sound of these words calmed me, and I felt comforted.

Link to Thesis:

Write a sentence or more that explains the way this example connects to the thesis of your essay:

> Her use of our family language was important to me at this time. It told me that she shared and understood my worries the way no one outside the family could. Hearing Vietnamese spoken when I was stressed gave me comfort and made me feel connected to my grandmother. Our special language is a resource my family is lucky to have.

Now put the three parts together. In the space below, write out your own topic sentence, the evidence you are including, and the overall connection to the thesis statement. Look over the three elements—topic sentence, evidence, and thesis connection—and make sure that they present a convincing explanation of your thoughts.

Follow-Up Activity

1. Study the thesis statement below. Then fill in the outline form for a possible body paragraph using the three parts of a well-developed paragraph presented above.

   Thesis Statement:

   Life on a college campus offers many opportunities for personal growth.

   A Body Paragraph

   Appropriate topic

   _____

   _____

   Evidence

   _____

   _____

   _____

   _____

   Link to thesis statement

   _____

   _____

   _____

   _____

2. Discuss with the class some other topic ideas and supporting evidence you could use if you were asked to write this essay.

A Basic Outline Form for an Essay That Presents a Thesis

Strong writers always create a basic plan of their essay to ensure that all its parts are complete and that they make logical sense. There are several ways to create a working plan for an essay.

Here is an outline form that you can use; it will work effectively for the kinds of essays assigned in *Write It .5*.

I. Introductory Paragraph:

A. Draft one or two opening sentences that give the reading selection's title, author, and main topic:

_____

_____

B. To plan your response to the first part of the writing topic, list the main points that will be included in your directed summary:

1.

2.

3.

4.

C. Write out your thesis statement. Be sure that it presents a clear position on the subject asked about in the writing topic State your thesis in your own words.

_____

_____

II. Body Paragraphs: For each body paragraph, plan the following parts:

A. Write down the main idea for the paragraph.

B. List the evidence you will use to support your topic idea (fact, example, etc.).

C. Tell how the evidence and your ideas link to the thesis statement.

(Repeat this part of the outline as often as necessary to plan all of your body paragraphs.)

III. Conclusion: Draft some general remarks you can make to close your essay. Perhaps you will remind your readers of the main argument of your paper—your opinion or point of view on the subject of your essay.

Drafting Your Essay

Once you have an outline or basic plan for your essay, including its specific and essential parts, you are ready to begin drafting it. Here are some helpful guidelines:

- Most people begin by drafting the introductory paragraph, but you may decide instead to begin with one of the body paragraphs.

- Remember that your thinking may develop as you draft your essay and that you may decide at some point to change or modify your thesis statement. Writers almost never keep the identical thesis statement they initially drafted because it is almost certain that drafting leads them to think even more deeply about their topic. Extended thinking usually brings new insights that a writer will want to include in his or her argument.

- Be sure that the evidence you use to support your topic idea and thesis statement is clear and specific.

- When you link the evidence to the thesis statement, be sure to explain fully and clearly how the evidence supports the thesis. The evidence parts of the argument are places where readers pay close attention to see if they understand you and to see if they find your ideas valid.

- Most important: Do not feel bound to the outline plan you began with at the draft stage of the writing process. Allow your thoughts to develop, and then capture those ideas in your essay—but do so in a systematic way. Always use the academic essay diagram to help you decide how to add new material to your essay.

A Rubric for Evaluating Student Essays

A rubric is a scoring tool that identifies the expectations for an assignment. A rubric divides the assignment into parts and gives descriptions of each part at varying levels of mastery. Rubrics are often used by instructors as grading guides that help ensure that their grading standards do not change over time or from student to student.

Rubrics also help students by giving them a clear set of guides to use as they complete assignments, and to give them valuable feedback on their graded work. Rubrics are an important part of academic culture, especially in courses that require a significant amount of writing. These rubrics identify the conventional standards of successful and effective writing in an academic setting. Here is the rubric that will be used in this course:

Grading Rubric

High Pass: (Highly satisfactory for BW3 students)
A paper in this range commands attention because of an insightful, cogent response to the text and contains few (or no) markers that indicate a student not fluent with English.

1. The paper has an impressive thesis or point of focus, elaborating that response with interesting ideas and well-chosen, persuasive supporting evidence.
2. The paper demonstrates the student's reading comprehension and analytical ability.
3. The paper's paragraphs are generally well organized and clearly pertinent to the point of focus.
4. A "High Pass" paper shows that the writer can use a variety of sentence patterns with relative ease, usually choose words precisely and aptly, and observe the conventions of written English with few errors.
5. Although rare instances of nonstandard English errors might be found in the paper's sentences and word choice, the sentences and diction are usually impressive, and the errors at this level can be corrected as the student takes English 4.

Pass: (Clearly satisfactory for BW 3 students)
A paper in this range provides a clearly acceptable response to the text, and ESL errors that occur are not the defining characteristic of the essay.

1. The paper has a strong thesis or point of focus, elaborating that response with appropriate examples and sensible reasoning.

2. The paper clearly and thoughtfully responds to the writing topic's demands, demonstrating the student's understanding of the reading selection and of essay-writing in general.

3. The paper's paragraphs are usually organized and appropriate to the point of focus.

4. Although limited ESL-type errors might be evident in the paper's sentences and word choice, the sentences and diction are usually clearly proficient, and the errors at this level are able to be corrected in English 4.

Low Pass: (Marginally satisfactory for BW 3 students)
A paper in this range provides an adequate response to the text (sometimes marginally so), and ESL errors do not impede understanding or occur so frequently as to be distracting.

1. The content of the paper is appropriate to the writing topic and demonstrates that the student can identify and write about the main ideas in the reading selection.

2. The paper has a point of focus (some sort of thesis), and a structure that includes support for that focus, but it may lack adequate development of ideas or of supporting evidence.

3. The paper shows evidence in most paragraphs that the writer understands how paragraphs should be organized.

4. Although a variety of nonstandard English errors may be evident in the construction of sentences or in word choice, these errors do not markedly impede understanding. Most sentences and diction are at least marginally acceptable. A pattern of mixed constructions, repeated errors in basic tense formation and agreement, and/or multiple serious errors in word choice and word formation are NOT acceptable at this level. Likewise, overly short essays that demonstrate comfort only with simplistic sentence patterns and limited vocabulary are not acceptable (these are often marked by stilted language).

High Fail: (Not satisfactory for BW3 students)
A paper in this range may provide an adequate response in terms of content; however, its dominant feature is the use of nonstandard English errors—though certainly not in the majority of the paper's sentences.
This grade range indicates a major problem in one or more of the following areas:

1. It may demonstrate some lack of understanding of the reading selection.

2. It may lack acceptable support, though there should be a clear attempt at producing a focused response.

3. It may contain an unacceptable number or variety of errors associated with ESL students. However, these errors will not be so pervasive as to appear in a majority of sentences. These papers are often characterized by an unevenness of sentence-level control or a limited ability to produce sentences beyond a particular style.

4. The paper's sentence-level errors are often part of a pattern: mixed constructions, basic errors in tense formation and agreement, and/or incorrect or inappropriate diction and word forms.

Fail: (Indicates major language difficulties for BW3 students)

A paper in this range may provide a basic (though perhaps limited) response in terms of content; however, its defining feature is the consistent use of ESL errors of several varieties and in the majority of the sentences. Where a paper fits in this range should be determined by the density of errors.

This grade range indicates a major problem in one or more of the following areas:

1. The paper often demonstrates a misreading of the reading selection.

2. It typically lacks support and/or a clear thesis.

3. It almost always contains an unacceptable number of serious sentence-level errors associated with ESL students: mixed constructions, basic errors in tense formation and agreement, and/or significant problems with word choice and word forms. The density, variety, seriousness, or frequency of these errors makes a higher grade inappropriate.

4. Often, there are instances when a student's phrasing and word order will seem like direct translation from the student's native language, instead of indicating an understanding of how to construct sentences in English.

Low Fail: (Indicates profound language deficiencies for BW3 students)

A paper in this range will often fail to provide any understandable response to the writing topic, and standard English language deficiencies may make the essay almost unreadable.

This grade range indicates a major problem in one or more of the following areas:

1. Almost no understanding of the reading selection.

2. Usually no significant support.

3. A pattern of ESL errors so pervasive that it blocks coherence and meaning.

Follow-Up Activity

1. Share with the class your ideas about how you could use the scoring rubric to help you write your essays. How might the rubric be helpful after you draft your paper? How might it be helpful after you receive your graded essay back from your instructor?

2. Read the following essay written by a college student. Then, working with a partner, with a small group, or with the class as a whole, use the scoring rubric to decide how the paper should be graded. Be sure that you can point to places in the essay to justify the grade you gave. Discuss your assessment of the essay with the class, and, if there is significant disagreement, offer your views.

Rejecting or Accepting Technology

Each an everyday we come up with new inventions, new technology that help make the world easier and more convenient place. In the essay "Accepting or rejecting innovation" by Jared Diamond, we see how people accept or reject certain inventions on the market. One technology we all use is a phone. We see how the newest phones come out and we automatically want the newest phone on stores. For example the iPhone they keep creating with different versions of the phone the iPhone 1, 2, 3, 4, and now 5 and sometimes there is not much difference between the versions. Like the iPhone 4 and the 4s they are exactly the same the only difference is that the 4s has SARI already integrated. But what helps customers accept or reject a new invention? Economy, prestige, vested interest are factors that help a consumer reject or accept a new invention. This essay helps you understand how a customer takes these three factors in to place well trying out a new invention. In this essay, we see how people look at the price before they buy it; that's when economy takes in to place. They see what brand it is and sometimes how good the product is doesn't count. What counts is the companies name, that's where the prestige comes in. Also, people see what they are used to and if the majority doesn't want to change some to a new invention they won't accept a new one that's where vested interest comes in to place. All of these come to a person's head before deciding how they feel towards a new invention out in the market.

Economy is a big factor that help a consumer decide if to accept or reject a new invention. The price and economical standing of a person matters when a new product is on the market. For example, if the price is extremely high, the consumer would double think itself to figure out in the product is really worth buying, if the price is really low the consumer might think the invention is not good enough if it's so cheap. So in other words the product has to be worth its value when it is brand new to the market. In other cases some people might not have a very good economic standing, the product and its price is fair and good but the consumer might not have enough money to purchase the product. Sometimes the idea is good, but money stands in the way of you trying it.

However economy isn't the only factor that takes in to place will purchasing a new product, prestige also takes in to place. In most cases the brand matters. For example, if we have two pairs of running shoes that have the work exactly the same they help your foot function and feel comfortable. Then you put the name Nike on one of them and increase the price. Most people will go on and buy the more expensive one simply because it has the name Nike on it. That is because people are used to brand names most people judge and care about what brand name you are wearing, not what the product functions for. In some rear cases it works the opposite. For example in the essay "the highs of low technology" by Johanne Mednick. In this essay we see how mednick explains that people start to admire her old bike because it's vintage. It's not a common bike, it not like any other because it's so old they don't make models like that anymore, as contrast to all the new models that there are tons of. The brand and the name matters to the consumer more than the product.

Last but not least, we also have a factor that takes in to place vested interest. For example, we have had the same keyboard for years and we don't manage to change it. Why? It will make our lives easier. Right? Yes, indeed it will make our live easier in the long run but it also means that people will have to get accustomed to a new thing professional writers will slow down because they would have to learn a whole new concept. New computers will have to be made to replace the old keyboards and lots of money would have to be invested on these acts. Therefore it cost too much money to do so and it's not that important for people to learn a new keyboard if they have already gotten use to one. The money and time invested matters to keep the usual going on rather than the new.

In conclusion all these factors take in to place when we want to buy a new product in the market. Let's face it we think of all of these things before purchasing a brand new product. Most of us try to save our money but still have the latest brands and products out there.

WRITING ASSIGNMENTS

Composition studies have identified four basic stages of the writing process—prewriting, drafting, revising, and editing. Research has taught us that writers who use these stages consciously and deliberately write more thoughtful and successful papers. Initially, you will find that using the writing process demands time and effort, but *Write It .5* will support that effort by giving you structured activities that help you to engage in systematic prewriting, drafting, and revising exercises. As you work through *Write It .5*, you will develop your own methods for using the writing process strategies you will learn in Part 3. Once you learn how to make these strategies work for you, you can and should rely on them whenever you are given a writing assignment. Soon you will be able to use them more efficiently and productively to critically read, think, and write in an academic setting.

Assignment 1

The issue in this first assignment unit asks you to think about what it means to be educated and why it is important. Begin by reading the lead selection by Malcolm X, "How I Discovered Words: A Homemade Education." Then, write an essay of your own that responds to the writing topic that follows Malcolm X's essay. Be sure to use the exercises and activities that are in this unit. They will guide you through the writing process—the prewriting, drafting, revising, and editing important to any writer when composing an academic argument. Much of the material that you produce as you complete these exercises will be usable, in some form, as part of your finished essay. We know that the more time and thought that you invest in these exercises, the more successful your essay will be.

How I Discovered Words: A Homemade Education   *Essay*

MALCOLM X

> *Malcolm X, born Malcolm Little, was one of the most influential Afri-*
> *can Americans in history. He was an American Muslim minister, a civil*
> *rights activist, and a gifted speaker. Throughout his relatively short adult*
> *life, he spoke, wrote, and worked for African American supremacy and*
> *self-determination. He encouraged African Americans to fight racism*
> *using all possible means, including violence. He was assassinated in 1965*
> *at the age of 39.*

I became increasingly frustrated at not being able to express what I wanted to convey in letters that I wrote, especially those to Mr. Elijah Muhammad. In the street, I had been the most articulate hustler out there—I had commanded attention when I said something. But now, trying to write simple English, I not only wasn't articulate, I wasn't even functional. How would I sound writing in slang, the way I would say it, something such as, "Look, daddy, let me pull your coat about a cat, Elijah Muhammad."

Many who today hear me somewhere in person or on television, or those who read something I've said, will think I went to school far beyond the eighth grade. This impression is due entirely to my prison studies.

It had really begun back in the Charlestown Prison, when Bimbi first made me feel envy of his stock of knowledge. Bimbi had always taken charge of any conversation he was in, and I had tried to emulate him. But every book I picked up had few sentences which didn't contain anywhere from one to nearly all of the words that might as well have been in Chinese. When I just skipped those words, of course, I really ended up with little idea of what the book said. So I had come to the Norfolk Prison Colony still going through only book-reading motions. Pretty soon, I would have quit even these motions, unless I had received the motivation that I did.

I saw that the best thing I could do was get hold of a dictionary—to study, to learn some words. I was lucky enough to reason also that I should try to improve my penmanship. It was sad. I couldn't even write in a straight line. It was both ideas together that moved me to request

(Continues)

a dictionary along with tablets and pencils from the Norfolk Prison Colony school.

I spent two days just riffling uncertainly through the dictionary's pages. I'd never realized so many words existed! I didn't know which words I needed to learn. Finally, just to start some kind of action, I began copying. In my slow, painstaking, ragged handwriting, I copied into my tablet everything printed on that first page, down to the punctuation marks.

I believe it took me a day. Then, aloud, I read back, to myself, everything I'd written on the tablet. Over and over, aloud, to myself, I read my own handwriting. I woke up the next morning, thinking about those words—immensely proud to realize that not only had I written so much at one time, but I'd written words that I never knew were in the world. Moreover, with a little effort, I also could remember what many of these words meant. I reviewed the words whose meanings I didn't remember. Funny thing, from the dictionary's first page right now, that "aardvark" springs to my mind. The dictionary had a picture of it, a long-tailed, long-eared, burrowing African mammal, which lives off termites caught by sticking out its tongue as an anteater does for ants.

I was so fascinated that I went on—I copied the dictionary's next page. And the same experience came when I studied that. With every succeeding page, I also learned of people and places and events from history. Actually, the dictionary is like a miniature encyclopedia. Finally, the dictionary's A section had filled a whole tablet—and I went on into the B's. That was the way I started copying what eventually became the entire dictionary. It went a lot faster after so much practice helped me to pick up handwriting speed. Between what I wrote in my tablet, and writing letters, during the rest of my time in prison I would guess I wrote a million words.

I suppose it was inevitable that as my word-base broadened, I could for the first time pick up a book and read and now begin to understand what the book was saying. Anyone who has read a great deal can imagine the new world that opened. Let me tell you something: From then until I left that prison, in every free moment I had, if I was not reading in the library, I was reading on my bunk. You couldn't have gotten me out of books with a wedge. Between Mr. Muhammad's teachings, my correspondence, my visitors—usually Ella and Reginald—and my reading of books, months passed without my even thinking about being imprisoned. In fact, up to then, I never had been so truly free in my life.

The Norfolk Prison Colony's library was in the school building. A variety of classes was taught here by instructors who came from such places as Harvard and Boston universities. The weekly debates between inmate teams were also held in the school building. You would be astonished to know how worked up convict debaters and audiences would get over subjects like "Should Babies Be Fed Milk?"

Available on the prison library's shelves were books on just about every general subject. Much of the big private collection that Parkhurst had willed to the prison was still in crates and boxes in the back of the library—thousands of old books. Some of them looked ancient: covers faded, old-time parchment-looking binding. Parkhurst, I've mentioned, seemed to have been principally interested in history and religion. He had the money and the special interest to have a lot of books that you wouldn't have in general circulation. Any college library would have been lucky to get that collection.

As you can imagine, especially in prison where there was heavy emphasis on rehabilitation, an inmate was smiled upon if he demonstrated an unusually intense interest in books. There was a sizable number of well-read inmates, especially the popular debaters. Some were said by many to be practically walking encyclopedias. They were almost celebrities. No university would ask any student to devour literature as I did when this new world opened to me, of being able to read and understand.

I read more in my room than in the library itself. An inmate who was known to read a lot could check out more than the permitted maximum number of books. I preferred reading in the total isolation of my own room. When I had progressed to really serious reading, every night at about ten P.M. I would be outraged with the "lights out." It always seemed to catch me right in the middle of something engrossing.

Fortunately, right outside my door was a corridor light that cast a glow into my room. The glow was enough to read by, once my eyes adjusted to it. So when "lights out" came, I would sit on the floor, where I would continue reading in that glow.

At one-hour intervals, the night guards paced past every room. Each time I heard the approaching footsteps, I jumped into bed and feigned sleep. And as soon as the guard passed, I got back out of bed onto the floor area of that light-glow, where I would read for another fifty-eight minutes—until the guard approached again. That went on until three

(Continues)

or four every morning. Three or four hours of sleep a night was enough for me. Often in the years in the streets I had slept less than that. . . .

I have often reflected upon the new vistas that reading opened to me. I knew right there in prison that reading had changed forever the course of my life. As I see it today, the ability to read awoke inside me some long-dormant craving to be mentally alive. I certainly wasn't seeking any degree, the way a college confers a status symbol upon its students. My homemade education gave me, with every additional book I read, a little bit more sensitivity to the deafness, dumbness, and blindness that was afflicting the black race in America. Not long ago, an English writer telephoned me from London, asking questions. One was, "What's your alma mater?" I told him, "Books." You will never catch me with a free fifteen minutes in which I'm not studying something I feel might be able to help the black man.

Writing Topic

According to Malcolm X, how does the meaning of getting an education refer to more than getting a college degree or training to get a good job? Do you agree with his understanding of why it is important to get an education? To support your position, be sure to use specific evidence taken from your own experience, observations, or reading.

Vocabulary and Dictionary Practice

Part I.

Look up the following words used in "How I Discovered Words." For each, write the two most common definitions on the lines provided, and include what part of speech each definition is (noun, verb, adjective, etc.). Then, under each of the two definitions, write a sentence that uses the word in a way that reflects that particular definition and part of speech.

1. articulate
2. hustler
3. functional
4. envy
5. emulate
6. riffle
7. inevitable
8. bunk
9. wedge
10. correspondence
11. parchment
12. rehabilitation
13. intense
14. devour
15. isolation
16. outrage
17. engross
18. feign
19. vista
20. dormant

1. **articulate**

   first definition: _____

   _____

part of speech: _____

sentence: _____

_____

second definition: _____

_____

part of speech: _____

sentence: _____

_____

2. **hustler**

first definition: _____

_____

part of speech: _____

sentence: _____

_____

second definition: _____

_____

part of speech: _____

sentence: _____

_____

3. **functional**

first definition: _____

_____

part of speech: _____

sentence: _____
_____

second definition: _____
_____

part of speech: _____

sentence: _____
_____

4. **envy**

first definition: _____
_____

part of speech: _____

sentence: _____
_____
_____

second definition: _____
_____

part of speech: _____

sentence: _____
_____

5. **emulate**

first definition: _____
_____

part of speech: _____

sentence: _____

_____

second definition: _____

_____

part of speech: _____

sentence: _____

_____

6. **riffle**

first definition: _____

_____

part of speech: _____

sentence: _____

_____

second definition: _____

_____

part of speech: _____

sentence: _____

_____

7. **inevitable**

first definition: _____

_____

part of speech: _____

sentence: _____

_____

second definition: _____

_____

part of speech: _____

sentence: _____

_____

8. **bunk**

first definition: _____

_____

part of speech: _____

sentence: _____

_____

second definition: _____

_____

part of speech: _____

sentence: _____

_____

9. **wedge**

first definition: _____

_____

part of speech: _____

sentence: _____

_____

second definition: _____

_____

part of speech: _____

sentence: _____

_____

10. **correspondence**

first definition: _____

_____

part of speech: _____

sentence: _____

_____

second definition: _____

_____

part of speech: _____

sentence: _____

_____

11. **parchment**

first definition: _____

_____

part of speech: _____

sentence: _____

_____

second definition: _____

_____

part of speech: _____

sentence: _____

_____

12. **rehabilitation**

first definition: _____

_____

part of speech: _____

sentence: _____

_____

second definition: _____

_____

part of speech: _____

sentence: _____

_____

13. **intense**

first definition: _____

_____

part of speech: _____

sentence: _____

_____

second definition: _____

_____

part of speech: _____

sentence: _____

_____

14. **devour**

first definition: _____

_____

part of speech: _____

sentence: _____

_____

second definition: _____

_____

part of speech: _____

sentence: _____

_____

15. **isolation**

first definition: _____

_____

part of speech: _____

sentence: _____

_____

second definition: _____

_____

part of speech: _____

sentence: _____

_____

16. **outrage**

    first definition: _____

    _____

    part of speech: _____

    sentence: _____

    _____

    second definition: _____

    _____

    part of speech: _____

    sentence: _____

    _____

17. **engross**

    first definition: _____

    _____

    part of speech: _____

    sentence: _____

    _____

    second definition: _____

    _____

    part of speech: _____

    sentence: _____

    _____

18. **feign**

    first definition: _____

    _____

part of speech: _____

sentence: _____

_____

second definition: _____

_____

part of speech: _____

sentence: _____

_____

19. **vista**

first definition: _____

_____

part of speech: _____

sentence: _____

_____

second definition: _____

_____

part of speech: _____

sentence: _____

_____

20. **dormant**

first definition: _____

_____

part of speech: _____

sentence: _____

_____

second definition: _____

_____

part of speech: _____

sentence: _____

_____

Part II.

A. Write down the sentence from "How I Discovered Words: A Homemade Education" that contains each of the following words.

B. Tell which one of the word's various definitions best fits the sentence.

C. Paraphrase the sentence without using the vocabulary word; in other words, write the sentence using your own words.

1. **articulate**

   A. _____

   _____

   B. _____

   _____

   C. _____

   _____

2. **hustler**

   A. _____

   _____

   B. _____

   _____

   C. _____

   _____

3. **functional**

   A. _____

   _____

   B. _____

   _____

   C. _____

   _____

4. **envy**

   A. _____

   _____

   B. _____

   _____

   C. _____

   _____

5. **emulate**

   A. _____

   _____

   B. _____

   _____

   C. _____

   _____

6. **riffle**

   A. _____

   _____

B. _____

_____

C. _____

_____

7. inevitable

A. _____

_____

B. _____

_____

C. _____

_____

8. bunk

A. _____

_____

B. _____

_____

C. _____

_____

9. wedge

A. _____

_____

B. _____

_____

C. _____

_____

10. **correspondence**

   A. _____

   _____

   B. _____

   _____

   C. _____

   _____

11. **parchment**

   A. _____

   _____

   B. _____

   _____

   C. _____

   _____

12. **rehabilitation**

   A. _____

   _____

   B. _____

   _____

   C. _____

   _____

13. **intense**

   A. _____

   _____

B. _____

_____

C. _____

_____

14. **devour**

A. _____

_____

B. _____

_____

C. _____

_____

15. **isolation**

A. _____

_____

B. _____

_____

C. _____

_____

16. **outrage**

A. _____

_____

B. _____

_____

C. _____

_____

17. **engross**

A. _____

_____

B. _____

_____

C. _____

_____

18. **feign**

A. _____

_____

B. _____

_____

C. _____

_____

19. **vista**

A. _____

_____

B. _____

_____

C. _____

_____

20. **dormant**

A. _____

_____

B. _____

_____

C. _____

_____

Part III.

For each of these words from "How I Discovered Words: A Homemade Education," tell something new and interesting you learned about the word from the dictionary. For example, you might have found the correct way to pronounce a word you were already familiar with from reading but not from speaking, or you might have learned that a word you thought of as entirely English came from a foreign language.

1. **articulate**

_____

_____

2. **hustler**

_____

_____

3. **emulate**

_____

_____

4. **riffle**

_____

_____

5. **bunk**

_____

_____

6. **wedge**

_____

_____

7. **engross**

_____

_____

8. **feign**

_____

_____

9. **dormant**

_____

_____

Follow-Up Activity

Write a self-review of your writing skills, identifying both what you do well as a writer and what you would like to improve. Your description must include at least three of the vocabulary words above. Share your self-assessment with a classmate and discuss strategies that might help you improve.

Doing a Careful Reading of "How I Discovered Words: A Homemade Education"

We hope that you come to realize the importance of working systematically with a reading selection to make sure that you understand its purpose and ideas. Use the following helpful techniques for doing a thoughtful reading of an essay; they will deepen your understanding of "How I Discovered Words: A Homemade Education" and generate some useful material for the draft you will eventually write when you respond to the writing topic.

As you work through these steps, try to commit them to memory so that they become a normal part of the writing process for you. Then, you can always use them to better comprehend any reading material you are interested in understanding well.

1. **Read the title.**
   - The title will tell you something about the reading's main topic.
   - It may also tell you something about Malcolm X's opinion on the topic.
   - Think about what you already know about the topic and what more you want to know.

2. **Learn about the author.**
   - Read the biographical information about Malcolm X at the top of the selection.
   - As you go through the remaining steps below, take note of how Malcolm X's life or work might connect with his topic.

3. **Read through the selection once quickly.**
   - Read quickly through the reading so that you get a general fresh impression of what it is about and what Malcolm X's attitude is toward the topic.
   - Notice the things—people, places, experiences, concepts, for example—he brings up to develop and support his opinion about the topic.

4. **Read again to identify the thesis.**
   - Now read the selection a second time, but more slowly and carefully, and *with a pen or highlighter in your hand.*
   - Find the thesis and underline it or write it in the margin. Remember, the thesis states Malcolm X's overall opinion on the topic of the reading. Often, the thesis is contained in a single sentence, but, in some cases, it takes several sentences to make the main argument of the reading selection clear. There are times, too, when the author does not state his or her thesis explicitly, but if you read the selection carefully, you should be able to state it and then write it in the margin.
   - To help, ask yourself, "What does Malcolm X seem to want readers to think about his topic?"

5. **Read slowly and methodically through the rest of the reading.**
   - Examine each body paragraph one at a time, and list or underline the kinds of evidence that Malcolm X uses to support his thesis.
   - Look in each body paragraph for a *topic sentence*—a sentence that both presents an idea and tells how it gives support to the reading's overall opinion.
   - As you read and study the selection, *be sure to write down any thoughts you have* about Malcolm X's opinion and supporting evidence.
   - It is your job to evaluate this evidence for its logic and validity, so be sure to *make notes in the margins* as you read.
   - *Mark the points* that you found interesting or convincing, and write a few words explaining your thoughts.
   - Note, too, any weaknesses you find.
   - When you look back at the notes you made in the margins, you should have a general idea of how convincing you found "How I Discovered Words: A Homemade Education" and what you found to be its strengths and weaknesses.

6. **Read again for review.**
   - Once you have thought through the reading selection, read it once more, looking for places where you don't quite understand what is being said.
   - Underline any terms that you aren't familiar with, and look them up in a dictionary.
   - Mark any places in the reading that don't fit with your understanding of the reading as a whole. Decide whether this is something that Malcolm X should have revised, or whether it is something that you need to read again because you don't understand it. You may find that you need to go back to Step 4 and begin working through the reading again.
   - Once you are certain that you understand the entire reading, you are prepared to discuss, summarize, and/or respond to the reading with your own essay.

Follow-Up Activity

Sitting with a classmate, compare the sentence each of you underlined— or wrote in the margin—as Malcolm X's thesis statement. If you disagree, discuss your choice and see if you can come to an agreement that makes sense to both of you.

Now share with one another the words from the reading selection that you didn't understand. Use an electronic or printed dictionary to find their meanings.

Discuss the results of this activity with the class. Compare your results and conclusions.

Questions to Review Your Understanding of "How I Discovered Words: A Homemade Education"

Answer the following questions to make sure that you have a clear understanding of Malcolm X's argument as a whole. Be sure to respond to each as thoroughly as you can.

Paragraph 1

When Malcolm X first came to prison, what difference did he notice between his ability to communicate on the street and by letters?

Paragraph 2

When Malcolm X spoke publicly after being in prison, what was the general impression of his level of education? What does he say explains the misconception?

Paragraph 3

Why did Malcolm X envy Bimbi and wish to be like him? Why couldn't he?

Paragraph 4

What things did Malcolm X request to help himself improve?

Paragraph 5
How did he spend his first two days with the new items he requested?

Paragraph 6
When did he first begin to feel a sense of pride and accomplishment?

Paragraph 8
Why does Malcolm X say that he had never before been as free as he was in prison?

Paragraphs 9–10
What kinds of educational resources were available in Norfolk Prison colony?

Paragraph 11
What activity could make an inmate into a celebrity?

Paragraphs 12–14

How did Malcolm X manage to read so many books while he was in prison?

Paragraph 15

In what ways did books change the life of Malcom X?

Responding to the Writing Topic

You have spent time with "How I Discovered Words: A Homemade Education" and should now have a good understanding of its ideas and overall message. It is important now to look at the writing topic at the bottom of this reading selection because the essay you write must directly answer the questions in the writing topic. Here it is again, but this time formatted so that each part of the topic is on its own line:

Writing Topic

According to Malcolm X, how does the meaning of getting an education refer to more than getting a college degree or training to get a good job?

Do you agree with his understanding of what it means to get an education?

To support your position, be sure to use specific evidence taken from your own experience, observations, or reading.

Here is a closer look at the writing topic's three parts:

- The first question asks you to summarize a specific aspect of "How I Discovered Words: A Homemade Education." As you read the question carefully, you will notice that it uses the question word **how**. Keep this word in mind because your response to the first question should explain **how** Malcolm X's definition of getting an education is about more than job training in an institution of higher learning or on the job itself. Your directed summary will tell exactly how education came to mean more to Malcolm X, and how he understands the meaning of that word.

- The second question in the writing topic asks what you think about his definition. Do you think the way that Malcolm X does, that education is not the same thing as career preparation? Is there more to becoming educated than learning job skills? Consider your responses carefully because they will reveal your opinion about the meaning of getting an education. This opinion will be stated as an assertion that answers the second question in the writing topic. This assertion will provide the thesis for your essay.

- The third part of the writing topic tells you to support your opinion – your thesis statement – with examples or other evidence taken from your own experiences, readings, or observations. This supporting material must be relevant and directly connect to the position you take in your essay on the definition of education. The activities that follow in this unit will guide you and help you find appropriate supporting material to use in your essay.

Follow-Up Activity

Think about something you learned on your own outside of a formal setting, the way Malcolm X learned to read. For example, you may have taught yourself to fish or to play chess. Write down the process you used to educate yourself. Tell a classmate about this activity and how this new knowledge changed your life.

Strategies to Help You Analyze a Reading Selection and Develop Your Ideas for Writing a Response

Now you are ready to build on the annotations you made in the reading selection and develop a more systematic analysis of "How I Discovered Words: A Homemade Education." We hope you realize how important prewriting is as a stage in the writing process. In addition to the prewriting guides that you were introduced to in Part 2, below you will find a list of additional prewriting techniques that—if you use them in a focused and sustained way—will lead you to a more systematic analysis of this or any reading selection. Use these strategies now on "How I Discovered Words: A Homemade Education" as you begin to form your own opinions and ideas. They will help to guide and clarify your thinking about Malcolm X's essay. They will also help you to put into words your own views on the topic he writes about—that getting an education is about more than simply ensuring an individual's future job and income.

Questioning

- Questions about the highlighting you did:
  Why did I underline this part of the reading?

  How is this information important to Malcolm X's point?

  What is the relationship between this information and the question I am being asked to write about?

- Questions about Malcolm X's ideas:
  What things in this essay do not make sense to me?

Where do I think Malcolm X should have explained further?

How do the examples in the essay relate to his point?

- Questions about "How I Discovered Words: A Homemade Education" that seem important: What are some of the things that Malcolm X says that I am happy to hear someone say?

What things that he says seem true to me?

What things that he says seem wrong to me?

What thing that he says is the most important to me?

What idea in this essay is completely new to me?

Freewriting

Use freewriting now to explore your responses to the questions above:

- Pick one or more of your answers to the questions you have already answered, and just begin to write about them.

- While you are doing this writing, do not stop or censor yourself; just let the words come.

- Do this for about five or ten minutes without thinking about spelling, grammar, word choice, or even the sense of what you are saying.

- When you have completed this activity, you will want to take a break.

- After your brief break, come back and read what you have written. Most of what you now have down on paper will not end up in your essay, but, as you read through your freewriting, you will find one or more sentences or ideas that seem interesting, important, or even compelling to you. Highlight these points and ideas. Are you beginning to develop your thoughts in a way that will shape your essay?

Listing

With this strategy, you simply list all of the thoughts and reactions you have noted so far. By looking down your list, you may see a pattern of ideas develop, one that you can use to develop an essay of your own.

- List all of the annotations you made for "How I Discovered Words: A Homemade Education."

- List the main ideas you can see in your answers to the questioning phase above.

- List any main ideas that developed from your responses to the follow-up activities above.

- Be sure to list all the items from your freewriting that you thought were interesting. As you make this list, other ideas may come to mind. Put them on your list as well.

Look over your list and group all the ideas that seem related to each other. See if you can find one related group of ideas that is longer than the others. These ideas may suggest what you want to say in response to the writing topic that follows Malcolm X's essay.

Shaping Your Ideas into a Rough Draft

By now, you should feel prepared to begin planning your rough draft. If you aren't, go back through some of the activities above and talk with classmates to see what they are thinking. Sometimes it takes a while before your ideas are formed enough; take as much time as you need to clarify your thoughts.

When you are ready to focus on your rough draft, you will have to think about each part of your essay and how you will compose it. Turn back to Part 2 and examine "A Suggested Structure for an Essay That Responds to Another Writer's Essay." Also, look again at the writing topic for "How I Discovered Words: A Homemade Education." Remind yourself that it asks you to do three things:

1. **Write a summary** that identifies Malcolm X's understanding of what it means to get an education.

   Remember that you have already worked on this in earlier activities. Look back now to the work you did. You may be able to use some of it below, when you write your essay's *directed summary*.

2. **Present your position** on this idea; do you agree with Malcolm X's view?

   This is your thesis statement, and it will unify your essay, so it's important that you write it out clearly. Turn back to the review questions you answered and the follow-up activities you did. What were your thoughts and ideas? You will use them below when you write a thesis statement. Remember that you can always revise it as you work on your rough draft.

3. **Support and develop your position** using specific evidence taken from your own experiences and readings. In other words, explain your thinking and why you have the view you present—and don't forget to include the specific "proof" that convinced you to take the position you take.

The explanation of your thoughts and the evidence that led you to draw those conclusions will make up nearly your entire essay. Look back to earlier exercises in this unit to remind yourself of some of the thinking you did about Malcolm X's argument. You will be able to use some of this as evidence to support your thesis. Remember it when you begin working on body paragraphs.

Drafting Your Directed Summary

Here is the first question in the writing topic:

> According to Malcolm X, how does the meaning of getting an education refer to more than getting a college degree or finding a good job?

Below are some strategies that will guide your response to this first question. Respond to each one as thoroughly and carefully as you can; then, use your answers and those you wrote in earlier activities to draft a directed summary that answers the first question. Notice that this question does *not* ask you to summarize the entire essay. Rather, it asks you to explain one aspect of Malcolm X's essay.

- First, review the writing topic for "How I Discovered Words: A Homemade Education," paying particular attention to the first question, which asks **how**, according to Malcolm X, **does the meaning of getting an education refer to more than getting a college degree or training to get a good job?** It will not be enough to tell about the way Malcolm X became educated; you will have to explain what specific things or qualities he gained from his studies.

- You might find it helpful to turn back to "How I Discovered Words: A Homemade Education" and mark the words that respond directly to the summary question. When writing your directed summary, be very careful to use your own words to *paraphrase* the ideas in his essay, or, when using his exact words, to place them inside of quotation marks.

- You should **avoid** using any of the following in a *directed summary*:

  1. a summary of the entire essay rather than a summary that pays attention only to the information and ideas required to answer the first question of the writing topic

  2. minor details or points that are irrelevant to the question

  3. your own thoughts, ideas, or opinions about the topic

  4. examples of your own or the author's, unless particularly necessary for an understanding of his point

Once you have written a directed summary, you will be ready to draft your essay's introductory paragraph. These steps will guide you:

- Introduce Malcolm X's essay by giving its title and the full name of the author. After the first mention to the author, you should refer to him by last name only.

- Follow the opening sentence or sentences with your directed summary of the essay.

- Last, present your thesis statement, or your answer to the second question of the writing topic. To develop your thesis statement, use the guides in the following section.

Follow-Up Activity 1

Write out a description of Malcolm X's study plan and method. Then, write a description of your own study plan and method.

Next, in a small group of your peers, compare and contrast the ways you and your classmates study to the way Malcolm X studied in prison. What things do you think all of you could learn from Malcolm X's study habits?

Follow-Up Activity 2

After the class has discussed the important points for "How I Discovered Words: A Homemade Education" that should be included in the directed summary, form small groups. Have each member of the group read his or her summary aloud; then, discuss the correctness and completeness of each summary.

Then, cut up your directed summary so that each strip of paper contains only one sentence. Exchange sentence strips with a partner. See if you can reassemble the directed summary so that it matches your partner's original version. Discuss any difficulties you had when you reassembled the summary. Determine whether some revision is needed.

Finally, edit your sentence list, and use it to rewrite your directed summary, revising where necessary.

Developing Your Thesis Statement

The second question in the writing topic asks you to *evaluate* Malcolm X's point of view on what it means to get an education. Do you agree with his idea that it includes a responsibility to others? *Weigh the evidence* he uses to support his position. Do you agree with his view? Your answer to this will be your essay's thesis statement.

Think of your thesis as needing three parts:

- the subject being considered
- Malcolm X's claim about the subject
- your opinion about the subject

Fill in your answer on the line below to form your thesis statement.

The issue, Malcolm X's idea about the issue, AND your opinion about the subject

_____

_____

After you have finished writing your sentence, review your statement to see that it does the following:

- identifies Malcolm X's argument
- makes clear your opinion about what he says

If either of these elements is missing, rewrite your thesis statement so that both are included.

Up to this point, you have been planning the draft of your introductory paragraph. Now that you have drafted your thesis statement, you can begin planning your body paragraphs. They will have to explain your ideas and give support to your thesis statement.

Follow-Up Activity

Write your definition of what it means to be an educated person. Then, give an example of someone you know personally whom you consider to be an educated person. Next, give an example of a historical or a current public figure who seems to be educated in terms of your definition. Share this information with a group of your classmates, and explain your choices to them. Then, compare your description of them with the description you would give for Malcolm X.

Developing Body Paragraphs for an Essay That Presents a Thesis

Reminders:

Body paragraphs make up the largest part of an essay.

- The job of each body paragraph is to develop one point that supports the thesis statement.
- Taken together, these points constitute the argument of the essay.
- Writing a good body paragraph can be easy once you understand the criteria that the body paragraph must fulfill.

Here is a review of the three most important requirements for paragraphs in an argumentative essay:

Parts of a Body Paragraph

An appropriate or suitable topic—one that supports the thesis statement

Evidence—for instance, a concrete fact, example or quotation—that demonstrates the point of the paragraph

A link to the thesis—sentences that show how and why the paragraph, including the evidence, relates to the thesis

A Basic Outline Form for an Essay That Presents a Thesis

Let's look back at all of the work you have done so far:

You have read and carefully annotated "How I Discovered Words: A Homemade Education."

You have analyzed its ideas.

You have written a directed summary in response to the first question in the writing topic.

You have thought about your own experiences and decided on your thesis statement.

You have drafted your essay's introduction.

All of that work should be gathered together now into a shape that will become your essay, your response to the writing topic for this reading selection by Malcolm X.

- Remember that you should follow the basic structure of an academic essay.
- To refresh your memory, turn back to Part 2 and review the diagram of the academic essay format.
- As you begin filling in this diagram form, you should be able to turn back to material you have already drafted as you worked through the exercises in this unit.
- Fill in the outline form below as fully as you can. A good plan will help you draft an essay that is clear and coherent.

I. Introductory Paragraph:

　　A. One or two opening sentences that give the reading selection's title, author, and main topic:

　　　　_____

　　　　_____

　　　　_____

　　B. The main points that you will include in the directed summary:

　　　　1.

　　　　2.

3.

4.

C. Your thesis statement. Be sure that it presents a clear position in response to the writing topic. State your thesis in your own words.

_____

_____

_____

II. Body Paragraphs: For each body paragraph that you will include in your essay, plan the following parts:

Write down the main point for the paragraph.

_____

_____

_____

List the evidence you will use to support the main point (fact, example, etc.).

_____

_____

_____

_____

_____

_____

Tell how the evidence and your ideas link to the thesis statement.

_____

_____

_____

_____

_____

_____

(Repeat this part of the outline as often as necessary to plan all of your body paragraphs.)

III. **Conclusion: What are some general remarks you can make to close your essay? Perhaps you will remind your readers of the main argument of your paper, for example.**

_____

_____

_____

_____

Drafting Your Essay

Now that you have a basic plan for the structure of your essay and a map of its various parts, you are ready to begin drafting.

- If your thinking changes as you write your draft, return to your outline and make necessary adjustments. Every time you decide to revise your outline and essay, remember that this is a good sign, a sign that your thinking is developing and becoming more thoughtful and convincing.

- Keep turning back to all of the activities in this unit as you draft your essay. Try to recall some of your reactions, thoughts, and ideas as you worked on these activities. This may help you to strengthen, expand on, or more fully develop your essay's argument.

Follow-Up Activity

Your draft will always benefit from careful rereadings, whether by you or someone else. Work with a classmate now to find areas in your draft that can be improved.

Use the following process to give and receive draft feedback.

1. Exchange a typed copy of your essay with one of your classmates.
2. Using a pen, mark your classmate's draft in the following manner:
    - Underline the subject of each sentence.
    - Use two lines to underline the verb in each sentence.
    - Identify the tense by writing it above the verb.
3. Using your highlighter:
    - If the subject and verb **do not agree**, highlight the sentence.
    - If the verb tense **is not correct**, highlight only the verb.
    - If the verb is irregular and improperly formed, highlight the verb.
    - If the sentence is a **fragment**, enclose it in parentheses.
    - If the sentence is a **run-on**, use a highlighter or a pen to draw two vertical lines between the independent clauses.
4. Using your pen, underline the essay's thesis.
    - If the thesis is clear, identifies a subject, and makes a claim about it, put a check in the margin.
    - If it needs more work or if you cannot find a thesis, put a dash in the margin.
5. Return the drafts and discuss your marks and suggestions.

Supplemental Reading

Going Home

PAK MUHAMMAD SUKMA

Pak Muhammad Sukma is a businessman with interests in the United States of America and Southeast Asia. He works primarily in the training and education of executives in international companies and has written articles and developed manuals to help the leadership in various firms understand and appreciate the cultural practices of corporations in countries other than their own. He holds degrees from both Syracuse University and the University of Indonesia.

A word means different things to different people and even to ourselves at different times of life. What I thought education meant when I was young and attending the University of Indonesia was quite different from the way I see it now.

I come from a *kampung* or community on the outskirts of Surakarta in Central Java. Surakarta is the modern name for the ancient royal capital of Solo, so it has a rich history—which meant nothing to me while I was growing up. I had heard all the stories about my grandmother's wedding a Dutchman and about her grandparents who were somehow related or connected to the Pakubuwonos. Apparently, marrying an *orang asing*, what you might call a *gringo* in Southern California, caused my family to be ostracized by the vestiges of Javanese royalty in the area, which explains why we did not get invited to the 2013 wedding of the daughter of the Sultan of Yogyakarta, a neighboring city. Rifts run deep in our culture.

But my story begins a little over fifteen years before these nuptials, when I was a student at the Engineering School of the University of Indonesia. I selected engineering as a major because my father was a mechanical engineer with the civil service, and my older brother served as an automotive engineer with the military. The men in my family prided themselves on being modern and "with it" in terms of Western science and technology. For us, education meant getting the training needed to get a high-paying job in science and technology.

An education meant the way to a career to me, too; however, while I am fascinated by the sciences and I love playing with tech gadgets, I soon discovered that I might do better in a different field of study. As to what that might be, I had no idea, so I continued to work toward a degree in electrical engineering.

My general dissatisfaction with my decision to become an electrical engineer partially explains why, when the student revolution of 1998 boiled over after then-President Suharto was elected to a seventh term in office and the military killed four students during a protest march, I was only too happy to get involved. In the beginning, the protests were about price increases brought about by an economic crisis, but the issue of vote-rigging was always in the background, and for this reason students demanded that the President step down. Admittedly, marching and chanting along with other students provided a great diversion from classes and homework assignments for most of us at the time. Looking back, I see that my discontentment in working through my classes in order to graduate and get a good job led me—almost accidentally—to expand my perspective and find a more satisfying way to view my studies and my understanding of what it means to get an education.

I noticed many things as I participated in the protest march, things that expanded my relatively simplistic view of the world. I noticed, for example, that there were certain individuals, both men and women, who would suddenly appear in different parts of any gathering and somehow get us more excited, and, looking back now, I recognize that they incited us to actions we might not have engaged in otherwise. But I realized, too, that our actions drew a great deal of attention and ultimately kept the situation alive in everyone's mind. Political leaders were forced to respond, and their political decisions were exposed to everyone for examination and consideration. Though I had joined the protest march for somewhat self-serving and immature reasons, I came away feeling as though my participation in the march had been important and perhaps had made at least a small difference in keeping the government accountable to the people it governed. Eventually, President Suharto stepped down, and the military returned order to society. Like student protests in many other parts of the world before and after, the events of the spring of 1998 became an indelible part of our education in Indonesia.

After my experience in Indonesia, I asked myself what I wanted to do next. Though many students were brought in for questioning after the march, to the best of my knowledge, none of those I knew suffered any misfortune. However, it was suggested to us that we might want to

(Continues)

investigate opportunities for study abroad, at least until things cooled down. I had acquaintances in various government ministries who had recently come back from such study programs, so I talked with them to get as much information as I could about study programs in Germany, Japan, and the United States. It turned out that Syracuse University in New York State was a favorite, and I heard that there was a well-established Indonesian community there. I applied, got accepted, and left home and country for Syracuse in the following year of 1999.

I did complete my BS in Electrical Engineering at Syracuse University. I already knew English fairly well but became quite fluent during my time there as an undergraduate. Nevertheless, this was not the full extent of my education, as I began to follow American politics closely and frequently compared what I learned of American politics to what I knew about the politics of my home country of Indonesia.

The outcome of the Bush-Gore presidential election bore certain similarities to what we Indonesians had gone through two years earlier. As you would expect, there were protests having to do with voting irregularities, especially in Florida, where each day of recounting chiseled away at the initial Al Gore lead. However, the turnout for protests in the United States was quite meager when compared to the crowd swell in Indonesia. Only about three hundred people showed up in Times Square for a National Pro-Democracy protest after Jesse Jackson called for an investigation into anomalies apparent in the Florida count. This contrasted with the more than twice that many pro-Bush voters coming out in Florida to support the final result, though it was thought that these were mainly out-of-towners bussed in by the GOP.

One of the things I learned from these two similar events is that the conditions of daily life in Indonesia compared to the United States brought about very different responses in each of these two countries when faced with political corruption. Perhaps the reason that Americans did not show more concern over the irregularities alleged in their election was that in late 1999 and early 2000 the United States economy was extremely robust, whereas Indonesia in 1997-1998 was in a deep recession, and the value of our currency fell precipitously. My experiences taught me that getting an education isn't about getting job training so as to be able to increase my income. The education that we receive in school is only a part of how I now define what it means to be well educated. Our knowledge gives us the ability to take social and political action rather than keeping our focus only on self-promotion.

I went on for additional degrees in psychology and economics. Since then, I have returned to Surakarta many times, where my education continues. Now I find the history of the place, both ancient and modern, to be just as fascinating as my iPhone and Xbox technologies.

Discussion Questions

1. Discuss the career Pak Mohammad Sukma prepared for at the University of Indonesia. Why did he select that course of study? Did he have any interest or ability in that field? What was his ultimate goal and his attitude toward? During this period, how do you think Sukma defined getting an education?

2. Explain the role that Sukma's extracurricular activities played in changing his understanding of the meaning of education. In what way is his new understanding similar to that of Malcolm X? In what way does it differ?

3. How does Malcolm X say that education changed his life? Do you think Sukma's life was changed more by his formal or his informal education? How does education change these writers' perspectives on race, culture, and the place where they were raised?

Courtesy of Pak Mohamed Sukma. Copyright © Kendall Hunt Publishing Company.

from *Narrative of the Life of Frederick Douglass*   *Essay*

FREDERICK DOUGLASS

Frederick Douglass was an African American writer, speaker, and social reformer who escaped from slavery to become a national leader of the abolitionist movement. He describes his experiences as a slave in his autobiography Narrative of the Life of Frederick Douglass, an American Slave *(1845), which became a bestseller and, in its time, played a significant role in promoting the cause of abolition. The following selection is an excerpt from that autobiography.*

My new mistress proved to be all she appeared when I first met her at the door,—a woman of the kindest heart and finest feelings.

(Continues)

She had never had a slave under her control previously to myself, and prior to her marriage she had been dependent upon her own industry for a living. She was by trade a weaver; and by constant application to her business, she had been in a good degree preserved from the blighting and dehumanizing effects of slavery. I was utterly astonished at her goodness. I scarcely knew how to behave towards her. She was entirely unlike any other white woman I had ever seen. I could not approach her as I was accustomed to approach other white ladies. My early instruction was all out of place. The crouching servility, usually so acceptable a quality in a slave, did not answer when manifested toward her. Her favor was not gained by it; she seemed to be disturbed by it. She did not deem it impudent or unmannerly for a slave to look her in the face. The meanest slave was put fully at ease in her presence, and none left without feeling better for having seen her. Her face was made of heavenly smiles, and her voice of tranquil music.

But, alas! this kind heart had but a short time to remain such. The fatal poison of irresponsible power was already in her hands, and soon commenced its infernal work. That cheerful eye, under the influence of slavery, soon became red with rage; that voice, made all of sweet accord, changed to one of harsh and horrid discord; and that angelic face gave place to that of a demon.

Very soon after I went to live with Mr. and Mrs. Auld, she very kindly commenced to teach me the A, B, C. After I had learned this, she assisted me in learning to spell words of three or four letters. Just at this point of my progress, Mr. Auld found out what was going on, and at once forbade Mrs. Auld to instruct me further, telling her, among other things, that it was unlawful, as well as unsafe, to teach a slave to read. To use his own words, further, he said, "If you give a nigger an inch, he will take an ell. A nigger should know nothing but to obey his master—to do as he is told to do. Learning would *spoil* the best nigger in the world. Now," said he, "if you teach that nigger (speaking of myself) how to read, there would be no keeping him. It would forever unfit him to be a slave. He would at once become unmanageable, and of no value to his master. As to himself, it could do him no good, but a great deal of harm. It would make him discontented and unhappy." These words sank deep into my heart, stirred up sentiments within that lay slumbering, and called into existence an entirely new train of thought. It was a new and special revelation, explaining dark and mysterious things, with which my youthful understanding had struggled, but struggled in vain. I now understood what had been to me a most perplexing difficulty—to wit, the white man's power to enslave the black man. It was a grand achievement, and I prized it highly. From that moment, I understood the pathway from slavery to freedom. It was just what I wanted, and I got it at a time when I the least expected it. Whilst I was saddened by the thought of losing the aid of my kind mistress, I was gladdened by the invaluable instruction which, by the merest accident, I had gained from my master. Though conscious of the difficulty of learning without a teacher, I set out with high hope, and a fixed purpose, at whatever cost of trouble, to learn how to read. The very decided manner with which he spoke, and strove to impress his wife with the evil consequences of giving me instruction, served to convince me that he was deeply sensible of the truths he was uttering. It gave me the best assurance that I might rely with the utmost confidence on the results which, he said, would flow from teaching me to read. What he most dreaded, that I most desired. What he most loved, that I most hated. That which to him was a great evil, to be carefully shunned, was to me a great good, to be diligently sought; and the argument which he so warmly urged, against my learning to read, only served to inspire me with a desire and determination to learn. In learning to read, I owe almost as much to the bitter opposition of my master, as to the kindly aid of my mistress. I acknowledge the benefit of both.

I lived in Master Hugh's family about seven years. During this time, I succeeded in learning to read and write. In accomplishing this, I was compelled to resort to various stratagems. I had no regular teacher. My mistress, who had kindly commenced to instruct me, had, in compliance with the advice and direction of her husband, not only ceased to instruct, but had set her face against my being instructed by any one else. It is due, however, to my mistress to say of her, that she did not adopt this course of treatment immediately. She at first lacked the depravity indispensable to shutting me up in mental darkness. It was at least necessary for her to have some training in the exercise of irresponsible power, to make her equal to the task of treating me as though I were a brute.

My mistress was, as I have said, a kind and tender-hearted woman; and in the simplicity of her soul she commenced, when I first went to live with her, to treat me as she supposed one human being ought to treat another. In entering upon the duties of a slaveholder, she did not seem to perceive that I sustained to her the relation of a mere chattel, and that for her to treat me as a human being was not only wrong, but dangerously so. Slavery proved as injurious to her as it did to me. When I went there, she was a pious, warm, and tender-hearted woman. There was no

(Continues)

sorrow or suffering for which she had not a tear. She had bread for the hungry, clothes for the naked, and comfort for every mourner that came within her reach. Slavery soon proved its ability to divest her of these heavenly qualities. Under its influence, the tender heart became stone, and the lamblike disposition gave way to one of tiger-like fierceness. The first step in her downward course was in her ceasing to instruct me. She now commenced to practise her husband's precepts. She finally became even more violent in her opposition than her husband himself. She was not satisfied with simply doing as well as he had commanded; she seemed anxious to do better. Nothing seemed to make her more angry than to see me with a newspaper. She seemed to think that here lay the danger. I have had her rush at me with a face made all up of fury, and snatch from me a newspaper, in a manner that fully revealed her apprehension. She was an apt woman; and a little experience soon demonstrated, to her satisfaction, that education and slavery were incompatible with each other.

From this time I was most narrowly watched. If I was in a separate room any considerable length of time, I was sure to be suspected of having a book, and was at once called to give an account of myself. All this, however, was too late. The first step had been taken. Mistress, in teaching me the alphabet, had given me the *inch*, and no precaution could prevent me from taking the *ell*.

The plan which I adopted, and the one by which I was most successful, was that of making friends of all the little white boys whom I met in the street. As many of these as I could, I converted into teachers. With their kindly aid, obtained at different times and in different places, I finally succeeded in learning to read. When I was sent of errands, I always took my book with me, and by going one part of my errand quickly, I found time to get a lesson before my return. I used also to carry bread with me, enough of which was always in the house, and to which I was always welcome; for I was much better off in this regard than many of the poor white children in our neighborhood. This bread I used to bestow upon the hungry little urchins, who, in return, would give me that more valuable bread of knowledge. I am strongly tempted to give the names of two or three of those little boys, as a testimonial of the gratitude and affection I bear them; but prudence forbids;—not that it would injure me, but it might embarrass them; for it is almost an unpardonable offence to teach slaves to read in this Christian country. It is enough to say of the dear little fellows, that they lived on Philpot Street, very near Durgin and Bailey's ship-yard. I used to talk this matter of slavery over with them. I would sometimes say to them, I wished I could be as free as they would be when they got to be men. "You will be free as soon as you are twenty-one, *but I am a slave for life!* Have not I as good a right to be free as you have?" These words used to trouble them; they would express for me the liveliest sympathy, and console me with the hope that something would occur by which I might be free.

I was now about twelve years old, and the thought of being *a slave for life* began to bear heavily upon my heart. Just about this time, I got hold of a book entitled *The Columbian Orator*. Every opportunity I got, I used to read this book. Among much of other interesting matter, I found in it a dialogue between a master and his slave. The slave was represented as having run away from his master three times. The dialogue represented the conversation which took place between them, when the slave was retaken the third time. In this dialogue, the whole argument in behalf of slavery was brought forward by the master, all of which was disposed of by the slave. The slave was made to say some very smart as well as impressive things in reply to his master—things which had the desired though unexpected effect; for the conversation resulted in the voluntary emancipation of the slave on the part of the master.

In the same book, I met with one of Sheridan's mighty speeches on and in behalf of Catholic emancipation. These were choice documents to me. I read them over and over again with unabated interest. They gave tongue to interesting thoughts of my own soul, which had frequently flashed through my mind, and died away for want of utterance. The moral which I gained from the dialogue was the power of truth over the conscience of even a slaveholder. What I got from Sheridan was a bold denunciation of slavery, and a powerful vindication of human rights. The reading of these documents enabled me to utter my thoughts, and to meet the arguments brought forward to sustain slavery; but while they relieved me of one difficulty, they brought on another even more painful than the one of which I was relieved. The more I read, the more I was led to abhor and detest my enslavers. I could regard them in no other light than a band of successful robbers, who had left their homes, and gone to Africa, and stolen us from our homes, and in a strange land reduced us to slavery. I loathed them as being the meanest as well as the most wicked of men. As I read and contemplated the subject, behold! that very discontentment which Master Hugh had predicted would follow my learning to read had already come, to torment and sting my soul to unutterable anguish. As I writhed under it, I would at times feel that learning to read had been a curse rather than a blessing. It had given me

(Continues)

a view of my wretched condition, without the remedy. It opened my eyes to the horrible pit, but to no ladder upon which to get out. In moments of agony, I envied my fellow-slaves for their stupidity. I have often wished myself a beast. I preferred the condition of the meanest reptile to my own. Any thing, no matter what, to get rid of thinking! It was this everlasting thinking of my condition that tormented me. There was no getting rid of it. It was pressed upon me by every object within sight or hearing, animate or inanimate. The silver trump of freedom had roused my soul to eternal wakefulness. Freedom now appeared, to disappear no more forever. It was heard in every sound, and seen in every thing. It was ever present to torment me with a sense of my wretched condition. I saw nothing without seeing it, I heard nothing without hearing it, and felt nothing without feeling it. It looked from every star, it smiled in every calm, breathed in every wind, and moved in every storm.

I often found myself regretting my own existence, and wishing myself dead; and but for the hope of being free, I have no doubt but that I should have killed myself, or done something for which I should have been killed. While in this state of mind, I was eager to hear any one speak of slavery. I was a ready listener. Every little while, I could hear something about the abolitionists. It was some time before I found what the word meant. It was always used in such connections as to make it an interesting word to me. If a slave ran away and succeeded in getting clear, or if a slave killed his master, set fire to a barn, or did any thing very wrong in the mind of a slaveholder, it was spoken of as the fruit of *abolition*. Hearing the word in this connection very often, I set about learning what it meant. The dictionary afforded me little or no help. I found it was "the act of abolishing;" but then I did not know what was to be abolished. Here I was perplexed. I did not dare to ask any one about its meaning, for I was satisfied that it was something they wanted me to know very little about. After a patient waiting, I got one of our city papers, containing an account of the number of petitions from the north, praying for the abolition of slavery in the District of Columbia, and of the slave trade between the States. From this time I understood the words *abolition* and *abolitionist*, and always drew near when that word was spoken, expecting to hear something of importance to myself and fellow-slaves. The light broke in upon me by degrees. I went one day down on the wharf of Mr. Waters; and seeing two Irishmen unloading a scow of stone, I went, unasked, and helped them. When we had finished, one of them came to me and asked me if I were a slave. I told him I was. He asked, "Are ye a slave for life?" I told him that I was. The good Irishman seemed to be deeply affected by the statement. He said to the other that it was a pity so fine a little fellow as myself should be a slave for life. He said it was a shame to hold me. They both advised me to run away to the north; that I should find friends there, and that I should be free. I pretended not to be interested in what they said, and treated them as if I did not understand them; for I feared they might be treacherous. White men have been known to encourage slaves to escape, and then, to get the reward, catch them and return them to their masters. I was afraid that these seemingly good men might use me so; but I nevertheless remembered their advice, and from that time I resolved to run away. I looked forward to a time at which it would be safe for me to escape. I was too young to think of doing so immediately; besides, I wished to learn how to write, as I might have occasion to write my own pass. I consoled myself with the hope that I should one day find a good chance. Meanwhile, I would learn to write.

The idea as to how I might learn to write was suggested to me by being in Durgin and Bailey's ship-yard, and frequently seeing the ship carpenters, after hewing, and getting a piece of timber ready for use, write on the timber the name of that part of the ship for which it was intended. When a piece of timber was intended for the larboard side, it would be marked thus—"L." When a piece was for the starboard side, it would be marked thus—"S." A piece for the larboard side forward, would be marked thus—"L. F." When a piece was for starboard side forward, it would be marked thus—"S. F." For larboard aft, it would be marked thus—"L. A." For starboard aft, it would be marked thus—"S. A." I soon learned the names of these letters, and for what they were intended when placed upon a piece of timber in the ship-yard. I immediately commenced copying them, and in a short time was able to make the four letters named. After that, when I met with any boy who I knew could write, I would tell him I could write as well as he. The next word would be, "I don't believe you. Let me see you try it." I would then make the letters which I had been so fortunate as to learn, and ask him to beat that. In this way I got a good many lessons in writing, which it is quite possible I should never have gotten in any other way. During this time, my copy-book was the board fence, brick wall, and pavement; my pen and ink was a lump of chalk. With these, I learned mainly how to write. I then commenced and continued copying the italics in *Webster's Spelling Book*, until I could make them all without looking on the book. By this time, my little Master Thomas had gone to school, and learned how to write, and had written over a number of copy-books. These had

(Continues)

been brought home, and shown to some of our near neighbors, and then laid aside. My mistress used to go to class meeting at the Wilk Street meetinghouse every Monday afternoon, and leave me to take care of the house. When left thus, I used to spend the time in writing in the spaces left in Master Thomas's copy-book, copying what he had written. I continued to do this until I could write a hand very similar to that of Master Thomas. Thus, after a long, tedious effort for years, I finally succeeded in learning how to write.

But to return to Mr. Freeland, and to my experience while in his employment. He, like Mr. Covey, gave us enough to eat; but, unlike Mr. Covey, he also gave us sufficient time to take our meals. He worked us hard, but always between sunrise and sunset. He required a good deal of work to be done, but gave us good tools with which to work. His farm was large, but he employed hands enough to work it, and with ease, compared with many of his neighbors. My treatment, while in his employment, was heavenly, compared with what I experienced at the hands of Mr. Edward Covey.

Mr. Freeland was himself the owner of but two slaves. Their names were Henry Harris and John Harris. The rest of his hands he hired. These consisted of myself, Sandy Jenkins, and Handy Caldwell. Henry and John were quite intelligent, and in a very little while after I went there, I succeeded in creating in them a strong desire to learn how to read. This desire soon sprang up in the others also. They very soon mustered up some old spelling-books, and nothing would do but that I must keep a Sabbath school. I agreed to do so, and accordingly devoted my Sundays to teaching these my loved fellow-slaves how to read. Neither of them knew his letters when I went there. Some of the slaves of the neighboring farms found what was going on, and also availed themselves of this little opportunity to learn to read. It was understood, among all who came, that there must be as little display about it as possible. It was necessary to keep our religious masters at St. Michael's unacquainted with the fact, that, instead of spending the Sabbath in wrestling, boxing, and drinking whisky, we were trying to learn how to read the will of God.

I held my Sabbath school at the house of a free colored man, whose name I deem it imprudent to mention; for should it be known, it might embarrass him greatly, though the crime of holding the school was committed ten years ago. I had at one time over forty scholars, and those of the right sort, ardently desiring to learn. They were of all ages, though mostly men and women. I look back to those Sundays with an amount of pleasure not to be expressed. They were great days to my soul. The work of instructing my dear fellow-slaves was the sweetest engagement with which I was ever blessed. We loved each other, and to leave them at the close of the Sabbath was a severe cross indeed. When I think that these precious souls are to-day shut up in the prison-house of slavery, my feelings overcome me, and I am almost ready to ask, "Does a righteous God govern the universe? and for what does he hold the thunders in his right hand, if not to smite the oppressor, and deliver the spoiled out of the hand of the spoiler?" These dear souls came not to Sabbath school because it was popular to do so, nor did I teach them because it was reputable to be thus engaged. Every moment they spent in that school, they were liable to be taken up, and given thirty-nine lashes. They came because they wished to learn. Their minds had been starved by their cruel masters. They had been shut up in mental darkness. I taught them, because it was the delight of my soul to be doing something that looked like bettering the condition of my race. I kept up my school nearly the whole year I lived with Mr. Freeland; and, beside my Sabbath school, I devoted three evenings in the week, during the winter, to teaching the slaves at home. And I have the happiness to know, that several of those who came to Sabbath school learned how to read; and that one, at least, is now free through my agency.

Discussion Questions

1. Discuss the education Frederick Douglass received from Mrs. Auld. What did she teach him? Why did she stop? How did the experience change her? Why does Douglas say the instruction he received, not from Mrs. Auld but from Mr. Auld, was "invaluable"? What is the most valuable instruction you have ever received? Explain.

2. Explain the steps in Douglass' plan to learn to read and write. Once he could read, what book had an "unexpected effect" on him? What was that effect? How would you have expected him to feel after reading these speeches and arguments related to slavery? What use could the skill of writing be to a slave like Douglass?

3. Describe the way Douglass spent his Sundays after learning to read. Compare the effects learning to read had on the slaves to the effect it had on Malcolm X. In what ways do you see Douglass, the other slaves, and Malcolm X imprisoned by illiteracy? In what ways do you think being unable to read in our society today is detrimental?

From *Narrative of the Life of Frederick Douglass* by Frederick Douglass, 1845.

Assignment 2

This unit's lead essay by Jared Diamond reflects on change. As in earlier units, the activities and exercises that follow Diamond's essay are there to guide you through the writing process so that you can fully comprehend the lead essay, develop your own insights about its topic, and capture those ideas fully and clearly in an essay of your own. Remember, the more carefully and thoroughly you use the supporting exercises and readings in the unit, the more thoughtful and successful your essay will be.

Accepting or Rejecting Innovation   *Essay*

JARED DIAMOND

> *Jared Diamond is a professor of geography at the University of California, Los Angeles. He began his scientific career in physiology and expanded into evolutionary biology and biogeography. He has been elected to the National Academy of Sciences, the American Academy of Arts and Sciences, and the American Philosophical Society. He has published more than six hundred articles and several books, including the* New York Times *bestseller* Guns, Germs, and Steel, *which was awarded a Pulitzer Prize.*

Once an inventor has discovered a use for a new technology, the next step is to persuade society to adopt it. Merely having a bigger, faster, more powerful device for doing something is no guarantee of ready acceptance. Innumerable such technologies were either not adopted at all or adopted only after prolonged resistance. Notorious examples include the world's continued rejection of an efficiently designed typewriter keyboard and Britain's long reluctance to adopt electric lighting. What is it that promotes an invention's acceptance by a society?

The first and most obvious factor is relative economic advantage compared with existing technology. While wheels are very useful in modern industrial societies, that has not been so in some other societies. Some advanced Native American cultures in ancient Mexico invented wheeled vehicles with axles for use as toys, but not for transport. That seems incredible to us, until we reflect that the peoples of ancient

Mexico lacked domestic animals to hitch to their wheeled vehicles, which therefore offered no advantage over human porters.

A second consideration is social value and prestige, which can override economic benefit—or lack thereof. Millions of people today buy designer jeans for double the price of equally durable generic jeans because the social cachet of the designer label counts for more than the extra cost. Similarly, Japan continues to use its horrendously cumbersome kanji writing system in preference to efficient alphabets or Japan's own efficient kana syllabary because the prestige attached to kanji is so great.

Still another factor is compatibility with vested interests. This book, like probably every other typed document you have ever read, was typed with a QWERTY keyboard, named for the left-most six letters in its upper row. Unbelievable as it may now sound, that keyboard layout was designed in 1873 as a feat of anti-engineering. It employs a whole series of perverse tricks designed to force typists to type as slowly as possible, such as scattering the commonest letters over all keyboard rows and concentrating them on the left side, where right-handed people have to use their weaker hand. The reason behind all of those seemingly counterproductive features is that the typewriters of 1873 jammed if adjacent keys were struck in quick succession, so that manufacturers had to slow typists down. When improvements in typewriters eliminated the problem of jamming, trials in 1932 showed that an efficiently laid-out keyboard would let us double our typing speed and reduce our typing effort by 95 percent. But QWERTY keyboards were solidly entrenched by then. The vested interest of hundreds of millions of QWERTY typists, typing teachers, typewriter and computer salespeople, and manufacturers have crushed all moves toward keyboard efficiency for over 60 years.

While the story of the QWERTY keyboard may sound funny, many similar cases of resistance to change based on financial interests or settled habits have involved much heavier economic consequences. Why does Japan now dominate the world market for transistorized electronic consumer products to a degree that damages the United States's balance of payments with Japan, even though transistors were invented and patented in the United States? Japan dominates the electronics market today because the Japanese company Sony bought transistor licensing rights from the American company Western Electric at a time when the American electronics consumer industry was churning out vacuum tube models and was therefore reluctant to compete with

(Continues)

its own products. Why were British cities still using gas street lighting into the 1920s, long after cities in the United States and Germany had converted to more efficient electric street lighting? British municipal governments rejected electric street lighting because they had invested heavily in gas lighting; to protect those investments, they placed regulatory obstacles in the way of competing electric light companies.

Writing Topic

What factors, according to Diamond, cause people to adopt technological innovations into their lives? To what extent do you think his ideas explain why people accept or reject innovations? Be sure to support your position using examples from your own experience, your observation of others, or your readings.

Vocabulary and Dictionary Practice

Part I.

Look up the following words used in "Accepting or Rejecting Innovation." If there is more than one definition, write both definitions on the lines below. For each definition, indicate the part of speech. Then, write a sentence of your own using the vocabulary word as that part of speech.

1. innovation
2. prolong
3. notorious
4. porter
5. cachet
6. syllabary
7. vested
8. perverse
9. counterproductive
10. churn

1. **innovation**:

first definition: _____

_____

part of speech: _____

sentence: _____

_____

second definition: _____

_____

part of speech: _____

sentence: _____

_____

2. **prolong**:

first definition: _____

_____

part of speech: _____

sentence: _____

_____

second definition: _____

_____

part of speech: _____

sentence: _____

_____

3. **notorious:**

first definition: _____

_____

part of speech: _____

sentence: _____

_____

second definition: _____

_____

part of speech: _____

sentence: _____

_____

4. **porter:**

first definition: _____

_____

part of speech: _____

sentence: _____

_____

second definition: _____

_____

part of speech: _____

sentence: _____

_____

5. **cachet:**

   first definition: _____

   _____

   part of speech: _____

   sentence: _____

   _____

   second definition: _____

   _____

   part of speech: _____

   sentence: _____

   _____

6. **syllabary:**

   first definition: _____

   _____

   part of speech: _____

   sentence: _____

   _____

second definition: _____

_____

part of speech: _____

sentence: _____

_____

7. **vested:**

first definition: _____

_____

part of speech: _____

sentence: _____

_____

second definition: _____

_____

part of speech: _____

sentence: _____

_____

8. **perverse:**

first definition: _____

_____

part of speech: _____

sentence: _____

_____

second definition: _____

_____

part of speech: _____

sentence: _____

_____

9. **counterproductive:**

first definition: _____

_____

part of speech: _____

sentence: _____

_____

second definition: _____

_____

part of speech: _____

sentence: _____

_____

10. **churn:**

first definition: _____

_____

part of speech: _____

sentence: _____

_____

second definition: _____

_____

part of speech: _____

sentence: _____

_____

Part II.

A. Write down each sentence from Diamond's essay that contains the following words.

B. Tell which one of the word's various definitions best fits the sentence.

C. Paraphrase the sentence without using the vocabulary word; in other words, write the sentence using your own words.

1. **innovation**

   A. _____

   _____

   B. _____

   _____

   C. _____

   _____

2. **prolong**

   A. _____

   _____

   B. _____

   _____

   C. _____

   _____

3. **notorious**

   A. _____

   _____

   B. _____

   _____

C. _____

_____

4. porter

A. _____

_____

B. _____

_____

C. _____

_____

5. cachet

A. _____

_____

B. _____

_____

C. _____

_____

6. syllabary

A. _____

_____

B. _____

_____

C. _____

_____

7. vested

A. _____

_____

B. _____

_____

C. _____

_____

8. perverse

A. _____

_____

B. _____

_____

C. _____

_____

9. counterproductive

A. _____

_____

B. _____

_____

C. _____

_____

10. churn

A. _____

_____

B. _____

_____

C. _____

_____

Part III.

For each of these words from "Accepting or Rejecting Innovation," tell something new and interesting you learned about the word from the dictionary. For example, you might have found the correct way to pronounce a word you were already familiar with from reading but not from speaking, or you might have learned that a word had a definition that you did not know.

1. **innovation**

_____

_____

2. **prolong**

_____

_____

3. **notorious**

_____

_____

4. **porter**

_____

_____

5. **cachet**

_____

_____

6. **syllabary**

_____

_____

7. **vested**

_____

_____

8. **perverse**

_____

_____

9. **counterproductive**

_____

_____

10. **churn**

_____

_____

Follow-Up Activity

1. Show the class a piece of technology that you have with you—for example, a cell phone or a computer. Tell them how you happen to have it, why you have it, how you use it, and how you would rate it over other models of the same kind. If you bought it yourself, explain why you chose it and whether you would make the same choice today. If it was a gift, tell the class how the giver happened to buy you that particular item.

2. After several or all of your classmates have presented, discuss the results. Do Diamond's ideas seem to be supported by the limited amount of evidence that your classmates have collected through these examples of their personal experiences?

3. Choose someone in your family and explain to the class his or her relationship with technology. Why do you think he or she feels this way?

4. If you were given enough money to buy any car you wish, tell your classmates which one you would choose and why. Try to think with an open mind before you answer so that you say more than "it's a good car." See if you can come up with at least five adjectives that describe why the car attracts you.

Doing a Careful Reading of "Accepting or Rejecting Innovation"

Use the following strategies and any others you choose to guide you through a systematic reading of Diamond's essay. For each step, write as much as you can. You don't yet know what may be of value as you work your way through Diamond's ideas, formulate your own, and ultimately respond in an essay of your own.

1. **Read the title.**
   - The title will tell you something about the reading selection's main topic.
   - It may also tell you something about Diamond's opinion on the topic.
   - Think about what you already know about the topic and what more you want to know.

2. **Learn about the author.**
   - Read the biographical information about Diamond at the top of the selection.
   - As you go through the remaining steps below, take note of how Diamond's life or work might connect with his topic.

3. **Read through the selection once quickly.**
   - Read quickly through the reading so that you get a general impression of what it is about and what Diamond's attitude is toward the topic.
   - Notice the things—people, places, experiences, concepts, for example—he brings up to develop and support his opinion about the topic.

4. **Read again to identify the thesis.**
   - Now read the selection a second time, but more slowly and carefully, and *with a pen or highlighter in your hand.*
   - Find the thesis and underline it or write it in the margin. Remember, the thesis states Diamond's overall opinion on the topic of the reading. Often, the thesis is contained in a single sentence, but, in some cases, it takes several sentences to make the main argument of the reading selection clear. There are times, too, when the author does not state his or her thesis explicitly, but, if you read the selection carefully, you should be able to state it and then write it in the margin.
   - To help, ask yourself, "What does Diamond seem to want readers to think about his topic?"

5. **Read slowly and methodically through the rest of the reading.**
   - Examine each body paragraph one at a time, and list or underline the kinds of evidence that Diamond uses to support his thesis.

- Look in each body paragraph for a *topic sentence*—a sentence that both presents an idea and tells how it gives support to the reading's overall opinion.
- As you read and study the selection, *be sure to write down any thoughts you have* about Diamond's opinion and supporting evidence.
- It is your job to evaluate this evidence for its logic and validity, so be sure to *make notes in the margins* as you read.
- *Mark the points* that you found interesting or convincing, and write a few words explaining your thoughts.
- Note, too, any weaknesses you find.
- When you look back at the notes you made in the margins, you should have a general idea of how convincing you found "Accepting or Rejecting Innovation" and what you found to be its strengths and weaknesses.

6. **Read again for review.**
   - Once you have thought through the reading selection, read it once more, looking for places where you don't quite understand what is being said.
   - Underline any terms that you aren't familiar with, and look them up in a dictionary.
   - Mark any places in the reading that don't fit with your understanding of the reading as a whole. Decide whether this is something that Diamond should have revised, or whether it is something that you need to read again because you don't understand it. You may find that you need to go back to Step 4 and begin working through the reading again.
   - Once you are certain that you understand the entire reading, you are prepared to discuss, summarize, and/or respond to the reading with your own essay.

Follow-Up Activity

Select two of the most important things in Diamond's essay that you marked. Tell the class why you think these two parts are important.

Questions to Review Your Understanding of "Accepting or Rejecting Innovation"

Answer the following questions as thoroughly and carefully as you can to ensure that you haven't missed any of the important aspects of Diamond's argument.

Paragraph 1
What question about society and inventions concerns Diamond?

Paragraph 2
What factor does Diamond say is most apparent?

Paragraph 3
According to Diamond, what considerations can be even more important than the financial ones?

Paragraph 4
Define the term "vested interests." According to Diamond, how can they sometimes become a factor?

Paragraph 5
What are some examples of slow change due to the above factors?

Responding to the Writing Topic

You should now have a good understanding of the ideas and overall message of "Accepting or Rejecting Innovation." Now look again at the writing topic that follows Diamond's essay, and begin thinking about how you will respond to it. For convenience, here it is with some of the important action words bolded:

Writing Topic

What factors, according to Diamond, **cause** people to adopt technological innovations into their lives? To what extent do you think his ideas **explain why** people accept or reject innovations? Be sure to **support your position** using examples from your own experience, your observation of others, or your readings.

You should always spend time taking apart a writing topic before you begin planning your essay. As with all previous essays in *Write It .5*, this writing topic has three basic parts. Rewrite them on the lines below:

1. _____

_____

2. _____

_____

3. _____

_____

Strategies to Help You Analyze a Reading Selection and Develop Your Ideas for Writing a Response

Now you are ready to build on the annotations you made in your careful reading of "Accepting and Rejecting Innovation." To develop a more systematic analysis, one that allows you to form your own opinions and ideas about those in Diamond's essay, use the prewriting guides that you were introduced to in Part 2. They will help to guide your thinking about Diamond's essay, but they will also help you to clarify and put into words your own views on the topic he writes about—what makes people accept innovation.

Questioning

- Questions about the highlighting you did:
  Why did I underline this part of the reading?

  How is this information important to Diamond's point?

  How can this information relate to the question I am being asked to write about?

- Questions about Diamond's ideas:
  What things in "Accepting and Rejecting Innovation" do not make sense to me?

  Where do I think Diamond should have given more explanation?

  How well do the examples in the essay relate to the point Diamond is making?

- Questions about "Accepting and Rejecting Innovation" that seem important:
  What are some of the things that Diamond says that I am happy to hear someone say?

What things that he says seem true to me?

What things that he says seem wrong to me?

What thing that Diamond says is most important to me?

What idea in this essay is completely new to me?

Freewriting

If you still feel that you have little to say to respond to Diamond's essay and topic, try some freewriting.

- Pick one or more of your answers to the questions you have already answered, and just begin to write about them.
- While you are doing this writing, do not stop or censor yourself; just let the words come.
- Do this for about five or ten minutes without thinking about spelling, grammar, word choice, or even the sense of what you are saying.
- When you have completed this activity, you will want to take a break.
- After your brief break, come back and read what you have written. Most of what you now have down on paper will not end up in your essay, but, as you read through your freewriting, you will find one or more sentences or ideas that seem interesting, important, or even compelling to you. Highlight these points and ideas.

Listing

With this strategy, you simply list all of the thoughts and reactions you have noted so far. By looking down your list, you may see a pattern of ideas develop, one that you can use to develop an essay of your own.

- List all of the annotations you made for "Accepting and Rejecting Innovation."
- List the main ideas you can see in your answers to the questioning phase above.
- List any main ideas that developed from your responses to the follow-up activities above.

- Be sure to list all the items from your freewriting that you thought were interesting. As you make this list, other ideas may come into your head. Put them on your list as well.

Study your list. Group all the ideas that seem related to each other. When you are done, one related group of ideas will probably be longer than the others. This group should give you a good start on what you want to say in your own essay in response to Diamond's essay.

Shaping Your Ideas into a Rough Draft

If you don't feel prepared at this point to plan your rough draft, go back through some of the activities above and talk with classmates to see what they are thinking. Continue to search for evidence because, as you do, you build a solid foundation from which to draw conclusions and formulate a thesis statement. Sometimes it takes a while before your ideas are fully formed; take as much time as you need to clarify your thoughts. Sometimes it helps to begin drafting. As you do, further insights may come to you.

When you are ready to focus on your rough draft, you will have to think about each part of your essay and how you will compose it. Turn back to Part 2 and examine "A Suggested Structure for an Essay That Responds to Another Writer's Essay." Also, look again at the writing topic for "Accepting and Rejecting Innovation." Remind yourself that it asks you to do three things:

1. Write a summary that identifies the issue that Diamond discusses and that explains how he views it.

   Remember that you have already worked on this in earlier activities when you annotated "Accepting or Rejecting Innovation" and when you answered comprehension questions and analyzed Diamond's ideas. Look back now to the work you did. You may be able to use some of it to help you collect the main ideas for your essay's *directed summary*.

2. Take a position on this idea; do you agree with Diamond's view?

   This part of the writing topic will lead you to your thesis statement, and your thesis statement will unify your essay, so it's important that you clearly express the position you want to take. Turn back to the review questions you answered and the follow-up activities you did. What were your thoughts and ideas? Collect them now so that you can use them as the basis for your working thesis statement. Remember that you can always revise it as you work on your rough draft.

3. Support and develop your position using specific evidence taken from your own experiences and readings. In other words, explain your thinking and why you have the view you present—and don't forget to include the specific "proof" that convinced you to take the position you take.

The explanation of your thoughts and the evidence that led you to draw those conclusions will make up nearly your entire essay. Look back to earlier exercises in this unit to remind yourself of some of the thinking you did. You will be able to use some of this as evidence to support your thesis. Remember it when you begin working on body paragraphs.

Now that you have collected your ideas and reviewed the writing topic for "Accepting and Rejecting Innovation," you are ready to refine your ideas and analysis into a rough draft. Use the sections that follow to guide you.

Drafting Your Directed Summary

- Begin drafting the directed summary by reviewing the writing topic for "Accepting or Rejecting Innovation," paying particular attention to the first question asked. The answer you give to this question is called a *directed summary* because it summarizes only the parts of Diamond's essay that answer this first question.

  As you learned in Part 2, the question that calls for a directed summary often opens with a question word such as *what, how,* or *why.* In Diamond's essay, the first question asks **"What factors**, according to Diamond, **cause** people to adopt technological innovations into their lives?" You will have to go back to his essay to find the information that tells *what factors cause* people to adopt innovations. It will not be enough to simply tell what these innovations are; you will also have to summarize *what factors cause people to adopt them,* according to Diamond.

- You might find it helpful to turn back to "Accepting or Rejecting Innovation" and mark the sentences that respond directly to the directed summary question. When writing your directed summary, be very careful to use your own words to *paraphrase* his ideas, as you learned to do in Part 2.

- You should avoid including any of the following in a *directed summary*:

  1. a summary of the entire essay rather than a summary that pays attention only to what is asked for in the first question of the writing topic

  2. minor details or points that are irrelevant to the question

  3. your own opinion or ideas

  4. examples of your own, and unless particularly helpful, those of the author

Once you have written a directed summary, you will be ready to draft your essay's introductory paragraph. These steps will help guide you:

- Introduce Diamond's essay by giving its title and the full name of its author.

- Follow these opening sentences with the directed summary.

- Last, present your thesis statement, or the answer to the second question in the writing topic. To develop your thesis statement, use the guides in the following section.

Follow-Up Activity

1. On the board, write the lists you developed in the activity above. Compare your lists with your classmates' lists and discuss.
2. Draft your directed summary.
3. Working in small groups or with a partner, take turns reading your directed summary aloud. Discuss the strengths and weaknesses of each summary.

Developing Your Thesis Statement

The second question in the writing topic asks you to form your own opinion regarding what causes people to accept innovation. Will you agree with Diamond? The question asks:

To what extent do you think his ideas explain why people accept or reject innovations?

Think of your thesis as needing three parts:

- the subject being considered
- Diamond's claim about the subject
- your opinion about the subject

You will have to provide a clear answer to this question because it will be the statement that unifies your essay and that the rest of your essay will explain and support. Use the following exercise to help you do this:

1. List the causes for accepting innovation that Diamond identifies in his essay.
2. After each one, write down a sentence or two that explains the causal relationship (where one thing causes another thing to happen) that Diamond puts forward.
3. List all the forms of new technology you can think of that are relatively new.
4. Look over your list and determine whether each has been accepted by society, or whether its acceptance is undecided.
5. For each item on your list, speculate as to why society has or has not accepted the new technology.
6. Look over your work and see if you agree with Diamond or if you want to make a different argument about why, overall, people accept or reject innovation.

Now use the following frame to help draft your thesis:

The subject and Diamond's idea about the subject/your opinion about the subject

_____

_____

_____

_____

After you have finished writing your sentence, review your statement to see that it contains the following elements:

- Diamond's point of view on the subject
- your point of view on the subject

If either of these elements is missing, rewrite your thesis statement so that both are included. Up to this point, you have been planning the draft of your introductory paragraph. Now that you have drafted your thesis statement, you can begin planning your body paragraphs. They will have to explain your ideas and give support to your thesis statement.

Developing Body Paragraphs for an Essay That Presents a Thesis

Reminders:

Body paragraphs make up the largest part of an essay.

- The job of each body paragraph is to develop one point that supports the thesis statement.

- Taken together, these points constitute the argument of the essay.

- Writing a good body paragraph can be easy once you understand the elements that the body paragraph must contain.

Here is a review of the three most important elements for paragraphs in an argumentative essay:

Parts of a Body Paragraph

An appropriate or suitable topic—one that supports the thesis statement

Evidence—for instance, a concrete fact, example, or quotation—that demonstrates the point of the paragraph

A link to the thesis—sentences that show how and why the paragraph, including the evidence, relates to the thesis

A Basic Outline Form for an Essay That Presents a Thesis

Let's look back at all of the work you have done so far:

You have read and carefully annotated "Accepting or Rejecting Innovation."

You have analyzed its ideas.

You have written a directed summary in response to the first question in the writing topic.

You have thought about your own experiences and decided on your thesis statement.

You have drafted your essay's introduction.

All of that work should be gathered together now into a shape that will become your essay, your response to the writing topic for "Accepting or Rejecting Innovation."

- Remember that you should follow the basic structure of an academic essay.
- To refresh your memory, turn back to Part 2 and review the diagram of the academic essay format.
- As you begin filling in this diagram form, you should be able to turn back to material you have already drafted as you worked through the exercises in this unit.
- Fill in the diagram form as fully as you can. A good plan will help you draft an essay that is clear and coherent.

I. Introductory Paragraph:

A. one or two opening sentences that give the reading selection's title, author, and main topic:

_____

_____

_____

B. the main points that will be included in the directed summary:

1.

2.

3.

4.

C. your thesis statement: Be sure that it presents a clear position in response to the writing topic. State your thesis in your own words.

_____

_____

_____

II. Body Paragraphs: For each body paragraph you will include in your essay, plan the following parts:

Write down the main point for the paragraph.

_____

_____

_____

List the evidence you will use to support your main point (fact, example, etc.).

_____

_____

_____

_____

_____

_____

Tell how the evidence and your ideas link to the thesis statement.

_____

_____

_____

_____

_____

_____

_____

_____

_____

_____

(Repeat this part of the outline as often as necessary to plan all of your body paragraphs.)

III. Conclusion: What are some general remarks you can make to close your essay? Perhaps you will remind your readers of the main argument of your paper, for example.

_____

_____

_____

Drafting Your Essay

Now that you have a basic plan for the structure of your essay and a map of its various parts, you are ready to begin drafting.

- If your thinking changes as you write your draft, return to your outline and make necessary adjustments. Every time you decide to revise your outline and essay, remember that this is a good sign, a sign that your thinking is developing and becoming more thoughtful and convincing.

- Keep turning back to all of the activities in this unit as you draft your essay. Try to recall some of your reactions, thoughts, and ideas as you worked on these activities. This may help you to strengthen, expand on, or more fully develop your essay's argument.

- In the space below, draft your essay's opening paragraph. First, look back to the main points that you listed in your outline, and to the thesis statement that you wrote. These elements will be important to include in your paragraph.

Follow-Up Activity

1. Have a classmate read your opening paragraph aloud. As you listen and follow along, mark the places that need more work. Discuss the paragraph with your classmate and decide what revisions you want to make.

Supplemental Reading

Cars and Their Enemies

JAMES Q. WILSON

James Q. Wilson completed his BA at the University of Redlands and his PhD in political science at the University of Chicago. From 1961 to 1987, he was the Shattuck Professor of Government at Harvard University. He published a number of books on America's governing institutions. His most recent book is titled American Politics, Then and Now *(2010).*

Imagine the country we now inhabit—big, urban, prosperous—with one exception: The automobile has not been invented. We have trains and bicycles, and some kind of self-powered buses and trucks, but no private cars driven by their owners for business or pleasure. Of late, let us suppose, someone has come forward with the idea of creating the personal automobile. Consider how we would react to such news.

Libertarians might support the idea, but hardly anyone else. Engineers would point out that such cars, if produced in any significant number, would zip along roads just a few feet—perhaps even a few inches—from one another; the chance of accidents would not simply be high; it would be certain. Public-health specialists would estimate that many of these accidents would lead to serious injuries and deaths. No one could say in advance how common they would be, but the best experts might guess that the number of people killed by cars would easily exceed the number killed by murderers. Psychologists would point out that if any young person were allowed to operate a car, the death rate would be even higher, as youngsters—those between the ages of sixteen and twenty-four—are much more likely than older persons to be impulsive risk-takers who find pleasure in reckless bravado. Educators would explain that, though they might try by training to reduce this youthful death rate, they could not be optimistic they would succeed.

Environmentalists would react in horror to the idea of automobiles powered by the internal combustion engine, apparently the most inexpensive method. Such devices, because they burn fuel incompletely, would eject large amounts of unpleasant gases into the air, such as carbon monoxide, nitrogen oxide, and sulfur dioxide. Other organic compounds, as well as clouds of particles, would also enter the atmosphere to produce unknown but probably harmful effects. Joining in this objection would be people who would not want their view spoiled by the creation of a network of roads.

Big-city mayors would add their own objections, though these would reflect their self-interest as much as their wisdom. If people could drive anywhere from anywhere, they would be able to live wherever they wished. This would produce a vast exodus from the large cities, led in all likelihood by the most prosperous—and thus the most tax-productive—citizens. Behind would remain people who, being poorer, were less mobile. Money would depart but problems remain.

Governors, pressed to keep taxes down and still fund costly health, welfare, educational, and criminal-justice programs, would wonder who would pay for the vast networks of roads that would be needed to carry automobiles. Their skepticism would be reinforced by the worries of police officials fearful of motorized thieves evading apprehension, and by the opposition of railroad executives foreseeing the collapse of their passenger business as people abandoned trains for cars.

Energy experts would react in horror at the prospect of supplying the gasoline stations and the vast quantities of petroleum necessary to fuel automobiles which, unlike buses and trucks, would be stored at home and not at a central depot and would burn much more fuel per person carried than some of their mass-transit alternatives.

In short, the automobile, the device on which most Americans rely for not only transportation but mobility, privacy, and fun, would not exist if it had to be created today. Of course, the car does exist, and has powerfully affected the living, working, and social spaces of America. But the argument against it persists. That argument dominates the thinking of academic experts on urban transportation and much of city planning. It can be found in countless books complaining of dreary suburban architecture, endless trips to and from work, the social isolation produced by solo auto trips, and the harmful effects of the car on air quality, noise levels, petroleum consumption, and road congestion.

Despite the criticisms, the use of the automobile has grown. In 1960, one-fifth of all households owned no car, and only one-fifth owned two; by 1990, only one-tenth owned no car, and over one-third owned two. In 1969, eighty percent of all urban trips involved a car, and only one-twentieth involved public transport; by 1990, car use had risen to eighty-four percent, and public transit had fallen to less than three percent. In 1990, three-fourths or more of the trips to and from work in nineteen out of our twenty largest metropolitan areas

(Continues)

were by a single person in an automobile. The exception was the New York metropolitan region, but even there—with an elaborate mass-transit system and a residential concentration high enough to make it possible for some people to walk to work—solo car use made up over half of all trips to work.

Suppose, however, that the anti-car writers were to win over the vastly more numerous pro-car drivers. Let us imagine what life would be like in a carless nation. People would have to live very close together so they could walk or, for healthy people living in sunny climes, bicycle to mass-transit stops. Living in close quarters would mean life as it is now lived in Manhattan. There would be few freestanding homes, many row houses, and lots of apartment buildings. There would be few private gardens except for flowerpots on balconies. The streets would be congested by pedestrians, trucks, and buses, as they were at the turn of the century before automobiles became common.

Moving about outside the larger cities would be difficult. People would be able to take trains to distant sites, but when they arrived at some attractive locale, it would turn out to be another city. They could visit the beach, but only (of necessity) crowded parts of it. They could go to a national park, but only the built-up section of it. They could see the countryside, but (mostly) through a train window. More isolated or remote locations would be accessible, but since public transit would provide the only way of getting there, the departures would be infrequent and the transfers frequent.

In other words, you could see the United States much as most Europeans saw their countryside before the automobile became an important means of locomotion. A train from London or Paris would take you to "the country" by way of a long journey through ugly industrial areas to those rural parts where either you had a home (and the means to ferry yourself to it) or there was a resort (that would be crowded enough to support a nearby train stop).

All this is a way of saying that the debate between car defenders and car haters is a debate between private benefits and public good. List the characteristics of travel that impose few costs on society and, in general, walking, cycling, and some forms of public transit will be seen to be superior. Non-car methods generate less pollution, use energy a bit more efficiently, produce less noise, and (with some exceptions) are safer. But list the characteristics of travel that are desired by individuals, and (with some exceptions) the car is clearly superior. The automobile is more flexible and punctual, supplies greater comfort, provides for carrying more parcels, creates more privacy, enables one to select fellow passengers, and, for distances over a mile or more, requires less travel time.

As a practical matter, of course, the debate between those who value private benefits and those who insist on their social costs is no real debate at all, since people select modes of travel based on individual, not social, preferences. That is why in almost every country in the world, the automobile has triumphed, and much of public policy has been devoted to the somewhat inconsistent task of subsidizing individual choices while attempting to reduce the costs attached to them. In the case of the automobile, governments have attempted to reduce exhaust pollution, make roadways safer, and restrict use (by tolls, speed bumps, pedestrian-only streets, and parking restrictions) in neighborhoods that attach a high value to pedestrian passage. Yet none of these efforts can alter the central fact that people have found cars to be the best means for getting about.

Take traffic congestion. Television loves to focus on grim scenes of gridlocked highways and angry motorists, but in fact people still get to work faster by car than by public transit. And the reason is not that car drivers live close to work and transit users travel a greater distance. According to the best estimates, cars outperform public transit in getting people quickly from their front doors to their work places. This fact is sometimes lost on car critics. Jane Holtz Kay, for example, writes that "the same number of people who spend an hour driving sixteen lanes of highway can travel on a two-track train line" (56). Wrong. Train travel is efficient *over a fixed, permanent route*, but people have to find some way to get to where the train starts and get to their final destination after the train stops. The *full* cost of moving people from home to work and back to the home is lower for cars than for trains. Moreover, cars are not subject to union strikes. The Long Island railroad or the bus system may shut down when workers walk off the job; cars do not.

The transportation argument rarely seems to take cognizance of the superiority of cars with respect to individual wants. Whenever there is a discussion about how best to move people about, mass-transit supporters typically overestimate, usually by a wide margin, how many people will leave their cars and happily hop onto trains or buses. So the real debate ought not be one between car enthusiasts and mass-transit advocates, but about ways of moderating the inevitable use of cars in order to minimize their deleterious effects.

(Continues)

Work Cited

Kay, Jane Holtz. *Asphalt Nation: How the Automobile Took Over America and How We Can Take It Back*. Berkeley: University of California Press, 1998. Print.

Discussion Questions

1. If the automobile were a recent innovation, who are the different groups that would possibly reject it, and what might the reasons be for their unwillingness to accept it? Discuss these reasons and their validity.

2. What are some reasons, including and in addition to those mentioned by James Q. Wilson, that the car was an accepted innovation? What does he mean when he says the use of the automobile comes down to a choice between private benefits and the public good?

3. In the end, where does Wilson believe we should concentrate our efforts regarding the use of cars? What ways can you think of to help accomplish this goal?

The Record Industry's Slow Fade

BRIAN HIATT AND EVAN SERPICK

Brian Hiatt and Evan Serpick are associate editors for Rolling Stone. *They wrote the following report in June 2007 in an attempt to understand the ongoing decline of the music industry and offer predictions from industry executives on the future of the music business. How has the industry fared since 2007?*

For the music industry, it was a rare bit of good news: Linkin Park's new album sold 623,000 copies in its first week this May—the strongest debut of the year. But it wasn't nearly enough. That same month, the band's record company, Warner Music Group, announced that it would lay off 400 people, and its stock price lingered at 58% of its peak from last June.

Overall CD sales have plummeted 16% for the year so far—and that's after seven years of near-constant erosion. In the face of widespread piracy, consumers' growing preference for low-profit-margin digital singles over albums, and other woes, the record business has plunged into a historic decline.

The major labels are struggling to reinvent their business models, even as some wonder whether it's too late. "The record business is over," says music attorney Peter Paterno, who represents Metallica and Dr. Dre. "The labels have wonderful assets—they just can't make any money off them." One senior music-industry source who requested anonymity went further: "Here we have a business that's dying. There won't be any major labels pretty soon."

In 2000, US consumers bought 785.1 million albums; last year, they bought 588.2 million (a figure that includes both CDs and downloaded albums), according to Nielsen Sound-Scan. In 2000, the ten top-selling albums in the US sold a combined 60 million copies; in 2006, the top ten sold just 25 million. Digital sales are growing—fans bought 582 million digital singles last year, up 65% from 2005, and purchased $600 million worth of ringtones—but the new revenue sources aren't making up for the shortfall.

More than 5,000 record-company employees have been laid off since 2000. The number of major labels dropped from five to four when Sony Music Entertainment and BMG Entertainment merged in

(Continues)

2004—and two of the remaining companies, EMI and Warner, have flirted with their own merger for years.

About 2,700 record stores have closed across the country since 2003, according to the research group Almighty Institute of Music Retail. Last year the eighty-nine-store Tower Records chain, which represented 2.5% of overall retail sales, went out of business, and Musicland, which operated more than 800 stores under the Sam Goody brand, among others, filed for bankruptcy. Around 65% of all music sales now take place in big-box stores such as Wal-Mart and Best Buy, which carry fewer titles than specialty stores and put less effort behind promoting new artists.

Just a few years ago, many industry executives thought their problems could be solved by bigger hits. "There wasn't anything a good hit couldn't fix for these guys," says a source who worked closely with top executives earlier this decade. "They felt like things were bad and getting worse, but I'm not sure they had the bandwidth to figure out how to fix it. Now, very few of those people are still heads of the companies."

More record executives now seem to understand that their problems are structural: The Internet appears to be the most consequential technological shift for the business of selling music since the 1920s, when phonograph records replaced sheet music as the industry's profit center. "We have to collectively understand that times have changed," says Lyor Cohen, CEO of Warner Music Group USA. In June, Warner announced a deal with the Website *Lala.com* that will allow consumers to stream much of its catalog for free, in hopes that they will then pay for downloads. It's the latest of recent major-label moves that would have been unthinkable a few years back: In May, one of the four majors, EMI, began allowing the iTunes Music Store to sell its catalog without the copy protection that labels have insisted upon for years. When YouTube started showing music videos without permission, all four of the labels made licensing deals instead of suing for copyright violations. To the dismay of some artists and managers, labels are insisting on deals for many artists in which the companies get a portion of touring, merchandising, product sponsorships, and other non-recorded-music sources of income.

So who killed the record industry as we knew it? "The record companies have created this situation themselves," says Simon Wright, CEO of Virgin Entertainment Group, which operates Virgin Megastores. While there are factors outside of the labels' control—from the rise of the Internet to the popularity of video games and DVDs—many in the industry see the last seven years as a series of botched opportunities. And among the biggest, they say, was the labels' failure to address online piracy at the beginning by making peace with the first file-sharing service, Napster. "They left billions and billions of dollars on the table by suing Napster—that was the moment that the labels killed themselves," says Jeff Kwatinetz, CEO of management company The Firm. "The record business had an unbelievable opportunity there. They were all using the same service. It was as if everybody was listening to the same radio station. Then Napster shut down, and all those 30 or 40 million people went to other [file-sharing services]."

It all could have been different: Seven years ago, the music industry's top executives gathered for secret talks with Napster CEO Hank Barry. At a July 15th, 2000, meeting, the execs—including the CEO of Universal's parent company, Edgar Bronfman Jr.; Sony Corporation head Nobuyuki Idei; and Bertelsmann chief Thomas Middelhof—sat in a hotel in Sun Valley, Idaho, with Barry and told him that they wanted to strike licensing deals with Napster. "Mr. Idei started the meeting," recalls Barry, now a director in the law firm Howard Rice. "He was talking about how Napster was something the customers wanted." The idea was to let Napster's 38 million users keep downloading for a monthly subscription fee—roughly $10—with revenues split between the service and the labels. But ultimately, despite a public offer of $1 billion from Napster, the companies never reached a settlement. "The record companies needed to jump off a cliff, and they couldn't bring themselves to jump," says Hilary Rosen, who was then CEO of the Recording Industry Association of America. "A lot of people say, 'The labels were dinosaurs and idiots, and what was the matter with them?' But they had retailers telling them, 'You better not sell anything online cheaper than in a store,' and they had artists saying, 'Don't screw up my WalMart sales.'" Adds Jim Guerinot, who manages Nine Inch Nails and Gwen Stefani, "Innovation meant cannibalizing their core business."

Even worse, the record companies waited almost two years after Napster's July 2nd, 2001 shutdown before licensing a user-friendly legal alternative to unauthorized file-sharing services: Apple's iTunes Music Store, which launched in the spring of 2003. Before that, labels started their own subscription services: PressPlay, which initially offered only Sony, Universal, and EMI music; and MusicNet, which had only EMI, Warner, and BMG music. The services failed. They were expensive, allowed little or no CD burning, and didn't work with many MP3 players then on the market.

(Continues)

Rosen and others see that 2001–03 period as disastrous for the business. "That's when we lost the users," Rosen says. "Peer-to-peer took hold. That's when we went from music having real value in people's minds to music having no economic value, just emotional value."

In the fall of 2003, the RIAA filed its first copyright-infringement lawsuits against file sharers. They've since sued more than 20,000 music fans. The RIAA maintains that the lawsuits are meant to spread the word that unauthorized downloading can have consequences. "It isn't being done on a punitive basis," says RIAA CEO Mitch Bainwol. But file-sharing isn't going away—there was a 4.4% increase in the number of peer-to-peer users in 2006, with about a billion tracks downloaded illegally per month, according to research group BigChampagne.

Despite the industry's woes, people are listening to at least as much music as ever. Consumers have bought more than 100 million iPods since their November 2001 introduction, and the touring business is thriving, earning a record $437 million last year. And according to research organization NPD Group, listenership to recorded music— whether from CDs, downloads, video games, satellite radio, terrestrial radio, online streams, or other sources—has increased since 2002. The problem the business faces is how to turn that interest into money. "How is it that the people that make the product of music are going bankrupt, while the use of the product is skyrocketing?" asks The Firm's Kwatinetz. "The model is wrong."

Kwatinetz sees other, leaner kinds of companies—from management firms like his own, which now doubles as a record label, to outsiders such as Starbucks—stepping in. Paul McCartney recently abandoned his longtime relationship with EMI Records to sign with Starbucks' fledgling Hear Music. Video-game giant Electronic Arts also started a label, exploiting the promotional value of its games, and the newly revived CBS Records will sell music featured in CBS TV shows.

Licensing music to video games, movies, TV shows, and online subscription services is becoming an increasing source of revenue. "We expect to be a brand licensing organization," says Cohen of Warner, which in May started a new division, Den of Thieves, devoted to producing TV shows and other video content from its music properties. And the record companies are looking to increase their takes in the booming music publishing business, which collects songwriting royalties from radio play and other sources. The performance-rights organization ASCAP reported a record $785 million in revenue in 2006, a 5% increase from 2005. Revenues are up "across the board," according to Martin Bandier, CEO of Sony/ATV Music Publishing, which controls the Beatles' publishing. "Music publishing will become a more important part of the business," he says. "If I worked for a record company, I'd be pulling my hair out. The recorded-music business is in total confusion, looking for a way out."

Nearly every corner of the record industry is feeling the pain. "A great American sector has been damaged enormously," says the RIAA's Bainwol, who blames piracy, "from songwriters to backup musicians to people who work at labels. The number of bands signed to labels has been compromised in a pretty severe fashion, roughly a third." Times are hard for record-company employees. "People feel threatened," says Rosen. "Their friends are getting laid off left and right." Adam Shore, general manager of the then-Atlantic Records-affiliated Vice Records, told *Rolling Stone* in January that his colleagues are having an "existential crisis." "We have great records, but we're less sure than ever that people are going to buy them" he says. "There's a sense around here of losing faith."

Discussion Questions

1. Sales of recordings are down, but people are listening to more music. What accounts for these two seemingly contradictory facts, according to Hiatt and Serpick? How would Diamond account for the contradiction?

2. Diamond argues that several factors are responsible for people's acceptance or rejection of innovation. How do some of these factors explain the decline of the record industry?

3. Explain why some people argue that music has no economic value to the artists, backup musicians, and record company employees who have lost their source of income because of file sharing. Why do you feel that this activity should or should not be illegal?

In Touch Too Much?

Essay

MARY MACVEAN

Mary MacVean has been an editor for the Los Angeles Times, *with assignments on subjects such as health and cooking. Some of her recent articles are "Concrete Hiking" (2016), "It Doesn't Have to Hurt" (2015), and "Is This the Funniest Workout in LA?" (2016).*

The big deadline for high school seniors to choose a college has passed, and parents' thoughts are turning toward the joy of less laundry or the agony of how to pay the bills—and perhaps toward how much they'll be in touch with their sons and daughters come September. It was not so long ago that parents drove a teenager to campus, said a tearful goodbye, and returned home to wait a week or so for a phone call from the dorm. Mom or Dad, in turn, might write letters—yes, with pens, on stationery.

But going to college these days means never having to say goodbye, thanks to near-saturation of cellphones, e-mail, instant messaging, texting, Facebook, and Skype. Researchers are looking at how new technology may be delaying the point at which college-bound students truly become independent from their parents, and how phenomena such as the introduction of unlimited calling plans have changed the nature of parent-child relationships, and not always for the better. Students walking from biology class to the gym can easily fill a few minutes with a call to Mom's office to whine about a professor's lecture. Dad can pass along family news via e-mail. Daily text messaging is not uncommon. How nice, you might think. And you might be right. Some research suggests that today's young adults are closer to their parents than their predecessors. But it's complicated. Sherry Turkle, a professor at the Massachusetts Institute of Technology whose specialty is technology and relationships, calls this a particular sort of "Huck Finn moment," in which Huck "takes his parents with him. We all sail down the Mississippi together."

From the electronic grade monitoring many high schools offer parents, it seems a small leap to keep electronic track of their (adult) children's schedules or to set reminders about deadlines or assignments. Professors have figured out that some kids are e-mailing papers home for parents to edit. And Skype and Facebook might be more than just chances to see a face that's missed at home; parents can peer into their little darling's messy dorm room or his messy social life. Experts said the change dates to 9/11, which upped parents' anxiety over being out of touch with their children. And the rising cost of college can threaten parents' willingness to let children make mistakes as they learn how to be adults. Many of today's college students have had so much of their schedule programmed, they may not know what to do with time and solitude, say Barbara Hofer, a Middlebury College psychology professor and author with Abigail Sullivan Moore of the book *The iConnected Parent*.

Researchers are looking at these changing relationships, formed in the last few years after parents got smartphones and Facebook accounts too—and learned how to use them. "There's a tremendous diversity in how kids handle this. Some maintain old rules. But for many, many young people, they grow up essentially with the idea that they don't have to separate from their parents," Turkle says. "It's about having an adolescence that doesn't include the kind of separation that we used to consider part of adolescence," she adds. "Something has become the norm that was considered pathological."

Hofer and colleagues surveyed students at Middlebury in Vermont and at the University of Michigan, two schools different in many ways. But at both, parents and students were in contact frequently, an average of more than thirteen times a week. "The one thing I've tried hard to do is not make this a helicopter story and not make it all negative," Hofer said in a telephone interview. "The quality of relationships that many students have with their parents is really quite remarkable. That's reported from parents and students." The complicated dance toward independence creates all sorts of tricky moments for both generations. The parents of today's college students were advised to get involved in the children's lives—to communicate, communicate, communicate. All that talk can signal a close, useful relationship, but it also can leave kids lacking what they need to fend for themselves. "The parent is on speed dial, the parent is on favorites. It's about having an adolescence that doesn't include the kind of separation that we used to consider part of adolescence," Turkle says. "It opens them up to real vulnerabilities now and later in life."

Parents are not always eager for such separation, Hofer said. "We just heard so many stories, campus after campus, of parents crossing boundaries," she said. By intervening in roommate disputes or sending daily text reminders of class work to be done, parents perpetuate a

(Continues)

feeling that the students needn't think for themselves because someone else is perfectly willing—even gleeful—to do it for them. Have you seen the TV commercial in which two young women try to deal with an abundantly overflowing washing machine? In the end, one of them calls dad. His advice? Unplug it. A parent might laugh and cry at the thought that a young adult couldn't figure that out. Hofer cited a student who said she wasn't homesick freshman year, but sophomore year her mother learned to use Skype and placed the computer on the kitchen floor so her daughter could see the family dog when it walked by. "That brought me right back into my mom's kitchen," the daughter told Hofer, and the young woman said she was homesick for the first time.

One recent evening, eight Pomona College students gathered around a table to talk about how "connected" they were to their parents. They were in touch through e-mail or text or Skype—technologies that some parents learned through their kids. Several said keeping in touch made the transition to college easier. Freshman Tim Kung, from San Diego, said his parents "were actually very considerate" about his desire to "unfriend" them from Facebook. Talking less frequently makes their conversations more meaningful, he said. It's tough for parents to avoid the temptation to step in when they learn from a Facebook post, as Edward Chuchla, whose daughter graduated in May from Pomona, put it in a telephone interview, "about how stressful it was writing Version 927 of a politics thesis." Sometimes, he said, he takes the bait. "If they post something provocative, we pick up the phone," he said. "We just call back to tell them we love them, and we're here if they need us."

Jamie Garcia, a freshman from Rosemead, said she's friends with her mother on Facebook, but added, "I'm not worried because she doesn't know how it works. She has like five friends." Her mother, Susan, however, is adept at texting. "I get a text from my mom every night, saying goodnight. So I text her back good night, like I'm alive; I made it through the day," Jamie said. Susan Garcia said later that she's reassured by the idea that she can reach her daughter easily. Even though Jamie moved only 35 miles and her family attends her softball games, they don't spend much time together, Susan Garcia said.

Katie Bent, a sophomore, calls home to Seattle weekly. "For me, I would love to be in contact with my parents very frequently, but I also feel like this is the time I'm supposed to be learning how to function without them," she said. "So last semester I completely destroyed my glasses at one point. That probably would have been a perfect time to deal with it, to find an optometrist in the area. What I did was call my mom, and said, 'Oh my God, Mom. What am I going to do?'" Mom found an optometrist. Katie's father, Sam, said that while he and his wife are much more in touch with Katie than he was with his own parents when he left home, he thinks it's important they not talk too often. "I know I don't call Katie unless I think it's important. She's in college; she's really busy. I don't call her up just to tell her a joke," he said. "In some sense, I'm glad she's not calling every day. She's learning to solve her own problems."

Caitlyn Hynes, the youngest of three children, has a lot of contact with her family in Upland—not only by phone or text, but also in person. Her father takes her to baseball lessons because she doesn't have a car. Caitlyn said her mother might call to say, "You should go to bed soon," which prompts Caitlyn to ask herself, "When am I actually going to be able to make these decisions for myself? I don't have two separate worlds, home and school. It's kind of like being in high school again. It's not like I don't want to hear from her, but more like needing a sense of independence."

Edward Chuchla wants to talk to his children, to feel close to them, to give counsel when asked. He and his wife also have tried to take the advice they got from the dean when they dropped off their daughter, Grace, at Pomona College four years ago: Back off; avoid being helicopter parents. "We're very careful to make sure communication happens on their terms," said Chuchla, whose son, Ben, is finishing his sophomore year at Dartmouth. Once, he said, he went too far. When his daughter left Pomona for a semester at Oxford, she had trouble getting permission to check books out of the library. The problem wasn't getting solved, so Chuchla e-mailed the foreign study office himself. When he heard from Grace, the message was, "I'll kill you if you do that again." Both generations are finding their way through the transition to adulthood as technological advances present even more new ways to connect. "We're all in this together," MIT's Turkle said. "We're all a little disoriented by these new possibilities together."

Discussion Questions

1. Why does Mary MacVean say that going away to college now means "never having to say good-bye"? Discuss the amount of time you spend communicating electronically with your parents and the topics of your conversations. How are these conversations different from or the same as the ones you had with them in high school?

(Continues)

2. When the article quotes Sherry Turkle, who suggests that the amount of college students' parent-child contact leads to a vulnerability later in life, what types of problems do you think she anticipates? Do you think she is right to be concerned? Why or why not?

3. Discuss which of Diamond's reasons for accepting innovations best explains this use of technology by parents and their college-age children. What are some reasons that this same technology might have been rejected by the same group?

From the *Los Angeles Times*, June 4, 2011 by Mary MacVean, Staff Writer. Copyright © 2011 by the Los Angeles Times. Reprinted by permission.

My Question

KEVIN KELLY

After attending the University of Rhode Island for a year, Kevin Kelly traveled extensively in Asia while working as a photographer, later publishing his photographs of little-known locales in the book Asia Grace. Kelly has worked as a writer, publisher, and editor for various publications but is probably best known for writing about digital culture and for cofounding and editing the online magazine Wired in 1993.

For most of my life I owned very little. I dropped out of college and for almost a decade wandered remote parts of Asia in cheap sneakers and worn jeans, with lots of time and no money. The cities I knew best were steeped in medieval richness; the lands I passed through were governed by ancient agricultural traditions. When I reached for a physical object, it was almost surely made of wood, fiber, or stone. I ate with my hands, trekked on foot through mountain valleys, and slept wherever. I carried very little stuff. My personal possessions totaled a sleeping bag, a change of clothes, a penknife, and some cameras. Living close to the land, I experienced the immediacy that opens up when the buffer of technology is removed. I got colder often, hotter more frequently, soaking wet a lot, bitten by insects faster, and synchronized more quickly to the rhythm of the day and seasons. Time seemed abundant.

After eight years in Asia, I returned to the United States. I sold what little I had and bought an inexpensive bicycle, which I rode on a 5,000-mile meander across the American continent, west to east. The highlight was gliding through the tidy farmland of the Amish in eastern Pennsylvania. Amish communities were the closest thing I could find on this continent to the state of minimal technology I had experienced in Asia. I admired the Amish for their selective possessions. Their unadorned homes were square bundles of contentment. I felt that my own life, unencumbered by fancy technology, was in parallel to theirs, and I intended to keep technology in my life to a minimum. I arrived on the East Coast owning nothing but my bicycle.

Growing up in suburban New Jersey in the 1950s and 1960s, I was surrounded by technology. But until I was 10, my family had no television, and when it did arrive in our household, I had no appetite for it. I saw how it worked on my friends. The technology of TV had

(Continues)

a remarkable ability to beckon people at specific times and then hold them enthralled for hours. Its creative commercials told them to acquire more technologies. They obeyed. I noticed that other bossy technologies, such as the car, also seemed to be able to get people to serve them, and to prod them to acquire and use still more technologies (freeways, drive-in theaters, fast food). I decided to keep technology to a minimum in my own life. As a teenager, I was having trouble hearing my own voice, and it seemed to me my friends' true voices were being drowned out by the loud conversations technology was having with itself. The less I participated in the circular logic of technology, the straighter my own trajectory could become.

When my cross-country bike ride ended, I was 27. I retreated to an out-of-the-way plot of cheap land in upstate New York with plenty of woods and no building codes. With a friend, I cut down oak trees to mill into lumber, and with these homemade beams we erected a house. We nailed each cedar shake onto the roof one by one. I have vivid memories of hauling hundreds of heavy rocks to build a retaining wall, which the overflowing creek tore down more than once. With my own hands I moved those stones many times. With yet more stones, we assembled a huge living-room fireplace. Despite the hard work, those stones and oak beams filled me with Amish contentment.

But I was not Amish. If you were going to cut down a huge tree, I decided, it was a good idea to use a chain saw. Any forest tribesman who could get his hands on one would agree. Once you gain your voice around technology and become more sure of what you want, it becomes obvious that some technologies are simply superior to others. If my travels in the old world had taught me anything, it was that aspirin, cotton clothing, metal pots, and telephones are fantastic inventions. They are *good*. People everywhere in the world, with very few exceptions, grab them when they can. Anyone who has ever held a perfectly designed hand tool knows that it can lift your soul. Airplanes had stretched my horizons; books had opened my mind; antibiotics had saved my life; photography had ignited my muse. Even the chain saw, which can cleanly slice through knotty burls too tough for a hand ax, had instilled in me a reverence for the beauty and strength of wood no other agent in the world could.

I became fascinated by the challenge of picking the few tools that might elevate my spirit. In 1980 I freelanced for a publication (the *Whole Earth Catalog*) that used its own readers to select and recommend appropriate tools picked out of the ocean of self-serving manufactured stuff. In the 1970s and '80s, the *Whole Earth Catalog* was, in essence, a user-generated website before the Web, before computers, employing only cheap newsprint. The audience was the authors. I was thrilled by the changes that simple, well-selected tools could provoke in people's lives.

At the age of 28, I started selling mail-order budget travel guides that published low-cost information on how to enter the technologically simple realms most of the planet lived in. My only two significant possessions at the time were a bike and sleeping bag, so I borrowed a friend's computer (an early Apple II) to automate my fledgling moonlight business, and I got a cheap telephone modem to transmit my text to the printer. A fellow editor at the *Whole Earth Catalog* with an interest in computers slipped me a guest account that allowed me to remotely join an experimental teleconferencing system being run by a college professor at the New Jersey Institute of Technology. I soon found myself immersed in something altogether bigger and wilder: the frontier of an online community. It was a new continent more alien to me than Asia, and I began to report on it as if it were an exotic travel destination. To my immense surprise, I found that these high-tech computer networks were not deadening the souls of early users like me; they were filling our souls. There was something unexpectedly organic about these ecosystems of people and wires. Out of complete nothingness, we were barn-raising a virtual commonwealth. When the Internet finally came along a few years later, it seemed almost Amish to me.

As computers moved to the center of our lives, I discovered something I had not noticed about technology before. In addition to technology's ability to satisfy (and create) desires, and to occasionally save labor, it did something else. It brought new opportunities. Right before my eyes I saw online networks connect people with ideas, options, and other people they could not possibly have met otherwise. Online networks unleashed passions, compounded creativity, amplified generosity. At the very cultural moment when pundits declared that writing was dead, millions began writing online more than they ever had written before. Exactly when the experts declared people would only bowl alone, millions began to gather together in large numbers. Online they collaborated, cooperated, shared, and created in myriad unexpected ways. This was new to me. Cold silicon chips, long metal wires, and complicated high-voltage gear were nurturing our best efforts as humans. Once I noticed how online computers stirred the muses

(Continues)

and multiplied possibilities, I realized that other technologies, such as automobiles, chain saws, biochemistry, and yes, even television, did the same in slightly different ways. For me, this gave a very different face to technology.

I was very active on early teleconference systems, and in 1984, based on my virtual online presence, I was hired by the *Whole Earth Catalog* to help edit the first consumer publication that reviewed personal computer software. (I believe I might have been the first person in the world hired online.) A few years later, I got involved in launching the first public gateway to the emerging internet, an online portal called the Well. In 1992, I helped found *Wired* magazine—the official bullhorn of digital culture—and curated its content for its first seven years. Ever since, I've hung out on the cusp of technological adoption. My friends now are the folks inventing supercomputers, genetic pharmaceuticals, search engines, nanotechnology, fiber-optic communications—everything that is new. I see the transforming power of technology everywhere I look.

Yet I don't have a PDA, a smartphone, or Bluetooth anything. I don't twitter. My three kids grew up without TV, and we still don't have broadcast or cable in our home. I don't have a laptop or travel with a computer, and I am often the last in my circle to get the latest must-have gadget. I ride my bike more often than I drive these days. I see my friends leashed to their vibrating handhelds, but I continue to keep the cornucopia of technology at arm's length so that I can more easily remember who I am. At the same time, I run a popular daily website called *Cool Tools*, which is a continuation of my long-ago *Whole Earth* job evaluating selected technology for the empowerment of individuals. A river of artifacts flows through my studio sent by vendors hoping for an endorsement; a fair number of those artifacts never leave. I am surrounded by stuff. Despite my wariness, I have chosen to deliberately position myself to keep the maximum number of technological options within my reach.

I acknowledge that my relationship with technology is full of contradictions. And I suspect they are your contradictions, too. Our lives today are strung with a profound and constant tension between the virtues of more technology and the personal necessity of less: Should I get my kid this gadget? Do I have time to master this labor-saving device? And more deeply: What *is* this technology taking over my life, anyway? What is this global force that elicits both our love and repulsion? How should we approach it? Can we resist it, or is each and every new technology inevitable? Does the relentless avalanche of new things deserve my support or my skepticism—and will my choice even matter?

I needed some answers to guide me through my technological dilemma. And the first question I faced was the most basic. I realized I had no idea what technology really *was*. What was its essence? If I didn't understand the basic nature of technology, then as each new piece of it came along, I would have no frame of reference to decide how weakly or strongly to embrace it.

My uncertainty about the nature of technology and my own con-flicted relationship with it sent me on a seven-year quest. My investiga-tions took me back to the beginning of time and ahead to the distant future. I delved deeply into technology's history, and I listened to futur-ists in Silicon Valley, where I live, spin out imaginative scenarios for what will come next. I interviewed some of technology's fiercest critics and its most ardent fans. I returned to rural Pennsylvania to spend more time with the Amish. I traveled to mountain villages in Laos, Bhutan, and western China to listen to the poor who lack material goods, and I visited the labs of rich entrepreneurs trying to invent things that every-one will consider essential in a few years.

The more closely I looked at the conflicting tendencies of technol-ogy, the bigger the questions became. Our confusion over technology usually starts with a very specific concern: Should we allow human cloning? Is constant texting making our kids dumb? Do we want auto-mobiles to park themselves? But as my quest evolved, I realized that if we want to find satisfying answers to those questions, we first need to consider technology as a whole. Only by listening to technology's story, divining its tendencies and biases, and tracing its current direction can we hope to solve our personal puzzles.

Discussion Questions

1. According to Kevin Kelly, how does technology change peo-ple's relationship with their environment and the earth's natural rhythms? Why do you or do you not consider the kind of synchron-icity he experienced to be important? Why would you or would you not personally like to spend some time wandering in an unfamiliar, remote place?

2. What are the inventions that Kelly thinks are "good" and that he willingly uses? Do his choices reflect any of the factors that Diamond says influence a society's reasons for adopting a new

(Continues)

technology? If so, explain which factor you feel underlies Kelly's use of these particular technologies. If not, how would you explain his embracing of these inventions?

3. Why do some people, including the author, feel that Kelly's relationship with technology is contradictory? How does Kelly explain his position on the use of technological inventions? If you had to ask the questions he asks before purchasing your latest technological items, what things would you have eliminated and what things would you still own? Explain.

4. What are the "big" questions regarding technology that Kelly identifies? What is his plan for answering them? How might factors that Diamond identifies change these answers?

Student Essay 1

Essay

"Accepting or Rejecting Innovation" is an essay written by Jared Diamond. The title is self-explanatory; you're either accepting or rejecting inventions. Diamond explains when new technology has been discovered that the next step is trying to persuade society to adopt it. The author is concerned with what promotes the acceptance of inventions by a society. He states three factors of what may cause people to either reject or accept new technologies. Also, he uses great examples to further explain his factors. According to Diamond, economic advantage, social value and prestige, and vested interests cause people to reject new technologies. To a great extent, I think his reasons for explaining why people reject new innovations of all kinds—new products, new ideas, and new ways of doing things.

Economic advantage causes people to reject new technology. The new inventions are supposed to make life less complicated, easier, or faster. However, the newer inventions cost a lot more money. In Wendell Berry's article titled *Why I Will Not Buy A Computer*, he explains his reasons for not buying a computer. One of Berry's reasons is that a computer would cost him more money. A step that comes with purchasing new innovations requires individuals to discard the "old model". However, he finds his writing tools more valuable than having a computer. His writing tools are the Royal Standard typewriter, and his wife. His wife works alongside with Berry; she critiques and reads his work. A computer wouldn't make his work better, be able to understand him, or be able to critique his work. Computers are even more expensive with all the advanced components, and programs being added. Some people would rather not spend money on expensive inventions. Some people would rather save their money. This is why economic advantage causes people to reject new technologies and why I agree to a great extent with Diamond.

People reject new technologies because of social value and prestige. In this generation, individuals are buying all the latest gadgets, clothes, and items to fit in. People do things because everyone else is doing, or buying that certain item. However, individuals like myself, feel like they can be different and choose not to follow what everybody else is doing and buying. For example, my father doesn't need to have a high-tech cell phone. My dad rocks his flip-phone, and has no problem with it. He feels as long as his phone can make calls and answer calls, then he's

(Continues)

just fine. People don't deal well with how-to manuals, and instruction manuals. People would rather just have everything simple and easy. For myself, I grew up in a Christian household. I was taught to not conform to the way of the world, and to be different than everybody else. It relates to the social value and prestige of new inventions. Individuals would be considered cool if they have a touch screen phone, and would be considered the opposite if you have a rinky-dink phone. Some people would rather not fall into what society is doing, and would rather be different. Because of social value and prestige, people reject new technologies.

Vested interests are another reason, which causes people to reject new technologies. Individuals will always try to come up with inventions. But some inventions would be pointless to have now. Some of the televisions being made now; what's the reason for owning three-dimensional television. People can only view disc movies on three-dimensional. Three-dimensional televisions should only be at movie theaters. Is it going to affect the people that don't have a three-dimensional TV? Will there be no channels for those without? Life would be the same without one. Today, society wants to make appliances, cell phones, and objects smarter than us. Society wants to make appliances that would be pointless to have. Every now and then, somebody's creating something that would just be a vested interest. Some of the inventions being made, people don't need them. Creating vested interests is another reason why people reject new inventions.

In conclusion, people don't need all the latest inventions to have a great life. The factors give explanations why people reject new inventions. I agree to a high extent, because people would rather save their money, be different, and just would rather have simple inventions that are easy to use. Honestly, the people that accept these inventions because of Diamond's reasons are constantly wasting their money, and always trying to fit in as the world changes. Life can still be good with simple inventions. Wendell Berry quoted, " I do not see that computers are bringing us one step nearer to anything that does matter to me: peace, economic justice, ecological health, political honesty, family and community stability, good work." people are worried about having the next big item when we should be worried about things that mean the most. Not only computers, but also all other gadgets, are making people less social, and creating less communication.

Use the following steps to evaluate the essay. For help, turn to Part 2 in this book to review the parts of an academic essay.

1. Check to see if the introduction gives the title of Diamond's essay and his name as the author.

2. Underline the sentences that make up the directed summary portion of the introduction. Check to see if the directed summary answers the first question of the writing topic.

3. Look for the thesis statement in the introduction (it should be the last sentence) and underline it twice. Does it give the subject of Diamond's essay, Diamond's point of view on the subject, and the student's point of view? If not, what is missing?

4. Look carefully at each body paragraph. For each paragraph, underline the topic sentence. Then, put boxes around the evidence (a specific example or fact). Finally, underline twice the sentence or sentences that link the paragraph to the thesis statement.

5. Which body paragraph is the best of the essay? What makes it the best?

6. Which body paragraph is the weakest? What does it need to be better?

7. Make a list of the three most important things you think need to be done to make this student's essay more successful.

Student Essay 2

Essay

INNOVATIONS ACCEPTED OR REJECTED

In "Accepting or Rejecting Innovation" by Jared Diamond the question of why some inventions are accepted by society is posed. Many factors come into play when discussing why inventions are accepted or not by society. Technology keeps advancing with new products coming out constantly, but not everyone buys new technology. People buy according to their preference, but not everyone chooses to buy new inventions. For the most part in today's time people do not want to fall behind on the latest gadgets. Therefore, people are constantly updating their technologies such as phones. People have become very dependent on gadgets and inventions that are meant to make our lives easier.

(Continues)

However, what is it about certain inventions that make people want to have the new products and what is popular. Some inventions are good, but do not get accepted by the people. Inventions are rejected because of influences they have on the economy affect, their prestige, and vested interest.

An invention that is really successful can have a positive affect on the economy, because of the circular flow of income and expenditures. If a company does very well with their products they will have more resources and more workers. Therefore, if there are more workers that means they have more money to spend back into the circular flow. On the opposing side there can be a good invention, but if it means having to spend money then it will not be accepted. A lack of resources can cause an invention to not be conventional. For example, some "Native American cultures in ancient Mexico invented wheeled vehicles with axels as toys" as Diamond stated, but not for real life use. They lacked the animals to be able to pull wheeled vehicles so they did not adapt that invention because it would not be beneficial to them. Inventions have to be profitable, and the companies of these inventions are most likely spending good money on marketing their products, and convincing people that they need their product. People are gullible and easily lured by ads into buying something that one does not even need, such as a newer version of a software or a car of the year. As technology keeps advancing so will inventions, which have an affect on the economy. If the affect is a negative one then people wont be interested in the invention.

Inventions or products that already hold a prestigious value are bound to not get rejected. People follow trends and the popular companies make products even more prestigious. For example, Starbucks coffee, Apple, and Nike, are all massive companies that have had huge success over time. When they were small companies first starting out they most likely did not have a lot off popularity. However, now we see people walking around in their Nike free runs with a Starbucks coffee in one hand and an iPhone in the other. The prestige of products and inventions make them even more wanted by people. If you ask someone if they would prefer a pair of Nike shoes over a pair of some other generic brand they would most likely pick the Nikes. The other pair of shoes would be rejected, because they do not hold up to the social value. People want the best and to be up to date on the latest fashions and technologies. If someone does not have an iPhone it is like they are missing out it seems like it is part of the norm to have what everyone else has. One has to stay up to date on all off the latest innovations, because we will be seen different. For example in "The Highs of Low Technology" by Johanne Mednick she uses her bike as a representation of how society looks at people who are living in the stone age per say. She has an old bike that she gets asked about often like where she got it because its old and something not seen anymore. Most people would probably want to be riding around a top of the line bike just because it is cool and what everyone else has. The newer bikes have many advancements that people see as necessary and are designed very well to appeal to the eye. Therefore, inventions and products with a quality name behind it will be accepted more easily, because of the prestige built up by the people.

The masses of the people are who the big companies are targeting to sell their inventions too, so they are constantly investing in producing innovations that people will likely pick up on. Some innovations may be admirable, however they will not do well in the market if the people or companies see that there is no profit. The ideas that are good but do not have a positive reaction with the people are usually because it means some sort of change or wasting money. Electric cars, for example, are good for the environment and would save money on gas. However, why do we not see electric cars in everyone's garages yet, well because electric cars do not satisfy people's needs. Electric cars also means that places to charge them are needed, and that would mean spending to have to install these charging spots. Gas stations already exist and it is what people are accustomed to, so changing to an electric car would be inconvenient. Electric cars do not go fast, and are not very appealing, so people do not accept them because they rather be driving a better looking car. Inventions that are rejected are usually ones that are unappealing and do not have benefit for the people. After all people buy what they want and need, and if certain products or innovations do not appeal to the buyers then it will not do well in the market.

The purpose of inventions is mainly to be an advancement and a positive thing to the consumers. That is why the people trying to get their inventions out need to make their products appeal to the people. The people have to see that the invention will benefit them in many ways, because if it does not it will simply be rejected. Many people claim to have the next big thing or ideas, but it usually takes time for an invention to be complete at its most beneficial selling point. Inventions as Diamond explains wont be accepted unless they have prestige or a positive affect in the economy. If the new products are not what

(Continues)

everyone is using they will most likely be rejected, because the of social status. In today's society we are lured by ads everywhere that are advertisements trying to sell us the latest things. Which makes it hard for people to ignore the latest technologies, however we only see ads for the already popular brands and inventions. Other inventions do not have a chance with the already existing ones, and are denied. There are many inventions, innovations, and advancements being made, but not all of them are successes. The inventions rejected do not meet the high standards of peoples needs. The way our society is and views things make inventions and technologies be accepted or rejected because of the nature of the consumers. We want the best brands and newest technologies that we dive into the pool of popular innovations. People want what others have and what is popular leading to the rejection of those unknown inventions, along with the economic standing and reputation of the new technologies.

Use the following steps to evaluate the essay. For help, turn back to Part 2 in this book to review the parts of an academic essay.

1. Check to see if the introduction gives the title of Diamond's essay and his name as the author.

2. Underline the sentences that make up the directed summary portion of the introduction. Check to see if the directed summary answers the first question of the writing topic.

3. Look for the thesis statement in the introduction (it should be the last sentence) and underline it twice. Does it give the subject of Diamond's essay, Diamond's point of view on the subject, and the student's point of view? If not, what is missing?

4. Look carefully at each body paragraph. For each paragraph, underline the topic sentence. Then, put boxes around the evidence (a specific example or fact). Finally, underline twice the sentence or sentences that link the paragraph to the thesis statement.

5. Which body paragraph is the best of the essay? What makes it the best?

6. Which body paragraph is the weakest? What does it need to be better?

7. Make a list of the three most important things you think need to be done to make this student's essay more successful.

Assignment 3

Use the activity pages and guidelines in this unit to read, annotate, analyze, and respond to the reading selection "Staying Put" and the writing topic that follows it. If you make full use of all of the guiding activity pages that follow, they will guide you through the writing process—the prewriting, drafting, revising, and editing that we hope you have come to see as indispensable. And, as in previous units, much of the material that you produce as you complete these activity pages will be usable, in some form, in the draft of your essay. The more time and thought you put into the unit as a whole, the more successful your essay will be.

Staying Put

Essay

SCOTT RUSSELL SANDERS

> *Scott Russell Sanders is a Distinguished Professor Emeritus of English at Indiana University. He has been awarded fellowships from the Guggenheim Foundation and the National Endowment for the Arts, and in 2012 he was elected to the American Academy of Arts and Sciences. He is a prolific writer of both fiction and nonfiction. His most recent books are* Divine Animal: A Novel *(2014), and a collection of eco-science fiction stories titled* Dancing in Dreamtime *(2016).*

As a boy in Ohio, I knew a farm family, the Millers, who not only saw but suffered from three tornadoes. The father, mother, and two sons were pulling into their driveway after church when the first tornado hoisted up their mobile home, spun it around, and carried it off. With the insurance money, they built a small frame house on the same spot. Several years later, a second tornado peeled off the roof, splintered the garage, and rustled two cows. The younger of the sons, who was in my class at school, told me that he had watched from the barn as the twister passed through, "And it never even mussed up my hair." The Millers rebuilt again, raising a new garage on the old foundation and adding another story to the house. That upper floor was reduced to kindling by

(Continues)

a third tornado, which also pulled out half the apple trees and slurped water from the stock pond. Soon after that, I left Ohio, snatched away by college as forcefully as by any cyclone. Last thing I heard, the family was preparing to rebuild yet again.

Why did the Millers refuse to move? I knew them well enough to say they were neither stupid nor crazy. After the garage disappeared, the father hung a sign from the mailbox that read: Tornado Alley. He figured the local terrain would coax future whirlwinds in their direction. Then why not move? Plain stubbornness was a factor: These were people who, once settled, might have remained at the foot of a volcano or on the bank of a flood-prone river or beside an earthquake fault. They had relatives nearby, helpful neighbors, jobs and stores and schools within a short drive, and those were all good reasons to stay. But the main reason they stayed, I believe, was that the Millers had invested so much of their lives in the land, planting orchards and gardens, spreading manure on the fields, digging ponds, building sheds, seeding pastures. This farm was not just so many acres of dirt, easily exchanged for an equal amount elsewhere; it was a particular place, intimately known, worked on, dreamed over, cherished.

Psychologists tell us that we answer trouble with one of two impulses, either fight or flight. I believe that the Millers exhibited a third instinct, that of staying put. When the pain of leaving behind what we know outweighs the pain of embracing it, or when the power we face is overwhelming and neither fight nor flight will save us, there may be salvation in sitting still. And if salvation is impossible, then at least, before perishing, we may gain a clearer vision of where we are. By sitting still, I do not mean the paralysis of dread, like that of a rabbit frozen beneath the dive of a hawk. I mean something like reverence, a respectful waiting, a deep attentiveness to forces much greater than our own. If indulged only for a moment, this reverent impulse may amount to little; but if sustained for months and years, as by the Millers on their farm, it may yield marvels. The Millers knew better than to fight a tornado, and they chose not to flee. Their commitment may have been foolhardy, but it was also grand. I suspect that most human achievements worth admiring are the result of such commitment, such devotion.

These tornado memories dramatize a choice we are faced with constantly: whether to go or stay, whether to move to a situation that is safer, richer, easier, more attractive, or to stick with what we have and make what we can of it. If the shine goes off our marriage, our house, our car, do we trade it for a new one? If the fertility leaches out of our soil, the creativity out of our job, the money out of our pockets, do we start over somewhere else? There are voices enough, both inner and outer, urging us to deal with difficulties by pulling up stakes and heading for new territory. I know them well, for they have been calling to me all my days. Claims for the virtues of moving on are familiar and seductive to Americans, this nation founded by immigrants and shaped by restless seekers. I wish to raise here a contrary voice, to say a few words on behalf of staying put, of learning the ground, of going deeper.

Exile usually suggests banishment, a forced departure from one's homeland. Famines and tyrants and wars do indeed force entire populations to flee; but most people who move, especially within the industrialized world, do so by choice. Novelist Salman Rushdie chose to leave his native India for England. In his book of essays *Imaginary Homelands*, he celebrates "the migrant sensibility": "The effect of mass migrations has been the creation of radically new types of human being: people who root themselves in ideas rather than places, in memories as much as in material things" (Rushdie 124). I quarrel with Rushdie because he articulates as eloquently as anyone the orthodoxy that I wish to counter: Rushdie's belief that movement is inherently good, staying put is bad; that uprooting brings tolerance, while rootedness breeds intolerance; that imaginary homelands are preferable to geographical ones; that to be modern, enlightened, fully of our time is to be displaced. Wholesale dis-placement may be inevitable; but we should not suppose that it occurs without disastrous consequences for the earth and for ourselves. People who root themselves in places are likelier to know and care for those places than are people who root themselves in ideas. When we cease to be migrants and become inhabitants, we might begin to pay enough heed and respect to where we are. By settling in, we have a chance of making a durable home for ourselves, our fellow creatures, and our descendants.

To become intimate with your home region, to know the territory as well as you can, to understand your life as woven into the local life does not prevent you from recognizing and honoring the diversity of other places, cultures, and ways. On the contrary, how can you value other places if you do not have one of your own? If you are not yourself *placed*, then you wander the world like a sightseer, a collector of sensations, with no gauge for measuring what you see. Local knowledge is the grounding for global knowledge.

(Continues)

Work Cited

Rushdie, Salman. *Imaginary Homelands: Essays and Criticism* 1981–1991. New York: Grant a-Viking Penguin, 1991. Print.

Writing Topic

According to Sanders, what are the benefits of "staying put"? Do you agree with his viewpoint? To support your position, be sure to use specific evidence taken from your own experiences, observations, or readings.

Vocabulary and Dictionary Practice

Part I.

Look up the following words used in "Staying Put." For each, write the two most common definitions on the lines provided, and include what part of speech each definition is (noun, verb, adjective, etc.). Then, under each of the two definitions, write a sentence that uses the word in a way that reflects that particular definition and part of speech.

1. hoist
2. rustle
3. kindling
4. slurp
5. cherish
6. salvation
7. perish
8. reverent
9. paralysis
10. foolhardy
11. leach
12. contrary
13. exile
14. sensibility
15. orthodox
16. heed
17. durable

  1. **hoist**

    first definition: _____

    _____

    part of speech: _____

    sentence: _____

    _____

second definition: _____

_____

part of speech: _____

sentence: _____

_____

2. **rustle**

first definition: _____

_____

part of speech: _____

sentence: _____

_____

second definition: _____

_____

part of speech: _____

sentence: _____

_____

3. **kindling**

first definition: _____

_____

part of speech: _____

sentence: _____

_____

second definition: _____

_____

part of speech: _____

sentence: _____

_____

4. **slurp**

first definition: _____

_____

part of speech: _____

sentence: _____

_____

second definition: _____

_____

part of speech: _____

sentence: _____

_____

5. **cherish**

first definition: _____

_____

part of speech: _____

sentence: _____

_____

second definition: _____

_____

part of speech: _____

sentence: _____

_____

6. **salvation**

first definition: _____

_____

part of speech: _____

sentence: _____

_____

second definition: _____

_____

part of speech: _____

sentence: _____

_____

7. **perish**

first definition: _____

_____

part of speech: _____

sentence: _____

_____

second definition: _____

_____

part of speech: _____

sentence: _____

_____

8. **reverent**

first definition: _____

_____

part of speech: _____

sentence: _____

_____

second definition: _____

_____

part of speech: _____

sentence: _____

_____

9. **paralysis**

first definition: _____

_____

part of speech: _____

sentence: _____

_____

second definition: _____

_____

part of speech: _____

sentence: _____

_____

10. **foolhardy**

first definition: _____

_____

part of speech: _____

sentence: _____

_____

second definition: _____

_____

part of speech: _____

sentence: _____

_____

11. **leach**

first definition: _____

_____

part of speech: _____

sentence: _____

_____

second definition: _____

_____

part of speech: _____

sentence: _____

_____

12. **contrary**

first definition: _____

_____

part of speech: _____

sentence: _____

_____

second definition: _____

_____

part of speech: _____

sentence: _____

_____

13. **exile**

first definition: _____

_____

part of speech: _____

sentence: _____

_____

second definition: _____

_____

part of speech: _____

sentence: _____

_____

14. **sensibility**

first definition: _____

_____

part of speech: _____

sentence: _____

_____

second definition: _____

_____

part of speech: _____

sentence: _____

_____

15. **orthodox**

   first definition: _____

   _____

   part of speech: _____

   sentence: _____

   _____

   second definition: _____

   _____

   part of speech: _____

   sentence: _____

   _____

16. **heed**

   first definition: _____

   _____

   part of speech: _____

   sentence: _____

   _____

   second definition: _____

   _____

   part of speech: _____

   sentence: _____

   _____

17. **durable**

   first definition: _____

   _____

part of speech: _____

sentence: _____

_____

second definition: _____

_____

part of speech: _____

sentence: _____

_____

Part II.

A. Write down the sentence from "Staying Put" that contains each of the following words.

B. Tell which one of the word's various definitions best fits the sentence.

C. Paraphrase the sentence without using the vocabulary word; in other words, write the sentence using your own words.

1. **hoist**

A. _____

_____

B. _____

_____

C. _____

_____

2. **rustle**

A. _____

_____

B. _____

_____

C. _____

_____

3. kindling

A. _____

_____

B. _____

_____

C. _____

_____

4. slurp

A. _____

_____

B. _____

_____

C. _____

_____

5. cherish

A. _____

_____

B. _____

_____

C. _____

_____

6. **salvation**

A. _____

_____

B. _____

_____

C. _____

_____

7. **perish**

A. _____

_____

B. _____

_____

C. _____

_____

8. **reverent**

A. _____

_____

B. _____

_____

C. _____

_____

9. **paralysis**

A. _____

_____

B. _____

_____

C. _____

_____

10. **foolhardy**

A. _____

_____

B. _____

_____

C. _____

_____

11. **leach**

A. _____

_____

B. _____

_____

C. _____

_____

12. **contrary**

A. _____

_____

B. _____

_____

C. _____

_____

13. **exile**

A. _____

_____

B. _____

_____

C. _____

_____

14. **sensibility**

A. _____

_____

B. _____

_____

C. _____

_____

15. **orthodox**

A. _____

_____

B. _____

_____

C. _____

_____

16. **heed**

A. _____

_____

B. _____

_____

C. _____

_____

17. **durable**

A. _____

_____

B. _____

_____

C. _____

_____

Part III.

For each of these words from "Staying Put," tell something new and interesting you learned about the word from the dictionary. For example, you might have found the correct way to pronounce a word you were already familiar with from reading but not from speaking, or you might have learned that a word you thought of as entirely English came from a foreign language.

1. **rustle**

_____

_____

2. **cherish**

_____

_____

3. **salvation**

_____

_____

4. **reverent**

_____

_____

5. **foolhardy**

_____

_____

6. **contrary**

_____

_____

7. **exile**

_____

_____

8. **sensibility**

_____

_____

9. **orthodox**

_____

_____

10. **heed**

_____

_____

Follow-Up Activity

Write a paragraph describing your day so far. Your description must include, underlined, at least four of the vocabulary words above. Share your paragraph with a classmate, and together write another sentence for your paragraph that contains a fifth word from the list above. The new sentence may come anywhere in the paragraph.

Doing a Careful Reading of "Staying Put"

We hope that you come to realize the importance of working systematically with a reading selection to make sure that you understand its purpose and ideas. Use the following helpful techniques for doing a thoughtful reading of an essay; they will deepen your understanding of "Staying Put" and generate some useful material for the draft you will eventually write when you respond to the writing topic.

As you work through these steps, try to commit them to memory so that they become a normal part of the writing process for you. Then, you can always use them to better comprehend any reading material you are interested in understanding well.

1. **Read the title.**
   - The title will tell you something about the reading's main topic.
   - It may also tell you something about Sanders's opinion on the topic.
   - Think about what you already know about the topic and what more you want to know.

2. **Learn about the author.**
   - Read the biographical information about Sanders at the top of the selection.
   - As you go through the remaining steps below, take note of how Sanders's life or work might connect with his topic.

3. **Read through the selection once quickly.**
   - Read quickly through the reading so that you get a general fresh impression of what it is about and what Sanders's attitude is toward the topic.
   - Notice the things—people, places, experiences, concepts, for example—he brings up to develop and support his opinion about the topic.

4. **Read again to identify the thesis.**
   - Now read the selection a second time, but more slowly and carefully, and *with a pen or highlighter in your hand.*
   - Find the thesis and underline it or write it in the margin. Remember, the thesis states Sanders's overall opinion on the topic of the reading. Often, the thesis is contained in a single sentence, but, in some cases, it takes several sentences to make the main argument of the reading selection clear. There are times, too, when the author does not state his or her thesis explicitly, but if you read the selection carefully, you should be able to state it and then write it in the margin.
   - To help, ask yourself, "What does Sanders want readers to think about his topic?"

5. **Read slowly and methodically through the rest of the reading.**
   - Examine each body paragraph one at a time, and list or underline the kinds of evidence that Sanders uses to support his thesis.
   - Look in each body paragraph for a *topic sentence*—a sentence that both presents an idea and tells how it gives support to the reading's overall opinion.
   - As you read and study the selection, *be sure to write down any thoughts you have* about Sanders's opinion and supporting evidence.
   - It is your job to evaluate this evidence for its logic and validity, so be sure to *make notes in the margins* as you read.
   - *Mark the points* that you found interesting or convincing, and write a few words explaining your thoughts.
   - Note, too, any weaknesses you find.
   - When you look back at the notes you made in the margins, you should have a general idea of how convincing you found "Staying Put" and what you found to be its strengths and weaknesses.

6. **Read again for review.**

- Once you have thought through the reading selection, read it once more, looking for places where you don't quite understand what is being said.
- Underline any terms that you aren't familiar with, and look them up in a dictionary.
- Mark any places in the reading that don't fit with your understanding of the reading as a whole. Decide whether this is something that Sanders should have revised, or whether it is something that you need to read again because you don't understand it. You may find that you need to go back to step 4 and begin working through the reading again.
- Once you are certain that you understand the entire reading, you are prepared to discuss, summarize, and/or respond to the reading with your own essay.

Follow-Up Activities

1. Survey the class to discover the number of students who "stayed put" to attend college and the number who relocated. As a class, create two lists: one of reasons to remain at home for college and another of reasons to relocate. Discuss the relative length and strength of each list. What outside factors might change or influence these lists?

2. Write one or two paragraphs telling about one of your favorite places. The place can be real or virtual. Be sure to explain as fully as you can just why this place is one of your favorite places to be. Describe it, explain some of the things you typically do in this place, tell how often you are able to go there and why, and include anything else you think is important. Then, sitting with a classmate, share your paragraph(s).

Questions to Review Your Understanding of "Staying Put"

Answer the following questions to make sure that you have a clear understanding of Sanders's argument as a whole. Be sure to respond to each as thoroughly as you can.

Paragraph 1

What natural disaster was experienced three times by the Miller family? How did they respond to these events?

Paragraph 2

What factors motivated the Millers' refusal to relocate?

Paragraph 3

What two instinctive responses to trouble do psychologists recognize? How do the Millers' reactions to their experiences correspond to these human impulses? What alternative instinct does the author, Scott Russell Sanders, believe that the Millers demonstrated?

Paragraph 4

What choice does Sanders believe we constantly face? What are some of the situations in which this choice is apparent? What do we, as a society, tend to believe is the correct choice when confronted with difficult situations? What choice does Sanders think might be better?

Paragraph 5

How do the author of "Staying Put" and Salman Rushdie disagree on the issue of migration?

Paragraph 6

How does the author feel that remaining local helps people better understand and appreciate the world?

Follow-Up Activity

Every American, unless his or her ancestors are all Native American, is either an immigrant or a descendent of immigrants, people who chose not to "stay put."

1. Make a list of reasons that you think make leaving a place essential. Explain each reason and give an example.

2. Make a list of other reasons why leaving is valid, in your opinion.

3. Make a list of unsound reasons for leaving.

4. Form small groups; compare your three lists with those of the other students in your group. Create a list of reasons that everyone in your group agrees are valid or relevant. Make another list of reasons that everyone agrees are invalid or irrelevant. Then, make a third list of the reasons your group could not put on either of the other two lists.

5. As a class, discuss the reasons on the third lists. Which items appeared on the lists of more than one group? Why is there such a difference of opinion when it comes to the reasons on this list?

Responding to the Writing Topic

You have spent time with "Staying Put" and should now have a good understanding of its ideas and overall message. It is important now to look again at the writing topic at the bottom of "Staying Put" because the essay you write must directly answer the questions in that topic. Here it is again, but this time formatted so that each part of the topic is on its own line:

Writing Topic

According to Sanders, what are the benefits of "staying put"?

Do you agree with his viewpoint?

To support your position, be sure to use specific evidence taken from your own experience, observations, or readings.

Here is a closer look at the writing topic's three parts:

- The first question asks you to summarize a specific aspect of "Staying Put." As you read the question carefully, you will notice that it uses the question word what. Keep this word in mind because your answer—your directed summary—must respond to this particular word. In other words, your summary must tell precisely *what* Sanders believes to be the benefits of "staying put."

- The second question in the writing topic asks for your opinion about Sanders's views. Do you agree that "staying put" has benefits? Do you think all of the "good" reasons Sanders offers for remaining actually result in beneficial outcomes? Do you think there are other benefits to "staying put" that Sanders does not mention? Do you think there are benefits to leaving? Do you think these benefits can or do outweigh those of staying? Your answers to these questions will help clarify your own position. Your thesis statement will result from your understanding of your own position.

- The third part of this writing topic reminds you that in building your essay, you must support your claim – your thesis statement – with examples; these examples can be taken from your own personal experience with "staying put" or leaving, your observation of others' either staying or leaving, or any reading you may have done related to remaining or going. The following activities will help you begin to find these examples. Be sure to keep notes on your ideas, your classmates' experiences shared in the classroom discussions, and the background readings you are assigned so that you can review and use this material to help you plan your essay.

Strategies to Help You Analyze a Reading Selection and Develop Your Ideas for Writing a Response

Now you are ready to build on the annotations you made in "Staying Put" and develop a more systematic analysis of its argument. To guide your writing process at this stage, look over the techniques below. Use them to form a deeper analysis of Sanders's ideas and your own. As you go through these strategies, you will begin to clarify your thinking about Sanders's essay. They will also help you to put into words your own views on the topic he writes about—that committing to a particular place is ultimately more rewarding both for ourselves and our communities.

Questioning

- Questions about the highlighting you did:
  Why did I underline this part of the reading?

  How is this information important to Sanders's point?

  What is the relationship between this information and the question I am being asked to write about?

- Questions about Sanders's ideas:
  What things in this essay do not make sense to me?

  Where do I think Sanders should have explained further?

  How do the examples in the essay relate to his point?

- Questions about "Staying Put" that seem important:
  What are some of the things that Sanders says that I am happy to hear someone say?

  What things that he says seem true to me?

  What things that he says seem wrong to me?

What thing that he says is the most important to me?

What idea in this essay is completely new to me?

Freewriting

Use freewriting now to explore your responses to the questions above:

- Pick one or more of your answers to the questions you have already answered, and just begin to write about them.
- While you are doing this writing, do not stop or censor yourself; just let the words come.
- Do this for about five or ten minutes without thinking about spelling, grammar, word choice, or even the sense of what you are saying.
- When you have completed this activity, you will want to take a break.
- After your brief break, come back and read what you have written. Most of what you now have down on paper will not end up in your essay, but, as you read through your freewriting, you will find one or more sentences or ideas that seem interesting, important, or even compelling to you. Highlight these points and ideas. Are you beginning to develop your thoughts in a way that will shape your essay?

Listing

With this strategy, you simply list all of the thoughts and reactions you have noted so far. By looking down your list, you may see a pattern of ideas develop, one that you can use to develop an essay of your own.

- List all of the annotations you made for "Staying Put."
- List the main ideas you can see in your answers to the questioning phase above.
- List any main ideas that developed from your responses to the follow-up activities above.
- Be sure to list all the items from your freewriting that you thought were interesting. As you make this list, other ideas may come to mind. Put them on your list as well.

Look over your list and group all the ideas that seem related to each other. See if you can find one related group of ideas that is longer than the others. These ideas may suggest what you want to say in response to the writing topic that follows Sanders's essay.

Shaping Your Ideas into a Rough Draft

By now, you should feel prepared to begin planning your rough draft. If you aren't, go back through some of the activities above and talk with classmates to see what they are thinking. Sometimes it takes a while before your ideas are formed enough; take as much time as you need to clarify your thoughts.

When you are ready to focus on your rough draft, you will have to think about each part of your essay and how you will compose it. Turn back to Part 2 and examine "A Suggested Structure for an Essay That Responds to Another Writer's Essay." Also, look again at the writing topic for "Staying Put." Remind yourself that it asks you to do three things:

1. **Write a summary** that identifies Sanders's argument regarding the benefits of staying put.

   Remember that you have already worked on this in earlier activities. Look back now to the work you did. You may be able to use some of it below, when you write your essay's *directed summary*.

2. **Present your position** on this idea; do you agree with Sanders's view?

   This is your thesis statement, and it will unify your essay, so it's important that you write it out clearly. Turn back to the review questions you answered and the follow-up activities you did. What were your thoughts and ideas? You will use them below when you write a thesis statement. Remember that you can always revise it as you work on your rough draft.

3. **Support and develop your position** using specific evidence taken from your own experiences and readings. In other words, explain your thinking and why you have the view you present—and don't forget to include the specific "proof" that convinced you to take the position you take.

   The explanation of your thoughts and the evidence that led you to draw those conclusions will make up nearly your entire essay. Look back to earlier exercises in this unit to remind yourself of some of the thinking you did about Sanders's argument. You will be able to use some of this as evidence to support your thesis. Remember it when you begin working on body paragraphs.

Drafting Your Directed Summary

Here is the first question in the writing topic:

According to Sanders, what are the benefits of "staying put"?

Notice that this question does **not** ask you to summarize the entire essay. Rather, it asks you to explain one aspect of Sanders's essay. The question word, the one your summary must answer directly, is **what**. You need to tell what specific benefits Sanders sees to "staying put." You do not want to include any other benefits there might be, only the ones Sanders identifies. Below are some questions that will help guide your response to the writing topic.

1. What choice does Sanders say people constantly face?

2. What qualities does Sanders believe make human achievements admirable?

3. What is the difference between people who root themselves in place and people who root themselves in ideas?

4. How does frequent movement from place to place impact neighborhoods?

5. According to Sanders, what kind of knowledge can come only from grounding in a particular place?

Now begin drafting your directed summary. You should **avoid** including any of the following in a directed summary:

1. a summary of the entire essay rather than a summary that pays attention only to what is asked for in the first question of the writing topic;

2. minor details or points that are irrelevant to the question;

3. your own opinion or ideas; and

4. examples of your own, and, unless particularly helpful, those of the author.

Follow-Up Activity

After you have written a draft of your summary, break up into small groups of three or four students. Look again at Sanders's essay. Together, study the first sentence of paragraph four. It highlights some of the qualities of the situations people seek when they move. Sanders is taking an opposing view. He is giving reasons for remaining in a situation and making the most of it. Because the writing topic asks for *only* the benefits of "staying put," there is no place in your summary for the advantages of moving to new locations. Exchange drafts, and take out a pen. Read your group member's draft. If any of the qualities mentioned in the first sentence of paragraph four appear in the draft, cross them out.

Developing Your Thesis Statement

The second question in the writing topic asks you to *evaluate* Sanders's point of view on the value of staying put, or committing to a place in spite of its drawbacks, limitations, or hardships. Do you agree with his idea that staying put reflects a deep sense of responsibility to self and to others? *Weigh the evidence* he uses to support his position. Do you agree with his view? Your answer to this will be your essay's thesis statement.

Think of your thesis as needing three parts:

• the issue being considered

• Sanders's claim about the issue

• your opinion about the issue

Fill in your answer on the line below to form your thesis statement.

The issue **and** Sanders's idea about the issue **and** your opinion about the issue

_____

_____

After you have finished writing your sentence, review your statement to see that it contains the following elements:

- identifies Sanders's argument
- makes clear your opinion about what he says

If either of these elements is missing, rewrite your thesis statement so that both are included.

Up to this point, you have been planning the draft of your introductory paragraph. Now that you have drafted your thesis statement, you can begin planning your body paragraphs. They will have to explain your ideas and give support to your thesis statement.

Developing Body Paragraphs for an Essay That Presents a Thesis

Reminders:

Body paragraphs make up the largest part of an essay.

- The job of each body paragraph is to develop one point that supports the thesis statement.
- Taken together, these points constitute the argument of the essay.
- Writing a good body paragraph can be easy once you understand the criteria that the body paragraph must fulfill.

Here is a review of the three most important requirements for paragraphs in an argumentative essay:

Parts of a Body Paragraph

An appropriate or suitable topic—one that supports the thesis statement

Evidence—for instance, a concrete fact, example, or quotation—that demonstrates the point of the paragraph

A link to the thesis—sentences that show how and why the paragraph, including the evidence, relates to the thesis

A Basic Outline Form for an Essay That Presents a Thesis

Let's look back at all of the work you have done so far:

You have read and carefully annotated "Staying Put."

You have analyzed its ideas.

You have written a directed summary in response to the first question in the writing topic.

You have thought about your own experiences and decided on your thesis statement.

You have drafted your essay's introduction.

All of that work should be gathered together now into a shape that will become your essay, your response to the writing topic for this reading selection by Sanders.

- Remember that you should follow the basic structure of an academic essay.
- To refresh your memory, turn back to Part 2 and review the diagram of the academic essay format.
- As you begin filling in this diagram form, you should be able to turn back to material you have already drafted as you worked through the exercises in this unit.
- Fill in the outline form below as fully as you can. A good plan will help you draft an essay that is clear and coherent.

I. Introductory Paragraph:

A. One or two opening sentences that give the reading selection's title, author, and main topic:

_____

_____

_____

B. The main points that you will include in the directed summary:

1.

2.

3.

4.

C. Your thesis statement. Be sure that it presents a clear position in response to the writing topic. State your thesis in your own words.

_____

_____

II. Body Paragraphs: For each body paragraph that you will include in your essay, plan the following parts:

Write down the main point for the paragraph.

_____

_____

_____

List the evidence you will use to support the main point (fact, example, etc.).

_____

_____

_____

_____

_____

_____

Tell how the evidence and your ideas link to the thesis statement.

_____

_____

_____

_____

_____

_____

_____

(Repeat this part of the outline as often as necessary to plan all of your body paragraphs.)

III. **Conclusion: What are some general remarks you can make to close your essay? Perhaps you will remind your readers of the main argument of your paper, for example.**

_____

_____

_____

Drafting Your Essay

Now that you have a basic plan for the structure of your essay and a map of its various parts, you are ready to begin drafting.

- If your thinking changes as you write your draft, return to your outline and make necessary adjustments. Every time you decide to revise your outline and essay, remember that this is a good sign, a sign that your thinking is developing and becoming more thoughtful and convincing.

- Keep turning back to all of the activities in this unit as you draft your essay. Try to recall some of your reactions, thoughts, and ideas as you worked on these activities. This may help you to strengthen, expand on, or more fully develop your essay's argument.

Follow-Up Activity

Your draft will always benefit from careful rereadings, whether by you or someone else. Work with a classmate now to find areas in your draft that can be improved.

Use the following process to give and receive draft feedback.

1. Exchange a typed copy of your essay with one of your classmates.
2. Using a pen, mark your classmate's draft in the following manner:
    - Underline the subject of each sentence.
    - Use two lines to underline the verb in each sentence.
    - Identify the tense by writing it above the verb.
3. Using your highlighter:
    - If the subject and verb **do not agree**, highlight the sentence.
    - If the verb tense **is not correct**, highlight only the verb.
    - If the verb is irregular and improperly formed, highlight the verb.
    - If the sentence is a **fragment**, enclose it in parentheses.
    - If the sentence is a **run-on**, draw two vertical lines between the independent clauses.
4. Using your pen, underline the essay's thesis.
    - If the thesis is clear, identifies a subject, and makes a claim about it, put a check in the margin.
    - If it needs more work or if you cannot find a thesis, put a dash in the margin.
5. Return the drafts and discuss your marks and suggestions.

Supplemental Reading

Why Staying Put Matters and Why It's So Hard

Essay

GRACY OLMSTEAD

Gracy Olmstead is a writer and an editor of The Federalist *and an associate editor of the* American Conservative. *Her articles have appeared in publications such as the* Washington Times, *the* Idaho Press Tribune, *the* Federalist, *and* Acculturated.

A lot of Americans are committed to staying close to home—but that doesn't mean all of them are happy about it. The newest *Heartland Monitor* poll considers where Americans live, and how they feel about their place. Responses were mixed, as the *Atlantic's* Gillian White reports: "Those who hail from rural areas and small towns were more likely to report staying in one area for multiple decades than their peers in larger metropolitan areas. Southern inhabitants were more likely to pick up and to move in 5 years or less, while those in the Mountain and Northeast regions were more likely to stay put."

Even though most Americans said that they liked the general direction their local areas were headed in, respondents had mixed feelings about the opportunities available in their areas for young people. Fifty percent of respondents said that they would not recommend their local area, while 42 percent said they would. City dwellers were the most apt to see their area as best for young people, with more than half saying they'd tell them to settle down there, while those in rural areas were less likely to encourage young people to come to their neck of the woods. . . . Even though they are aware of the problems in cities and towns where they live, most Americans aren't considering moving any time soon. Sixty-one percent of respondents said the probability of relocation was not very likely—with 41 percent saying it wasn't likely at all.

A lot of people make decisions to move (or not move) based on job opportunities. Also, there's the college dynamic: Higher-educated young people are more likely to pick up and move, either before or after they finish their education. As the *New York Times* noted last October, "about a million [college graduates] cross state lines each year, and these so-called young and the restless don't tend to settle down until their mid-30s" (Miller).

(Continues)

Staying put—fully inhabiting, loving, and stewarding the place in which you live—is a conservative idea in many respects. It's interwoven with the idea of civic care and involvement, the importance of commitment to the political, economic, and cultural well-being of a community. But it is also, increasingly, an option that makes financial sense. Although metropolitan areas offer more jobs and higher salaries, they also often mean exorbitantly priced housing and longer commutes, as well as expensive groceries, household items, and childcare.

That said, being mobile and moving to a new place also offer greater independence, financial security, lifestyle options, and economic incentives. City dwellers live in a vibrant intellectual and cultural environment, with a plethora of restaurants, theaters, and museums at their disposal. They can spend more time with their peers: The city is more likely to be overflowing with young, like-minded professionals than small-town Iowa is. New buildings, attractive downtowns, and thriving commerce areas are all more likely to be present—and will contrast starkly with America's ghostlike heartland towns.

It's tough to make a case for the small town, and it's tough to stay in a small town. So why do people do it?

White talked to Marilyn Brown, a woman who's decided to stay in Cleveland despite growing crime and lack of opportunity. "I don't have a great big family. We're all right here together," she told White. And in addition to the family incentives, White writes, "Brown's reticence is partially because she doesn't think that a move would eliminate the hassles she faces in Cleveland, but instead just introduce different ones. 'Everybody is having problems with one thing or another.'"

Many people have realized that mobility takes a long-term toll on their family and community life. Not only that, moving to a place for recreational or consumeristic purposes is a sapping and exorbitant lifestyle choice, in a time when employment opportunities are still tenuous, especially for younger Americans. Staying "close to home" is more attractive when you know that there will be a safety net, a support group, and a community in that place—to help you even through times of financial difficulty.

But Brown's answer also reminds us that there is no such thing as a perfect place. We will never live in the city or town of our dreams. The grass will always be greener on the other side of the fence. That's why committing to a place—its people, its quirks, its flaws as well as its strengths—is one of the most freeing options we have. It is in planting ourselves that we can learn to thrive.

Works Cited

"Americans' Local Experiences." Poll. Allstate/National Journal *Heart-land Monitor* Poll 22 (1st Quarter 2015). Web. 1 Mar. 2015. <http://heartlandmonitor.com/americans-local-experiences/>.

Miller, Claire Cain. "Where Young College Graduates Are Choosing to Live." *New York Times.com*. New York Times Company, 20 Oct. 2014. Web. 1 Mar. 2015. <https://www.nytimes.com/2014/10/20/upshot/where-young-college-graduates-are-choosing-to-live.html?_r=2&abt=0002&abg=1>.

White, Gillian. "Staying Close to Home, No Matter What." *The Atlantic.com*. Atlantic Monthly Group, 18 Mar. 2015. Web. 1 Mar. 2015. https://www.theatlantic.com/business/archive/2015/03/staying-close-to-home-no-matter-what/387736/>.

Discussion Questions

1. What conclusions might you draw from the *Heartland Monitor* poll researching where Americans live, and how they feel about their place of residence?

2. In what way, according to Gracy Olmstead, is "staying put" a conservative idea? Why do you feel that the connecting ideas she cites do or do not apply only to the place one is and not to the place one might move to?

3. Pick some passages from Olmstead's article, and tell how they parallel the argument Russell Scott Sanders makes in "Staying Put."

Stay Put?

Essay

SARAH SKWIRE

Sarah Skwire received a BA from Wesleyan University and an MA and a PhD in literature from the University of Chicago. She has published articles and a writing textbook titled Writing with a Thesis *(2007). She is currently a literary editor for the Foundation for Economic Education (FEE), and a member of the FEE Faculty Network, a group of researchers, writers, and educators who are dedicated to the importance of human liberty.*

Earlier this week, I read a column by Gracy Olmstead published in the *American Conservative*. It was called "Why Staying Put Matters." Her argument that we should stay where we are, learn to flourish where we were born, and invest our time and our lives in our local communities troubled me, though I wasn't quite sure why.

With her article on my mind, I got into my car to drive to Chicago from Indianapolis. I thought about Olmstead's article all through the three-hour drive, which goes through 180-some miles of farmland, punctuated by the occasional wind farm. Anyone making the drive may find it hard to believe that anything as big as Chicago could be so nearby. Then the traffic begins to thicken, the billboards increase in frequency, and out of nowhere the skyline appears.

Having arrived, I am writing this column from the 29th floor of the Sofitel hotel in the Chicago Loop. When I look out my window, I have a stunning view of the Hancock building. Just behind it is Lake Michigan. I see new and old buildings in a stunning range of architectural styles. There's a highly wrought Gothic church just to my right. To my left, I see a series of office towers and apartment buildings that look like a child's drawing of a cityscape. I can even see a rooftop garden and some overly optimistic patio furniture. Chicago is a miracle.

Driving to Chicago, I always feel a little like Carrie Meeber in the first chapter of Theodore Dreiser's *Sister Carrie* as she comes to Chicago from her small town to seek her fortune. To the child, to the genius with imagination, or to the wholly untraveled, the approach to a great city for the first time is a wonderful thing, particularly if it be evening—that mystic period between the glare and gloom of the world when life is changing from one sphere or condition to another. Ah, the promise of the night. What does it not hold for the weary! What old illusion of hope is not here forever repeated! Says the soul of the toiler to itself, "I shall soon be free. I shall be in the ways and the hosts of the merry. The streets, the lamps, the lighted chamber set for dining, are for me. The theatre, the halls, the parties, the ways of rest and the paths of song—these are mine in the night" (Dreiser 12). Leaving aside our moral assessments of the choices Carrie makes as she explores the challenges of life in Chicago and climbs over any number of people to achieve success, we can all share her wonder when we think about our first sight of our first big city.

Now mind you, I'm fond of small towns and the things they offer as well. In mid-sized Indianapolis, I enjoy replicating some of that small-town culture. I keep a garden in my backyard so I can grow tomatoes. I make jam and pickles. I talk over the backyard fence to my neighbors. I brake for yard sales and for kids with lemonade stands. And there's no better way to understand America than to visit a small town's Fourth of July parade. Please don't write to my editors and tell them that I have cast aspersions on your beloved Paris, France—or Paris, Indiana. I like them both. But I don't like Olmstead's argument. Worried by a recent poll about the American tendency to relocate, she urges her readers to stay where they are and to bloom where they're planted. She writes, "Staying put—fully inhabiting, loving, and stewarding the place in which you live—is a conservative idea in many respects. It's interwoven with the idea of civic care and involvement, the importance of commitment to the political, economic, and cultural wellbeing of a community. But it is also, increasingly, an option that makes financial sense" (Olmstead).

Cities, Olmstead notes, are full of expensive things like restaurants and theaters, "new buildings, attractive downtowns, and thriving commerce areas." They're also loaded with young professionals to socialize with. But these are just shallow temptations. "We will never live in the city or town of our dreams. The grass will always be greener on the other side of the fence. That's why committing to a place—its people, its quirks, its flaws as well as its strengths—is one of the most freeing options we have" (Olmstead). Stay put. Don't change. How much better can it be anywhere else?

Reading Olmstead's article made me think instantly of F. A. Hayek's essay "Why I Am Not a Conservative." In it, he points out that "one of the fundamental traits of the conservative attitude is a fear of change, a timid distrust of the new as such" (Hayek 45). I have rarely seen a more thoroughgoing example of this kind of timidity than in

(Continues)

Olmstead's piece. Stay where you are because it is where you are. If you leave in order to pursue economic opportunity, a wider range of social networks, a more appealing set of choices in restaurants and stores, or maybe just the chance to stay on the 29th floor of the Sofitel, you are betraying yourself.

But humans have always relocated in order to better their economic position or to find freedom or for countless other reasons that are as varied as the people behind them. Since when have conservatives tried to discourage others from taking responsibility for improving their own lives? I will leave aside any comments about how, if my mother's ancestors hadn't hopped a boat from England in 1620, they'd have been imprisoned for heresy, or if my father's forebears had decided to "fully inhabit" their small towns in Russia and Poland, the entire family would have been wiped out in one pogrom or another. I'm fairly sure Olmstead didn't mean to suggest that the kind of stasis she recommends for Americans should apply to those in other countries who wish to seek a better life here.

But why, then, should it apply to any of us? The best stories always begin with travel. Whether it is Abraham called by God to "go from your land, from your birthplace and from your father's house, to the land which I will show you," Bilbo Baggins setting out for adventure with a band of dwarfs, or Huck Finn setting out on a raft, exploring new places teaches us about others and about ourselves. We may, like Bilbo, come back home to the Shire eventually. Or we may, like Huck, light out for the territories. But whichever way our stories end, they will be richer and fuller for our having had the bravery to explore.

I don't think we should try to stop that. I don't think we should even wish that we could. But then, I didn't cry when my daughters learned to ride their bikes. I cheered them on and watched them go.

Works Cited

Dreiser, Theodore. *Sister Carrie*. New York: Norton, 1991. Print.

Hayek, F. A., *The Constitution of Liberty*. Chicago: The University of Chicago Press, 1960. Print.

Olmstead, Gracy. "Why Staying Put Matters and Why It's So Hard." *The American Conservative.com*. American Ideas Institute, 19 Mar. 2015. Web. 19 Mar. 2015. <http://www.theamericanconservative.com/olmstead/why-staying-put-matters-and-why-its-so-hard/>.

Discussion Questions

1. Why does Sarah Skwire feel that Gracy Olmstead's argument arises out of "timidity" rather than reason? Explain your reason for thinking Skwire is being fair or unfair. How does Skwire's later comment that she is "fairly" sure Olmstead was not referring to immigrants make her case stronger or weaker?

2. What relationship does Skwire suggest exists between travel and story? What examples does she use to support this point? What do the examples she chooses imply about those who choose to leave? By contrast, what do they suggest about about those who stay?

3. Do you think that Skwire adequately rebuts Olmstead's point about leaving being a betrayal of the self? Explain. Where do you think Russell Scott Sanders would stand on this issue of self-betrayal? Why?

The States That College Graduates Are Most Likely to Leave

Essay

QUOCTRUNG BUI

Quoctrung Bui has worked at Planet Money on NPR *and* the Federal Reserve Board *in Washington, DC. He is currently a graphics editor for the* New York Times, *where he frequently writes about social science and policy.*

This year's election has forced Americans to take notice of class divisions between workers. And while these divisions may at first ring of lazy stereotypes—the rural Rust Belt worker without a college degree and the coastal urban college-educated worker—they're rooted in a real dynamic. Many of the most skilled workers—young people with college degrees—are leaving struggling regions of America for cities, specifically for cities in Southern and coastal states.

There are clear economic reasons for their choice. Dense metro areas tend to produce more jobs and make workers more productive. Wages, for all kinds of workers, are also higher. In theory, these incentives should prompt workers of all levels of education to move to metro areas. But moving outside one's region is relatively rare these days, and even more rare for someone without a college degree.

Moving is actually quite uncommon in advanced economies. The United States has been one of the exceptions. It has one of the highest rates of internal migration among advanced economies, and it has since at least the middle of the 19th century. A study conducted by Joseph P. Ferrie comparing thousands of American and British census records between 1850 and 1880 showed that nearly two-thirds of American men moved across county lines, while only a quarter of British men did ("The End of American Exceptionalism" 20).

For America's first century, internal migration was largely driven by farming—moving west to new land. But toward the end of the 19th and in the early 20th century, migration began to be driven by people moving to American cities—small and large. This pattern added a twist after World War II, when more people began moving outside their local region, particularly to the Sun Belt (Ferrie, "Historical Statistics of the U.S." 12). Before the 1940s, roughly 15 percent of

Americans lived outside a census division in which they were born, and by 1970 that had jumped to 25 percent (Ferrie. Historical Statistics of the U.S., 14).

But in the 1980s, according to Molloy, Smith, and Wozniak, people started moving less. Internal migration has been in gradual decline ever since across all demographic groups. In the 1980s, 3 percent of men moved across state lines each year; over the last decade, that figure has dropped to 1.7 percent. The decline is similar for women. Between 2001 and 2010, the demographic groups with the lowest rate of interstate migration were people with less than a high school diploma (1 percent) or nothing beyond a high school diploma (1.2 percent). Migration rates for college-educated people were roughly twice that (34).

In the regional competition for the most skilled and most mobile workers in America, noncoastal states are at a disadvantage. Although they have some large cities, they tend to be farther from other large cities than is the case in the coastal areas. The economists Stuart Rosenthal and William Strange looked at the benefits of density and found that they tend to dissipate over distances greater than five miles (375). ("The End of American Exceptionalism" 19).

This advantage provided by clusters of cities is helpful for coastal states, which tend to contain many big metro areas, such as San Diego, Los Angeles, San Jose, and San Francisco in California, or the so-called Acela corridor stretching from Washington to Boston. But it can be bad news for inland areas with one or two large cities that are farther apart: Omaha and Kansas City, Missouri, say; or Cleveland and Columbus, Ohio.

The flows of young college graduates out of a state can often be replaced by flows of young college graduates moving in. The problem that many interior states face is that young college graduates moving into the state aren't keeping up with those that are leaving.

"Lots of talented young people all over the country are eager to see new sights—what is different, and a problem for Michigan is that we have an unusually low rate of immigration," says Charley Ballard, a regional economist at Michigan State University, in an e-mail.

Keeping young college graduates would help alleviate the effects of globalization and technological change on these local economies. It's not surprising that many states with net losses in their young and college-educated populations also showed some big gains for Donald J. Trump relative to Mitt Romney's performance in 2012.

(Continues)

The map shows the total net migration figures for those with a college degree under 40 between 2000 and 2015. (People who grew up in one state, went to college in another, and then moved somewhere else are counted as migrating from the state where they attended college.) Generally, Rust Belt and Midwest states such as Ohio, Michigan, and Iowa, and Plains states such as South Dakota and Nebraska have seen the largest net losses in younger, college-educated people (IPUMS-USA, University of Minnesota).

The places that are gaining college graduates tend to be coastal and Southern states such as California, Maryland, Texas, and South Carolina. Two exceptions to this trend are New York and Massachusetts, states that also produce a large number of college graduates to begin with (IPUMS-USA, University of Minnesota).

One reason that inland states have a reasonable case for disappointment at not keeping their young college graduates is that they're helping to pay to educate them. A majority of college graduates get their degrees from public universities, which are partly funded by state governments. Of course, this doesn't diminish the other important benefits that public universities bring to each state's economy, but if states are losing more college graduates than they are holding or bringing in, they're effectively subsidizing other states' skilled labor forces.

Cities in these states do have some advantages. The cost of living is lower, mostly because housing is cheaper. Outdoor recreation is often more accessible. Still, these areas are in a bind: Without jobs to offer, luring young college-educated people is hard. At the same time, it's hard to create jobs without a college-educated labor force.

To Mr. Ballard, it's not clear that one policy proposal exists that could jump-start the process. "It really is a chicken-and-egg problem," he says. "I don't think there's anybody out there that thinks there's some quick, easy solution."

In the days when cities competed for manufacturing, advertising low wages and reliable utilities was often enough to draw businesses. Mr. Ballard pins his hopes of attracting more young, college-educated workers to Michigan on efforts to market cultural amenities and natural beauty. He points to the Grand Rapids ArtPrize, an arts festival that awards half a million dollars to artists, as something that has brought some cultural cachet to that city, Michigan's second largest.

"It's not all about jobs," Mr. Ballard says. "You've got to have it be a place where people want to live."

Works Cited

Ferrie, Joseph P. "The End of American Exceptionalism? Mobility in the U.S. Since 1850." PDF file. <http://faculty.wcas.northwestern.edu/~fe2r/papers/Exceptionalism.pdf>.

IPUMS-USA, University of Minnesota. "Where Young College Graduates Tend to Move: Net Migration of College Educated People under 40, 2000-2015. *NYTimes.com*. The New York Times Company, 22 Nov. 2016. Map.

Molloy, Raven, Christopher L. Smith, and Abigail Wozniak. *Internal Migration in the United States*. Finance and Economics Discussion Series. Cambridge, MA: National Bureau of Economic Research, 2011. PDF file. <http://www.nber.org/papers/w17307.pdf>.

_____. "Historical Statistics of the U.S., Millennial Edition: Internal Migration." PDF file. <http://faculty.wcas.northwestern.edu/~fe2r/papers/essay.pdf>.

Rosenthal, Stuart S., and William C. Strange. "The Attenuation of Human Capital Spillovers." *Journal of Urban Economics* 64 (2008): 373-389. Print.

Discussion Questions

1. Discuss America's changing internal migration patterns and their driving forces in the country's first century, the late 19th and early 20th century, post-World War II, the 1980s, and the present.

2. What are some of the reasons identified by Quoctrung Bui for young, educated people to leave the inland states? Discuss the impact of this migration on the non-coastal states. What are some of the advantages these places can offer to compensate for their lack of exciting social and economic opportunities? What further things do you think they can do or need to do to make college graduates stay home? When you graduate, will you return to the place where you were raised? Why or why not?

3. If he were given the opportunity to be the commencement speaker at a public university in an inland state, what do you think Scott Russell Sanders would say to the students about going out into the world?

Assignment 4

Read the following essay and the writing topic that follows it. Then, use the exercises and activities that follow to move through the writing process and develop your own essay in response to the argument Jane Jacobs presents in "Learning Responsibility on City Sidewalks."

Learning Responsibility on City Sidewalks

JANE JACOBS

Architectural and social critic Jane Jacobs opposed the conventional wisdom of most architects and city planners in the 1950s and 1960s by championing the value of human interaction on "lively" city streets, streets like those of Jacobs's own New York City neighborhood of Greenwich Village. The following passage, adapted from Jacobs's influential book The Death and Life of Great American Cities *(1961), presents one important aspect of her argument.*

On a recent walk home, I passed a block of Puerto Rican families. Twenty-eight children of all ages were playing on the sidewalk without any event more serious than a squabble over a bag of candy. They were under the casual surveillance of adults, who were primarily visiting in public with each other. The surveillance was only seemingly casual, however, as was proved when the candy squabble broke out and peace and justice were quickly reestablished. The identities of the adults kept changing because some kept putting their heads out the windows, others kept coming in and going on errands, and others passed by and lingered a little. But the number of adults stayed fairly constant between eight and eleven during the hour I watched. Arriving home, I noticed a similar scene at our end of our block: In front of the tailor's, our apartment-house, the laundry, the pizza place, and the fruit man's store, twelve children were playing on the sidewalk in sight of fourteen adults.

Lively sidewalks have positive aspects for city children's play, and these are at least as important as safety and protection. The people of cities can, and on lively diversified sidewalks they do, supervise the incidental play of children and assimilate the children into city society. They do it in the course of carrying on their other pursuits. To waste the normal presence of adults on lively sidewalks and to bank instead (however idealistically) on hiring substitutes for them, is frivolous in the extreme. It is frivolous not only socially but also economically, because cities have desperate shortages of money and of personnel for more interesting uses of the outdoors than playgrounds. City planners do not seem to realize how high a ratio of adults is needed to rear children. Nor do they seem to understand that parks and recreational equipment do not rear children. These can be useful adjuncts, but only people can rear children and assimilate them into civilized society. It is folly to build cities in a way that wastes this normal, casual manpower for child rearing and either leaves this essential job too much undone—with terrible consequences—or makes it necessary to hire substitutes like playground monitors. The myth that playgrounds and grass and hired guards or supervisors are innately wholesome for children and that city streets, filled with ordinary people, are innately evil for children, boils down to a deep contempt for ordinary people.

In real life, only from the ordinary adults on city sidewalks do children learn—if they learn at all—the first fundamental of successful city life: People must take a modicum of public responsibility for each other, even if they have no ties of kinship or friendship. This is a lesson nobody learns by being told. It is learned from the experience of having other people without ties of kinship or close friendship take a modicum of public responsibility for you. When Mr. Lacey, the locksmith, bawls out one of my sons for running into the street, and then later reports the transgression to my husband as he passes the locksmith shop, my son gets more than an overt lesson in safety. He also gets, indirectly, the lesson that Mr. Lacey, with whom we have no ties other than street propinquity, feels responsible for him to a degree. The boy who goes unrescued in the elevator of a high-rise housing project learns the opposite lesson from his experience. So do the children in housing projects who squirt water into house windows and on passersby, and go unrebuked because they are anonymous children in anonymous grounds.

The lesson that city dwellers have to take responsibility for what goes on in the city streets is taught again and again to children on the sidewalks that enjoy a local public life. They can absorb it astonishingly early. They show they have absorbed it by taking it for granted that

(Continues)

they, too, are part of the management. They volunteer—before they're asked—directions to people who are lost; they tell a man he will get a ticket if he parks where he thinks he is going to park; they offer unsolicited advice to the building superintendent to use rock salt instead of a chopper to attack the ice on the sidewalk. The presence or absence of this kind of street bossiness in city children is a fairly good tip-off to the presence or absence of responsible adult behavior toward the sidewalk and the children who use it. The children are imitating adult attitudes. This has nothing to do with income. Some of the poorest parts of cities do the best by their children in this respect. And some do the worst.

This is instruction in civic responsibility that people hired to look after children cannot teach, because the essence of this responsibility is that you do it without being hired. It is a lesson that parents, by themselves, are powerless to teach. If parents take minor public responsibility for strangers or neighbors in a society where nobody else does, this simply means that the parents are embarrassingly different and meddlesome, not that this is the proper way to behave. Such instruction must come from society itself, and in cities, if it comes, it comes almost entirely during the time children spend at incidental play on the sidewalks.

Writing Topic

According to Jacobs, what valuable lesson do children learn on city sidewalks, and how do they learn this lesson? What do you think of her argument? To support your position, be sure to use specific evidence taken from your own experience, observations, or reading, including the readings at the end of this unit.

Vocabulary and Dictionary Practice

Part I.

Look up the following words used in "Learning Responsibility on City Sidewalks." For each, write the two most common definitions on the lines provided, and include what part of speech each definition is (noun, verb, adjective, etc.). Then, under each of the two definitions, write a sentence that uses the word in a way that reflects that particular definition and part of speech.

1. squabble
2. surveillance
3. linger
4. tailor
5. diversified
6. incidental
7. assimilate
8. adjunct
9. folly
10. casual
11. innately
12. modicum
13. transgression
14. overt
15. propinquity
16. rebuke (note: the actual word used is "unrebuked")
17. anonymous
18. unsolicited
19. bossy
20. meddlesome

1. word: **squabble**

   first definition: _____

   _____

   part of speech: _____

sentence: _____

_____

second definition: _____

_____

part of speech: _____

sentence: _____

_____

2. word: **surveillance**

first definition: _____

_____

part of speech: _____

sentence: _____

_____

second definition: _____

_____

part of speech: _____

sentence: _____

_____

3. word: **linger**

first definition: _____

_____

part of speech: _____

sentence: _____

_____

second definition: _____

_____

part of speech: _____

sentence: _____

_____

4. word: **tailor**

first definition: _____

_____

part of speech: _____

sentence: _____

_____

second definition: _____

_____

part of speech: _____

sentence: _____

_____

5. word: **diversified**

first definition: _____

_____

part of speech: _____

sentence: _____

_____

second definition: _____

_____

part of speech: _____

sentence: _____

_____

6. word: **incidental**

first definition: _____

_____

part of speech: _____

sentence: _____

_____

second definition: _____

_____

part of speech: _____

sentence: _____

_____

7. word: **assimilate**

first definition: _____

_____

part of speech: _____

sentence: _____

_____

second definition: _____

_____

part of speech: _____

sentence: _____

_____

8. word: **adjunct**

   first definition: _____

   _____

   part of speech: _____

   sentence: _____

   _____

   second definition: _____

   _____

   part of speech: _____

   sentence: _____

   _____

9. word: **folly**

   first definition: _____

   _____

   part of speech: _____

   sentence: _____

   _____

   second definition: _____

   _____

   part of speech: _____

   sentence: _____

   _____

10. word: **casual**

    first definition: _____

    _____

part of speech: _____

sentence: _____

_____

second definition: _____

_____

part of speech: _____

sentence: _____

_____

11. word: **innately**

first definition: _____

_____

part of speech: _____

sentence: _____

_____

second definition: _____

_____

part of speech: _____

sentence: _____

_____

12. word: **modicum**

first definition: _____

_____

part of speech: _____

sentence: _____

_____

second definition: _____

_____

part of speech: _____

sentence: _____

_____

13. word: **transgression**

first definition: _____

_____

part of speech: _____

sentence: _____

_____

second definition: _____

_____

part of speech: _____

sentence: _____

_____

14. word: **overt**

first definition: _____

_____

part of speech: _____

sentence: _____

_____

second definition: _____

_____

part of speech: _____

sentence: _____

_____

15. word: **propinquity**

first definition: _____

_____

part of speech: _____

sentence: _____

_____

second definition: _____

_____

part of speech: _____

sentence: _____

_____

16. word: **rebuke**

first definition: _____

_____

part of speech: _____

sentence: _____

_____

second definition: _____

_____

part of speech: _____

sentence: _____

_____

17. word: **anonymous**

   first definition: _____

   _____

   part of speech: _____

   sentence: _____

   _____

   second definition: _____

   _____

   part of speech: _____

   sentence: _____

   _____

18. word: **unsolicited**

   first definition: _____

   _____

   part of speech: _____

   sentence: _____

   _____

   second definition: _____

   _____

   part of speech: _____

   sentence: _____

   _____

19. word: **bossy**

   first definition: _____

   _____

part of speech: _____

sentence: _____

_____

second definition: _____

_____

part of speech: _____

sentence: _____

_____

20. word: **meddlesome**

first definition: _____

_____

part of speech: _____

sentence: _____

_____

second definition: _____

_____

part of speech: _____

sentence: _____

_____

Part II.

Write down the sentence from the reading selection that contains the following words. Tell which one of the word's various definitions best fits the sentence. Paraphrase the sentence without using the vocabulary word; in other words, write the sentence using your own words.

1. word: **squabble**

   original sentence: _____

   _____

   definition: _____

   _____

   paraphrase: _____

   _____

2. word: **surveillance**

   original sentence: _____

   _____

   definition: _____

   _____

   paraphrase: _____

   _____

3. word: **linger**

   original sentence: _____

   _____

   definition: _____

   _____

   paraphrase: _____

   _____

4. word: **tailor**

   original sentence: _____

   _____

definition: _____

_____

paraphrase: _____

_____

5. word: **diversified**

original sentence: _____

_____

definition: _____

_____

paraphrase: _____

_____

6. word: **incidental**

original sentence: _____

_____

definition: _____

_____

paraphrase: _____

_____

7. word: **assimilate**

original sentence: _____

_____

definition: _____

_____

paraphrase: _____

_____

8. word: **adjunct**

   original sentence: _____

   _____

   definition: _____

   _____

   paraphrase: _____

   _____

9. word: **folly**

   original sentence: _____

   _____

   definition: _____

   _____

   paraphrase: _____

   _____

10. word: **casual**

    original sentence: _____

    _____

    definition: _____

    _____

    paraphrase: _____

    _____

11. word: **innately**

   original sentence: _____

   _____

   definition: _____

   _____

   paraphrase: _____

   _____

12. word: **modicum**

   original sentence: _____

   _____

   definition: _____

   _____

   paraphrase: _____

   _____

13. word: **transgression**

   original sentence: _____

   _____

   definition: _____

   _____

   paraphrase: _____

   _____

14. word: **overt**

   original sentence: _____

   _____

definition: _____

_____

paraphrase: _____

_____

15. word: **propinquity**

original sentence: _____

_____

definition: _____

_____

paraphrase: _____

_____

16. word: **rebuke**

original sentence: _____

_____

definition: _____

_____

paraphrase: _____

_____

17. word: **anonymous**

original sentence: _____

_____

definition: _____

_____

paraphrase: _____

_____

18. word: **unsolicited**

original sentence: _____

_____

definition: _____

_____

paraphrase: _____

_____

19. word: **bossy**

original sentence: _____

_____

definition: _____

_____

paraphrase: _____

_____

20. word: **meddlesome**

original sentence: _____

_____

definition: _____

_____

paraphrase: _____

_____

Part III.

Choose ten words from the essay and tell something new and interesting you learned about the words from the dictionary. For example, you might have found the correct way to pronounce a word you were already familiar with from reading but not from speaking, or you might have learned that a word you thought of as entirely English came from another language.

word: **squabble**

_____

_____

word: **surveillance**

_____

_____

word: **linger**

_____

_____

word: **tailor**

_____

_____

word: **diversified**

_____

_____

word: **incidental**

_____

_____

word: **assimilate**

_____

_____

word: **adjunct**

_____

_____

word: **folly**

_____

_____

word: **casual**

_____

_____

word: **innately**

_____

_____

word: **modicum**

_____

_____

word: **transgression**

_____

_____

word: **overt**

_____

_____

word: **propinquity**

_____

_____

word: **rebuke**

_____

_____

word: **anonymous**

_____

_____

word: **unsolicited**

_____

_____

word: **bossy**

_____

_____

word: **meddlesome**

_____

_____

Follow-Up Activity

Write a five-sentence description of your favorite place to relax. Your description must include at least three of the vocabulary words above. Read your description aloud to the class.

Doing a Careful Reading of "Learning Responsibility on City Sidewalks"

By now, you should be aware of the importance of working systematically with a reading selection to make sure that you understand its purpose and ideas. If you have worked on Assignments 1, 2, and 3, you have practiced with some helpful techniques for doing a thoughtful reading of an essay; use them again now to better understand Jacobs's essay.

The steps are reproduced here, but your goal should be to memorize them so that they become a normal part of the writing process for you.

1. **Read the title.**
   - The title will tell you something about the reading's main topic.
   - It may also tell you something about Jacobs's opinion on the topic.
   - Think about what you already know about the topic and what more you want to know.

2. **Learn about the author.**
   - Read the biographical information about Jacobs at the top of the selection.
   - As you go through the remaining steps below, take note of how Jacobs's life or work might connect with her topic.

3. **Read through the selection once quickly.**
   - Read quickly through the reading so that you get a general impression of what it is about and what Jacobs's attitude is toward the topic.
   - Notice the things—people, places, experiences, concepts, for example—she brings up to develop and support her opinion about the topic.

4. **Read again to identify the thesis.**
   - Now read the selection a second time, but more slowly and carefully, and *with a pen or highlighter in your hand.*
   - Find the thesis and underline it or write it in the margin. Remember, the thesis states Jacobs's overall opinion on the topic of the reading. Often, the thesis is contained in a single sentence, but, in some cases, it takes several sentences to make the main argument of the reading selection clear. There are times, too, when the author does not state his or her thesis explicitly, but, if you read the selection carefully, you should be able to state it and then write it in the margin.
   - To help, ask yourself, "What does Jacobs seem to want readers to think about her topic?"

5. **Read slowly and methodically through the rest of the reading.**
   - Examine each body paragraph one at a time, and list or underline the kinds of evidence that Jacobs uses to support her thesis.

- Look in each body paragraph for a *topic sentence*—a sentence that both presents an idea and tells how it gives support to the reading's overall opinion.

- As you read and study the selection, *be sure to write down any thoughts you have* about Jacobs's opinion and supporting evidence.

- It is your job to evaluate this evidence for its logic and validity, so be sure to *make notes in the margins* as you read.

- *Mark the points* that you found interesting or convincing, and write a few words explaining your thoughts.

- Note, too, any weaknesses you find.

- When you look back at the notes you made in the margins, you should have a general idea of how convincing you found "Learning Responsibility on City Sidewalks" and what you found to be its strengths and weaknesses.

6. **Read again for review.**

- Once you have thought through the reading selection, read it once more, looking for places where you don't quite understand what is being said.

- Underline any terms that you aren't familiar with, and look them up in a dictionary.

- Mark any places in the reading that don't fit with your understanding of the reading as a whole. Decide whether this is something that Jacobs should have revised, or whether it is something that you need to read again because you don't understand it. You may find that you need to go back to Step 4 and begin working through the reading again.

- Once you are certain that you understand the entire reading, you are prepared to discuss, summarize, and/or respond to the reading with your own essay.

Follow-Up Activity

Close this book. Then, on a sheet of paper, try writing down the six steps for a careful reading, using your memory and your own words.

- When you are finished, open the book to this page and see how you did.

- Take careful note of any steps you left out.

- Looking over your list, put a star next to the steps that are most helpful to you, and briefly explain why.

- Consider more carefully the steps that you did not star, and think about how you might alter them so that they would be more helpful.

Discuss the results of this activity with the class. Compare your results and conclusions.

Questions to Review Your Understanding of "Learning Responsibility on City Sidewalks"

Answer the following questions to make sure that you have a clear understanding of Jacobs's argument as a whole. Be sure to respond to each as thoroughly as you can.

Paragraph 1

In the scene described, what two groups of people are on the sidewalk? Identify some of the activities of each group. Describe the interaction between the two groups.

Paragraph 2

According to Jacobs, what are the benefits of "lively sidewalks"?

Paragraph 2

What does Jacobs think is wrong with the way city planners think about parks and recreation equipment?

Paragraph 3

Describe the process that Jacobs believes teaches children to be responsible members of society.

Paragraph 4

What kinds of behavior show that children have learned to be responsible, according to Jacobs?

Paragraph 5

Why does Jacobs feel that parents and teachers alone cannot teach civic responsibility?

Follow-Up Activity

Tell about a time you were in a public place (in a grocery store, on an airplane) and saw a child misbehaving. Did you say anything to the child? Explain the scene, and your response, to members of your class.

Responding to the Writing Topic

You should now have a good understanding of the ideas and overall message of "Learning Responsibility on City Sidewalks." You are ready to look again at the writing topic and begin thinking about how you will respond to it. Here it is again, this time with each of three requirements on its own line:

Writing Topic

According to Jacobs, what valuable lesson do children learn on city sidewalks, and how do they learn this lesson? What do you think of her argument? To support your position, be sure to use specific evidence taken from your own experience, observations, or reading, including the readings at the end of this unit.

Here is a closer look at the writing topic's three parts:

- The first question asks you to summarize a specific aspect of "Learning Responsibility on City Sidewalks." As you read it carefully, you will notice that it has two question words, **what** and **how**. Keep them in mind because they should shape your response to this question. In other words, your directed summary should tell both "what" and "how." When examining a writing topic, you should always underline the question words (who, what, when, where, why, and how), to help you focus on answering the exact question asked.

- The second question in the writing topic asks what you think about the way children learn civic responsibility. Do you think, as Jacobs does, that traditional authority figures are not the only ones responsible for teaching children to be good citizens? Are these lessons only learned the way Jacobs claims, or are there other ways to teach civic responsibility? Your answer to this part of the writing topic will become the thesis of your essay because it will provide an assertion that tells the reader your opinion about the topic.

- The third part of the writing topic asks you to support your claim—your thesis—with clear examples taken from your own experiences. The following activities will help you begin to find these examples. Be sure to keep notes on your ideas, your classroom discussions, and any background readings you do so that you can turn back to them for material as you plan your essay.

Follow-Up Activity

1. Make a list of five verbs that you would use to describe what happens on Jacobs's city sidewalks. Compare your list with those of your classmates. What activities were on everyone's list? What activities were noticed by only one person?

2. Make a list of five verbs that you would use to describe what happens in the area around your home. Compare your list to the one you made about city sidewalks. Explain to a classmate the reason for the similarity or difference between your two lists.

3. Compare your list about your home with your classmates' lists. How many different kinds of living environments can you identify in your class?

4. Form small groups, and have each member of the group identify the person in his or her life most responsible for teaching about civic responsibility. Each member should describe the role of this person. Was the person a parent or teacher? Do the experiences learning about civic responsibility seem to support or contradict Jacobs?

5. Think about your life and the decisions you have made or will make (such as going to college, getting married, choosing a career, having children). How does having a sense of civic responsibility influence your decisions on such important matters?

Strategies to Help You Analyze a Reading Selection and Develop Your Ideas for Writing a Response

We hope you realize that prewriting strategies are an important and productive part of the writing process. If you use them in a focused and sustained way, they lead you to a more systematic analysis of any reading selection. Use these strategies now on "Learning Responsibility on City Sidewalks" as you begin to form your own opinions and ideas. They will help to guide and clarify your thinking about Jacobs's essay. They will also help you to put into words your own views on the topic she writes about—that everyone should take responsibility for each other, including children, even if they are not relatives or friends.

Questioning

- Questions about the highlighting you did:
  Why did I underline this part of the reading?

  How is this information important to Jacobs's point?

  What is the relationship between this information and the question I am being asked to write about?

- Questions about Jacobs's ideas:
  What things in this essay do not make sense to me?

  Where do I think Jacobs should have explained further?

  How do the examples in the essay relate to her point?

- Questions about "Learning Responsibility on City Sidewalks" that seem important:

  What are some of the things that Jacobs says that I am happy to hear someone say?

  What things that she says seem true to me?

  What things that she says seem wrong to me?

  What thing that she says is most important to me?

  What idea in this essay is completely new to me?

Freewriting

Use freewriting now to explore your responses to the questions above:

- Pick one or more of your answers to the questions you have already answered, and just begin to write about them.
- While you are doing this writing, do not stop or censor yourself; just let the words come.
- Do this for about five or ten minutes without thinking about spelling, grammar, word choice, or even the sense of what you are saying.
- When you have completed this activity, you will want to take a break.
- After your brief break, come back and read what you have written. Most of what you now have down on paper will not end up in your essay, but, as you read through your freewriting, you will find one or more sentences or ideas that seem interesting, important, or even compelling to you. Highlight these points and ideas. Are you beginning to develop your thoughts in a way that will shape your essay?

Listing

With this strategy, you simply list all of the thoughts and reactions you have noted so far. By looking down your list, you may see a pattern of ideas develop, one that you can use to develop an essay of your own.

- List all of the annotations you made for "Learning Responsibility on City Sidewalks."
- List the main ideas you can see in your answers to "Questioning," above.
- List any main ideas that developed from your responses to the follow-up activities above.
- Be sure to list all the items from your freewriting that you thought were interesting. As you make this list, other ideas may come to you. Put them on your list as well.

Look over your list and group all the ideas that seem related to each other. See if you can find one related group of ideas that is longer than the others. These ideas may suggest what you want to say in response to Jacobs's essay.

Shaping Your Ideas into a Rough Draft

By now, you should feel prepared to begin planning your rough draft. If you aren't, go back through some of the activities above, and talk with classmates to see what they are thinking. Sometimes it takes a while before your ideas are formed enough; take as much time as you need to clarify your thoughts.

When you are ready to focus on your rough draft, you will have to think about each part of your essay and how you will compose it. Turn back to Part 2 and examine "A Suggested Structure for an Essay That Responds to Another Writer's Essay." Also, look again at the writing topic for "Learning Responsibility on City Sidewalks." Remind yourself that it asks you to do three things:

1. Write a summary that identifies the way in which children develop social responsibility by socializing on city sidewalks, rather than in parks or their own yard, according to Jacobs. Explain her ideas as well as you can.

   Remember that you have already worked on this in earlier activities. Look back now to the work you did. You may be able to use some of it below, when you write your essay's *directed summary*.

2. Take a position on this idea; do you agree with Jacobs's view?

   This is your thesis statement, and it will unify your essay, so it's important that you write it out clearly. Turn back to the review questions you answered, and the follow-up activities you did. What were your thoughts and ideas? You will use them below when you write a thesis statement. Remember that you can always revise it as you work on your rough draft.

3. Support and develop your position using specific evidence taken from your own experiences and readings. In other words, explain your thinking and why you have the view you present—and don't forget to include the specific evidence from your experience or your reading that convinced you to take the position you take.

The explanation of your thoughts and the evidence that led you to draw those conclusions will make up nearly your entire essay. Look back to earlier exercises in this unit to remind yourself of some of the thinking you did as you considered whether playing on our city sidewalks gives children valuable training in becoming good citizens. You will be able to use some of this as evidence to support your thesis. Remember it when you begin working on body paragraphs.

Drafting Your Directed Summary

Here are some questions that will help you answer the first part of the writing topic. Answer each one as thoroughly and carefully as you can; then, use your answers and those you wrote in earlier activities to draft a directed summary. Begin drafting the directed summary by reviewing the writing topic for "Learning Responsibility on City Sidewalks," paying particular attention to the first question asked.

> According to Jacobs, what valuable lesson do children learn on city sidewalks, and how do they learn this lesson?

- The answer you give to this question is called a *directed summary* because it summarizes only the parts of Jacobs's essay that answer this first question.

- As you learned in Part 2, the question that calls for a directed summary often opens with a question word such as *what, how,* or *why*. In the writing topic for Jacobs's essay, the first question asks, *what* valuable lessons the children learn when playing on neighborhood streets? You will have to go back to the essay to find the information that tells *what* these lessons are. You will also have to consider *how* children learn these lessons, according to Jacobs. For example, notice her idea about the way adults respond to children playing on the street and how the adult reactions to the children's behavior educate the children.

- Be sure to turn back to the essay itself and mark the sentences that answer this first writing topic question. Don't rely on your memory alone. Also, review your own responses and classroom discussion notes to "Questions to Review Your Understanding." You will most likely discover that you have already found important information that you can use in your directed summary.

You should avoid including any of the following in a directed summary:

1. minor details or points that are irrelevant to the question,

2. your own opinion or ideas, and

3. examples of your own, and, unless particularly helpful, those of the author.

Follow-Up Activity

1. As the class as a whole discusses the important points from "Learning Responsibility on City Sidewalks" that need to be included in the directed summary, make a numbered list on the board of the essential elements necessary to form a complete and accurate directed summary of this essay. Also, remind each other of the list of items to avoid in a directed summary, and make sure none of them are on the list you have created.

2. Form small groups and exchange drafts of your summaries. Read your partner's summary out loud to the group. With a different colored pen from the one used to write the draft, have the group help you put a number after the sentence that corresponds to each number on the board. Have the group also note any sentences in the summary that are on the previous list of things to avoid in a directed summary.

3. Return the summaries to their authors. Look at your own. Check to see which elements are omitted from your summary and what material is included unnecessarily; then, revise.

Developing Your Thesis Statement

The second question in the writing topic asks you to *evaluate* Jacobs's point of view on the benefits that come from allowing children to play on city sidewalks and *weigh the evidence* she uses to support her position. Do you agree with her view on the training of children? Your answer to this will be your essay's thesis statement.

Think of your thesis as needing three parts:

- the subject being considered
- Jacobs's claim about the subject
- your opinion about the subject

Fill in your answer on the line below to form your thesis statement.

_____

_____

After you have finished writing your sentence, review your statement to see that it contains the following elements:

- identifies Jacobs's argument
- makes clear your opinion about what she says

If either of these elements is missing, rewrite your thesis statement so that both are included.

Up to this point, you have been planning the draft of your introductory paragraph. Now that you have drafted your thesis statement, you can begin planning your body paragraphs. They will have to explain your ideas and give support to your thesis statement.

Developing Body Paragraphs for an Essay That Presents a Thesis

Reminders:
Body paragraphs make up the largest part of an essay.

- The job of each body paragraph is to develop **one** point that supports the thesis statement.
- Taken together, these points constitute the argument of the essay.
- Writing a good body paragraph can be easy once you understand the criteria that the body paragraph must fulfill.

Here is a review of the three most important requirements for paragraphs in an argumentative essay:

Parts of a Body Paragraph

An appropriate or suitable point—one that supports the opinion in the thesis statement

Evidence—for instance, a concrete fact, example, or quotation—that demonstrates the point of the paragraph

A link to the thesis—sentences that show how and why the paragraph, including the evidence, relates to the thesis

A Basic Outline Form for an Essay That Presents a Thesis

Let's look back at all of the work you have done so far:

You have read and carefully annotated "Learning Responsibility on City Sidewalks."

You have analyzed its ideas.

You have written a directed summary in response to the first question in the writing topic.

You have thought about your own experiences and decided on your thesis statement.

You have drafted your essay's introduction.

All of that work should be gathered together now into a shape that will become your essay, your response to the writing topic for Jacobs's essay.

- Remember that you should follow the basic structure of an academic essay.
- To refresh your memory, turn back to Part 2 and review the diagram of the academic essay format.
- As you begin filling in this diagram, you should be able to turn back to material you have already drafted as you worked through the exercises in this unit.
- Fill in the outline form below as fully as you can. A good plan will help you draft an essay that is clear and coherent.

I. Introductory Paragraph:

A. One or two opening sentences that give the reading selection's title, author, and main topic:

_____

_____

_____

B. The main points that will be included in the directed summary:

1.

2.

3.

4.

C. Your thesis statement. Be sure that it presents a clear position in response to the writing topic. State your thesis in your own words.

_____

_____

_____

II. **Body Paragraphs: For each body paragraph that you will include in your essay, plan the following parts:**

Write down the main point of the paragraph.

_____

_____

_____

List the evidence you will use to explain and support the main point (fact, example, etc.).

_____

_____

_____

_____

_____

Tell how the evidence and your ideas link to the thesis statement.

_____

_____

_____

_____

_____

_____

_____

_____

_____

(Repeat this part of the outline as often as necessary to plan all of your body paragraphs.)

III. Conclusion: What are some general remarks you can make to close your essay? Perhaps you will remind your readers of the main argument of your paper, for example.

_____

_____

_____

Drafting Your Essay

Now that you have a basic plan for the structure of your essay and a map of its various parts, you are ready to begin drafting.

- If your thinking changes as you write your draft, return to your outline and make necessary adjustments. Every time you decide to revise your outline and essay, remember that this is a good sign, a sign that your thinking is developing and becoming more thoughtful and convincing.

- Keep turning back to all of the activities in this unit as you draft your essay. Try to recall some of your reactions, thoughts, and ideas as you worked on these activities. Doing this may help you to strengthen, expand on, or more fully develop your essay's argument.

Follow-Up Activity

Your draft will always benefit from careful rereadings, by you or someone else. Work with a classmate now to find areas in your draft that can be improved.

Use the following process to give and receive draft feedback.

1. Exchange a typed copy of your essay with one of your classmate's.
2. Using a pen and a highlighter, mark your classmate's draft in the following manner:
   - Using your pen, underline the subject of each sentence.
   - Use two lines to underline the verb in each sentence.
   - Identify the tense by writing it above the verb.
3. Using your highlighter:
   - If the subject and verb **do not agree**, highlight the sentence.
   - If the verb tense **is not correct**, highlight only the verb.
   - If an irregular verb is **improperly** formed, highlight the verb.
   - If the sentence is a **fragment**, enclose it in parentheses.
   - If the sentence is a **run-on**, draw two vertical lines between the independent clauses.
4. Using your pen, underline the essay's thesis.
   - If it is clear, if it identifies a subject, and if it states an opinion about it, put a check in the margin.
   - If it needs more work or if you cannot find a thesis, put an X in the margin.
5. Return the drafts and discuss your marks and suggestions.

Supplemental Reading

It Takes a Whole Village to Raise a Child. Igbo and Yoruba (Nigeria) Proverb

Essay

REV. JOSEPH G. HEALEY

Joseph G. Healey is an American teacher and writer. He earned his BA in communication from Maryknoll Seminary, and his MA in theology from the University of Missouri. He spent a number of years doing missionary work in Africa, and became familiar with traditional proverbs of several African cultures. He has recorded many of his experiences in scholarly papers and books, including Small Christian Communities/Basic Ecclesial Communities: Theology of One World *(2012) and* Building the Church as Family of God: Evaluation of Small Christian Communities in Eastern Africa *(2013).*

This Igbo and Yoruba (Nigeria) proverb exists in different forms in many African languages. The basic meaning is that child upbringing is a communal effort. The responsibility for raising a child is shared with the larger family (sometimes called the extended family). Everyone in the family participates, especially the older children, aunts and uncles, grandparents, and even cousins. It is not unusual for African children to stay for long periods with their grandparents or aunts or uncles. Even the wider community, such as neighbors and friends, gets involved. Children are considered a blessing from God for the whole community. This communal responsibility in raising children is also seen in the Sukuma (Tanzania) proverb "One knee does not bring up a child" and in the Swahili (East and Central Africa) proverb "One hand does not nurse a child."

In general, this Nigerian proverb conveys the African worldview that emphasizes the values of family relationships, parental care, self-sacrificing concern for others, sharing, and even hospitality. This is very close to the Biblical worldview as seen in Scripture texts related to unity and cooperation (Ecclesiastes 4:9,12) and a mother's self-sacrificing love (Isaiah 49:15–16).

The multiple uses of this Nigerian proverb show the timeliness and relevance of African proverbs in today's world. In 1996, Hillary Clinton, the wife of the President of the United States, published a book

(Continues)

on children and family values titled *It Takes a Village* and based on this proverb. That same year, Maryknoll Father Don Sybertz and I published the first edition of our book *Towards an African Narrative Theology* (now available from Paulines Publications Africa, in Nairobi, Kenya, and Orbis Books, in Maryknoll, New York). In chapter three on "Community," we used this Nigerian proverb and many other African proverbs and sayings on the values of community, unity, cooperation, and sharing. In Dallas, Texas, there was a controversy over four security guards that whipped some kids who broke into a mall. The parents of the kids said that the guards had no right to discipline their kids, but the guards said that they did what they did because "the village raises the children."

The Anglican Archbishop John Sentamu of York, England, at a consultation in Swanwick, England, stated in September 2005, "As *It takes a whole village to raise a child* so it takes *the whole global village to eradicate poverty*. It starts with each of us personally. For example, do we buy Fairtrade goods?"

Discussion Questions

1. Identify and explain the various African proverbs that exist in African languages (Sukuma, Swahili, and Igbo and Yoruba). What idea do they all have in common?

2. Give some examples that the author says show that these African proverbs are both timely and relevant for today's world. Which of these examples do you think works best or fails to work to support his point? Explain your answer.

3. What is the connection between the philosophy of these proverbs and the purchasing of fair trade goods?

(Note: Fair trade is a social movement that promotes the development of products that are sustainable—that is, products that give environmental, social, and economic benefits. Fair trade focuses mainly on developing countries, and on creating a fairer trading system by raising the prices of goods coming from developing countries into developed countries.)

Why We Need to Talk to Strangers

CLAIRE MCCARTHY, MD

Claire McCarthy is an Assistant Professor of Pediatrics at Harvard Medical School and a pediatrician at Boston Children's Hospital. She is also a writer, and her work has appeared in publications such as Harvard Health Publications, family magazines, newspapers such as the Huffington Post, *and* Thriving, *a blog associated with Boston Children's Hospital and targeted for parents. The following article is from her blog.*

I remember a warm September day at the playground 22 years ago. I was there with my 19-month-old daughter and newborn son. Zack was hungry, so I sat down on a bench to nurse him—but every time I got him settled, Michaela ran away from me. Far away, out-of-view away (she was a quick little thing). The playground was fenced in, but there were lots of ways for a toddler to get hurt there. Finally, a lovely woman with a preschooler came over and offered to watch Michaela so that I could feed Zack. I was beyond grateful. I nearly cried. If it were now instead of 22 years ago, I wonder, would someone offer to help—or would they call child protective services instead, saying that I wasn't watching my toddler?

I've been thinking about that September day ever since I read a great post called "Would You Call 911 on Another Parent?" by Tracy Cutchlow. Instead of offering to help when they see a child alone, she says, people are calling the cops. "What's missing," she says, "is the sense that we're all responsible for everyone's children." And this, she says, comes from not knowing each other. I agree—but I think it's more than that.

Recently, someone did call child protective services about one of my patients, a child with special health care needs. He or she said that the child's mother was neglecting her. Her mother wasn't neglecting her; there was a very simple explanation for what the neighbor saw. But instead of asking about it, instead of getting to know the family and seeing if they needed help, the neighbor called the authorities, resulting in an upsetting, humiliating, and ultimately unnecessary investigation.

What has become of us?

Now, I am definitely not saying that we shouldn't take action if we see something that worries us or makes us think that a child might be

(Continues)

neglected or abused. But unless we think that there is imminent danger to the child (or to us if we intervene), or we are physically unable to do something ourselves, our first and only action doesn't need to be calling the authorities. The action could be, as Crutchlow says, keeping an eye on the child alone in the car until the parent gets back. Or keeping an eye on the child alone in the playground—and instead of calling the cops if she says her mom is at work, talking to neighbors about helping the family with child care. But we don't do these things. I don't think it's because we aren't as nice as we were 22 years ago. And it's not because our neighborhoods are more dangerous, because they're not. I think it's because our culture has shifted; minding your own business (or calling the cops) is fine, knocking on a stranger's door or helping someone else's kid off the jungle gym is creepy.

Again: What has become of us?

Crutchlow is right; we don't get to know people enough. But even more, *we don't think we should*. It's safer and more acceptable to be insular, to talk to only those you know, to make friends only with those who are somehow connected to us (and then with caution). It's like we tell our children: Don't talk to strangers. But if we never talk to strangers, they stay strangers. And that's a problem. If people stay strangers, we never find out if all the things we think about them are true or not. We don't get to find out if the parent at the park is actually neglectful—or just stressed out and overwhelmed. We don't get to find out if the person who never says anything at school pick-up is actually a snob—or just shy, or hard-of-hearing or non-English speaking. We don't find out anything, and so what we imagine becomes real. This is not just sad, but can have terrible consequences; just look at everything that is happening in Ferguson, Missouri.

And if people stay strangers, we lose the chance to help them—and to be helped by them. We lose the chance to help frazzled young parents like the one I was 22 years ago. We lose the chance to help prevent child abuse, connect a family to resources and support, be a role model, or find one. We lose the chance to make friends, end someone's loneliness (or our own), make a difference. When we live in silos and never venture out of them, the world can't help but be a harder and sadder place. That can't be what we want; that can't be who we want to be.

So, the next time you see something that worries you, or someone having trouble, stop and think: *Is there something that I personally can do, right now, to help?* And the next time you see someone you see often but don't know, introduce yourself. Bring cookies to new neighbors (you don't have to bake them)—or old neighbors you've never met. Hold the door for a parent pushing a stroller, or smile instead of scowl at the fussy toddler in the grocery carriage—and chat with her parent. Reach out a hand instead of reaching for your phone to call 911. Talking to strangers isn't just a nice thing to do, it's a necessary thing to do. It's the only way to turn things around.

Discussion Questions

1. What specific event from her past proves to Claire McCarthy that society has changed in the last twenty-two years? In what ways does she believe people and society are still the same? Explain your reason for thinking that she is either correct or naïve.

2. Under what circumstances does the author believe that we have an obligation to intervene and report concerns about someone else's child? Describe some specific details of a situation that you might observe that would fit one or both of McCarthy's requirements for taking action.

3. Using a quotation from this article, briefly state the problem McCarthy identifies. What kind of world does she say is created by this problem? What solution does she propose? Tell your reasons for deciding to participate or not to participate in the action she recommends.

Actually, It Doesn't Take a Village

Essay

DIANE SWANBROW

Diane Swanbrow is director of communications at the University of Michigan's Institute for Social Research. She speaks and writes on a variety of subjects, including American culture, cultural anthropology, and philosophy.

"In the African villages that I study in Mali, children fare as well in nuclear families as they do in extended families," says U-M researcher Beverly Strassmann, professor of anthropology and faculty associate at the U-M Institute for Social Research (ISR). "There's a naïve belief that villages raise children communally, when in reality children are raised by their own families, and their survival depends critically on the survival of their mothers." Strassmann's recently published studies provide the first empirical data on two theoretical pillars of the belief that it takes a village to raise a child. One of these pillars is the grandmother hypothesis—the idea that a child is more likely to survive if a grandmother is nearby. The other is cooperative breeding theory, based on animal behavior studies that have shown that in a wide variety of birds, including scrub jays, and many mammals, such as the mongoose, adults may delay their own reproduction to help raise the offspring of others.

"Some researchers have suggested that humans may also be a cooperatively breeding species," says Strassmann, who views human behavior from the perspective of evolutionary biology. "But the evidence I found shows that this is not always the case and that there can be quite a lot of competition and coercion within families." Cooperative breeding is not the universal, evolved pattern. Instead, there is huge diversity in the array of successful family systems in humans. For example, in the United States, there is a huge proportion of nuclear families and single moms. Look at Bill Clinton and Barack Obama. Certainly, many children of single mothers not only survive but thrive.

"Cooperative breeding does help [us] to understand nineteenth-century European societies, for example, in Ireland, where marriage was postponed to the late twenties or even thirties due to the scarcity of farms to inherit," Strassman says. "In these societies, celibate individuals often worked on the farms of siblings as helpers and can be compared to cooperatively breeding birds that delay reproduction and act as helpers at their parents' nest when the habitat is saturated and all nest sites are taken. However, cooperative breeding does not fit many other societies, such as the one I study in Africa."

In a study published this summer in the *Proceedings of the National Academy of Sciences*, Strassmann analyzed data on child survival in various family structures from her ongoing, twenty-five-year study of the Dogon people of Mali, West Africa, a traditional, agricultural society in which resources are scarce and mortality is high. Like many human groups in the past, Dogon society is patrilineal, with a tight-knit web of kinship established through fathers. The Dogon practice polygyny and do not use contraception; Dogon women give birth to nine children, on average, over their lifetimes (Strassmann 10894). Strassmann's study is the only research on the subject to date that looks at future possibilities and that controls for confounding variables, such as family wealth and family structure, that could affect child survival. In the seventeen hundred Dogon children she followed, Strassmann found that children were over four times more likely to die by age five if their mothers were dead (10896).

"In the Dogon, it is mothers alone who are critical for getting children past the early-life bottleneck in survival," Strassmann says. "Adding an extra adult to the family did not improve a child's survival. Although it's important to note that these findings are about child survival up to age five, they don't speak to the value of having grandparents later on. Children were fifty-two percent less likely to die if their paternal grandparents were dead. Why? Because in a patrilineal society, the paternal grandparents are likely to live with the child, competing for scarce resources." Also, "The grandmother hypothesis does not take into account that grandmothers may need help themselves, not just among groups like the Dogon but in societies like our own."

In another study, published this summer in *Human Nature*, Strassmann and ISR researcher Wendy Garrard further investigated the validity of the grandmother hypothesis. This study involved a meta-analysis of published studies done over several centuries in seventeen patrilineal societies in Africa, Asia, Europe, and North America. "Our analysis showed that the grandparents who actually lived with their grandchildren did not have a beneficial effect on the grandchildren's survival," Strassmann says. "Grandparents who did not live with the grandchildren sometimes did have a positive effect because they were not competing for scarce resources."

In her study of the Dogon, Strassmann found that children's risk of death is higher in polygynous than in monogamous families (10897).

(Continues)

This reflects the hazard of living with unrelated females whose own children are competing with the children of co-wives for limited resources. Supporting this finding, Strassmann cites "Hamilton's Rule," established by British evolutionary biologist W. D. Hamilton in the 1960s (10898). It is the first formal, mathematical description of kin selection theory, the idea that the degree to which we are willing to invest our resources in another person depends, in part, on the degree of genetic kinship we share with them.

But kinship cuts both ways, according to Strassmann. "Our results also suggest that kin competition is an important aspect of human family systems," she says. "Genetic conflicts of interest occur even within the family. This competition starts before birth, with maternal genes allocating resources strategically between present and future offspring. The competition extends throughout childhood with sibling rivalry." At reproductive maturity, kin compete for the resources needed for mating and parental effort. And finally, in old age, net producers eventually become net consumers who compete with other family members for food and shelter.

According to University of Michigan research, it doesn't take a village to raise a child after all.

Work Cited

Strassmann, Beverly I. u Cooperation and Competition in a Cliff-Dwelling People. Proceedings of the National Academy of Sciences of the United States of America 108 Supplement 2 (2011): 10894 901. Print.

Discussion Questions

1. Why do you think, as the author asserts, the belief that it takes a whole village to raise a child is commonly accepted as truth? What responsibility does this belief place on the community? What evidence have you seen or not seen that local institutions, such as churches and city governments, attempt to act according to this belief?

2. What is "cooperative breeding"? Discuss the example pointed out in the article of a society that might be thought about in terms of this concept. What particular factors made this society adopt such behavior? Does it continue there to this day? Why or why not? Discuss the ways the Dogon people of Mali are different in terms of cooperative breeding from the nineteenth-century Irish. Discuss the country, or a

community in it, of you or your family's origin in terms of evidence of cooperative breeding. Be sure to refer in your discussion to such factors as age of marriage and number of offspring.

3. Discuss the importance of kin relationships, particularly mothers, paternal grandparents, and grandmothers, to the survival of a child.

Won't You Be My Neighbor?

Essay

PETER LOVENHEIM

Lovenheim is the author of In the Neighborhood: The Search for Community on an American Street, One Sleepover at a Time *(2010), the culmination of a project he discusses in the following essay, originally published in the* New York Times *on June 23, 2008. He teaches writing at Rochester Institute of Technology and is also the author of* Portrait of a Burger as a Young Calf: The Story of One Man, Two Cows, and the Feeding of a Nation *(2002).*

The alarm on my cell phone rang at 5:50 a.m., and I awoke to find myself in a twin bed in a spare room at my neighbor Lou's house. Lou was eighty-one. His six children were grown and scattered around the country, and he lived alone, two doors down from me. His wife, Edie, had died five years earlier. "When people learn you've lost your wife," he told me, "they all ask the same question. 'How long were you married?' And when you tell them fifty-two years, they say 'Isn't that wonderful!'"

Lou had said he gets up at six, but after ten more minutes, I heard nothing from his room down the hall. Had he died? He had a heart ailment but generally was in good health. With a full head of silver-gray hair, bright hazel-blue eyes, and a broad chest, he walked with the confident bearing of a man who had enjoyed a long and satisfying career as a surgeon.

The previous evening, as I'd left home, the last words I heard before I shut the door had been, "Dad, you're crazy!" from my teenage daughter. Sure, the sight of your fifty-year-old father leaving with an overnight bag to sleep at a neighbor's house would embarrass any teenager, but "crazy"? I didn't think so. There's talk today about how as a society we've become fragmented by ethnicity, income, city versus suburb, red state versus blue. But we also divide ourselves with invisible dotted lines. I'm talking about the property lines that isolate us from the people we are physically closest to: our neighbors.

A calamity on my street in a middle-class suburb of Rochester several years ago got me thinking about this. One night, a neighbor shot and killed his wife and then himself; their two middle-school-age children ran screaming into the night. Though the couple had lived on our street for seven years, my wife and I hardly knew them. We'd see them jogging together. Sometimes our children would carpool.

Some of the neighbors attended the funerals and called on relatives. Someone laid a single bunch of yellow flowers at the family's front door, but nothing else was done to mark the loss. Within weeks, the children had moved with their grandparents to another part of town. The only indication that anything had changed was the "For Sale" sign on the lawn.

A family had vanished, yet the impact on our neighborhood was slight. How could that be? Did I live in a community or just in a house on a street surrounded by people whose lives were entirely separate? Few of my neighbors, I later learned, knew others on the street more than casually; many didn't know even the names of those a few doors down.

According to social scientists, from 1974 to 1998, the frequency with which Americans spent a social evening with neighbors fell by about one-third. Robert Putnam, the author of *Bowling Alone*, a groundbreaking study of the disintegration of the American social fabric, suggests that the decline actually began twenty years earlier, so that neighborhood ties today are less than half as strong as they were in the 1950s.

Why is it that in an age of cheap long-distance rates, discount airlines, and the Internet, when we can create community anywhere, we often don't know the people who live next door? Maybe my neighbors didn't mind living this way, but I did. I wanted to get to know the people whose houses I passed each day—not just what they do for a living and how many children they have, but the depth of their experience and what kind of people they are.

What would it take, I wondered, to penetrate the barriers between us? I thought about childhood sleepovers and the insight I used to get from waking up inside a friend's home. Would my neighbors let me sleep over and write about their lives from inside their own houses?

A little more than a year after the murder-suicide, I began to telephone my neighbors and send e-mail messages; in some cases, I just walked up to the door and rang the bell. The first one turned me down, but then I called Lou. "You can write about me, but it will be boring," he warned. "I have nothing going on in my life—nothing. My life is zero. I don't do anything."

(Continues)

That turned out not to be true. When Lou finally awoke that morning at six, he and I shared breakfast. Then he lay on a couch in his study and, skipping his morning nap, told me about his grandparents' immigration, his Catholic upbringing, his admission to medical school despite anti-Italian quotas, and how he met and courted his wife, built a career, and raised a family. Later, we went to the YMCA for his regular workout; he mostly just kibitzed with friends. We ate lunch. He took a nap. We watched the business news. That evening, he made us dinner and talked of friends he'd lost, his concerns for his children's futures, and his own mortality. Before I left, Lou told me how to get into his house in case of an emergency, and I told him where I hide my spare key. That evening, as I carried my bag home, I felt that in my neighbor's house lived a person I actually knew. I was privileged to be his friend until he died, just this past spring.

Remarkably, of the eighteen or so neighbors I eventually approached about sleeping over, more than half said yes. There was the recently married young couple, both working in business; the real estate agent and her two small children, and the pathologist married to a pediatrician who specializes in autism. Eventually, I met a woman living three doors away, the opposite direction from Lou, who was seriously ill with breast cancer and in need of help. My goal shifted: Could we build a supportive community around her—in effect, patch together a real neighborhood? Lou and I and some of the other neighbors ended up taking turns driving her to doctors' appointments and watching her children.

Our political leaders speak of crossing party lines to achieve greater unity. Maybe we should all cross the invisible lines between our homes and achieve greater unity in the places we live. We probably don't need to sleep over; all it might take is to make a phone call, send a note, or ring a bell. Why not try it today?

Discussion Questions

1. What are the "invisible dotted lines" that Peter Lovenheim says exist in our communities today? What facts or statistics does he use to support his assertion that these lines are real? Think about the place where you grew up. What facts or examples can you give to show that Lovenheim's lines were or were not there?

2. What steps does the author take to erase the lines, "penetrate the barriers," where he lives? What does his teenage daughter think about his plan? Why do you think that his daughter's assessment was right or wrong?

3. Discuss the way Lovenheim's actions and their results are related to the African proverbs about child rearing.

Assignment 5

Lewis Thomas's "The Iks"

As in the previous unit on "Learning Responsibility on City Sidewalks," this unit takes you through the writing process, helping you analyze Lewis Thomas's ideas and write an essay of your own in response to his ideas. This unit will take you through the writing process using the strategies that you were introduced to in Part 2 and that you practiced in Assignment 4. As you work through these strategies again in Assignment 5, see if you can use them more deliberately this time. In other words, personalize these strategies and make them yours. For each activity, ask yourself what the goal of the lesson is and how you can best use each activity or exercise to maximize its benefits for you. Remember that, ultimately, you are working through each page in this unit in order to produce the best, most successful essay that you can. Try to determine how each page can help you to accomplish that goal.

The Iks

LEWIS THOMAS

"The Iks," by physician-scientist Lewis Thomas, was originally published in the New England Journal of Medicine *in the early 1970s. It is part of a collection of 29 essays that center on science, but that range in focus from molecules, to organisms, to organisms' organization in societies, and even to the search for life forms not of the Earth. Thomas's consistent idea throughout the collection is that there are many replications between the enclosed unit of a cell and the complex interactions of a society. Thomas's belief, one that comes out of his life of study in the sciences, is that we humans are a very young species and just beginning to learn about how to get along with one another to ensure our survival. His optimism about our future is based on his belief that, like other much older species have done, we will continue our social development and learn better ways to get along.*

The small tribe of Iks, formerly nomadic hunters and gatherers in the mountain valleys of northern Uganda, have become celebrities, literary symbols for the ultimate fate of disheartened, heartless mankind at large. Two disastrously conclusive things happened to them: The government decided to have a national park, so they were compelled by law to give up hunting in the valleys and become farmers on poor hillside soil, and then they were visited for two years by an anthropologist who detested them and wrote a book about them.

The message of the book is that the Iks have transformed themselves into an irreversibly disagreeable collection of unattached, brutish creatures, totally selfish and loveless, in response to the dismantling of their traditional culture. Moreover, this is what the rest of us are like in our inner selves, and we will all turn into Iks when the structure of our society comes all unhinged.

The argument rests, of course, on certain assumptions about the core of human beings, and is necessarily speculative. You have to agree in advance that man is fundamentally a bad lot, out for himself alone, displaying such graces as affection and compassion only as learned habits. If you take this view, the story of the Iks can be used to confirm it. These people seem to be living together, clustered in small, dense villages, but they are really solitary, unrelated individuals with no evident use for each other. They talk, but only to make ill-tempered demands

(Continues)

and cold refusals. They share nothing. They never sing. They turn the children out to forage as soon as they can walk, and desert the elders to starve whenever they can, and the foraging children snatch food from the mouths of the helpless elders. It is a mean society.

They breed without love or even casual regard. They defecate on each other's doorsteps. They watch their neighbors for signs of misfortune, and only then do they laugh. In the book they do a lot of laughing, having so much bad luck. Several times they even laughed at the anthropologist, who found this especially repellent (one senses, between the lines, that the scholar is not himself the world's luckiest man). Worse, they took him into the family, snatched his food, defecated on his doorstep, and hooted dislike at him. They gave him two bad years.

It is a depressing book. If, as he suggests, there is only Ikness at the center of each of us, our sole hope for hanging onto the name of humanity will be in endlessly mending the structure of our society, and it is changing so quickly and completely that we may never find the threads in time. Meanwhile, left to ourselves alone, solitary, we will become the same joyless, zestless, untouching lone animals.

But this may be too narrow a view. For one thing, the Iks are extraordinary. They are absolutely astonishing, in fact. The anthropologist has never seen people like them anywhere, nor have I. You'd think, if they were simply examples of the common essence of mankind, they'd seem more recognizable. Instead, they are bizarre, anomalous. I have known my share of peculiar, difficult, nervous, grabby people, but I've never encountered any genuinely, consistently detestable human beings in all my life. The Iks sound more like abnormalities, maladies.

I cannot accept it. I do not believe that the Iks are representative of isolated, revealed man, unobscured by social habits. I believe their behavior is something extra, something laid on. This unremitting, compulsive repellence is a kind of complicated ritual. They must have learned to act this way; they copied it, somehow. I have a theory, then. The Iks have gone crazy. The solitary Ik, isolated in the ruins of an exploded culture, has built a new defense for himself. If you live in an unworkable society, you can make up one of your own, and this is what the Iks have done. Each Ik has become a group, a one-man tribe on its own, a constituency.

Now everything falls into place. This is why they do seem, after all, vaguely familiar to all of us. We've seen them before. This is precisely the way groups of one size or another, ranging from committees to nations, behave. It is, of course, this aspect of humanity that has lagged behind the rest of evolution, and this is why the Ik seems so primitive. In his absolute selfishness, his incapacity to give anything away, no matter what, he is a successful committee. When he stands at the door of his hut, shouting insults at his neighbors in a loud harangue, he is a city addressing another city. Cities have all the Ik characteristics. They defecate on doorsteps, in rivers and lakes, their own or anyone else's. They leave rubbish. They detest all neighboring cities, give nothing away. They even build institutions for deserting elders out of sight.

Nations are the most Ik-like of all. No wonder the Iks seem familiar. For total greed, rapacity, heartlessness, and irresponsibility there is nothing to match a nation. Nations, by law, are solitary, self-centered, withdrawn into themselves. There is no such thing as affection between nations, and certainly no nation ever loved another. They bawl insults from their doorsteps, defecate into whole oceans, snatch all the food, survive by detestation, take joy in the bad luck of others, celebrate the death of others, live for the death of others.

That's it, and I shall stop worrying about the book. It does not signify that man is a sparse, inhuman thing at his center. He's all right. It only says what we've always known and never had enough time to worry about, that we haven't yet learned how to stay human when assembled in masses. The Ik, in his despair, is acting out this failure, and perhaps we should pay closer attention. Nations have themselves become too frightening to think about, but we might learn some things by watching these people.

Writing Topic

According to Thomas, why can the behavior of individual Iks be compared to the behavior of "groups of one size or another, ranging from committees to nations"? What do you think of his argument? Support your answer with examples from your own experience, your observation of others, or your readings.

Vocabulary and Dictionary Practice

Part I.

"The Iks" uses several words that may be new for you. Here are ten that you should familiarize yourself with in order to fully understand Thomas's ideas. Add to this list any other words in the reading selection that you do not know.

For each word on the list, write the two most common definitions on the lines provided and include what part of speech each definition is (noun, verb, adjective, etc). Then, under each of the two definitions, write a sentence that uses the word in a way that reflects that particular definition and part of speech.

1. dismantle
2. speculative
3. zest
4. anomalous
5. malady
6. obscured
7. unremitting
8. constituency
9. harangue
10. rapacity

1. **dismantle**

   first definition: _____

   _____

   part of speech: _____

   sentence: _____

   _____

   second definition: _____

   _____

   part of speech: _____

   sentence: _____

   _____

2. **speculative**

  first definition: _____

  _____

  part of speech: _____

  sentence: _____

  _____

  second definition: _____

  _____

  part of speech: _____

  sentence: _____

  _____

3. **zest**

  first definition: _____

  _____

  part of speech: _____

  sentence: _____

  _____

  second definition: _____

  _____

  part of speech: _____

  sentence: _____

  _____

4. **anomalous**

  first definition: _____

  _____

part of speech: _____

sentence: _____

_____

second definition: _____

_____

part of speech: _____

sentence: _____

_____

5. **malady**

first definition: _____

_____

part of speech: _____

sentence: _____

_____

second definition: _____

_____

part of speech: _____

sentence: _____

_____

6. **obscured**

first definition: _____

_____

part of speech: _____

sentence: _____

_____

second definition: _____

_____

part of speech: _____

sentence: _____

_____

7. **unremitting**

first definition: _____

_____

part of speech: _____

sentence: _____

_____

second definition: _____

_____

part of speech: _____

sentence: _____

_____

8. **constituency**

first definition: _____

_____

part of speech: _____

sentence: _____

_____

second definition: _____

_____

part of speech: _____

sentence: _____

_____

9. **harangue**

first definition: _____

_____

part of speech: _____

sentence: _____

_____

second definition: _____

_____

part of speech: _____

sentence: _____

_____

10. **rapacity**

first definition: _____

_____

part of speech: _____

sentence: _____

_____

second definition: _____

_____

part of speech: _____

sentence: _____

_____

Part II.

A. Write down each sentence from Thomas's essay that contains the following words.

B. Tell which of the word's various definitions best fits the sentence.

C. Paraphrase the sentence without using the vocabulary word; in other words, write the sentence using your own words.

1. **dismantle**

   A. _____

   _____

   B. _____

   _____

   C. _____

   _____

2. **speculative**

   A. _____

   _____

   B. _____

   _____

   C. _____

   _____

3. **zest**

   A. _____

   _____

   B. _____

   _____

   C. _____

   _____

4. **anomalous**

A. _____

_____

B. _____

_____

C. _____

_____

5. **malady**

A. _____

_____

B. _____

_____

C. _____

_____

6. **obscured**

A. _____

_____

B. _____

_____

C. _____

_____

7. **unremitting**

A. _____

_____

B. _____

_____

C. _____

_____

8. **constituency**

A. _____

_____

B. _____

_____

C. _____

_____

9. **harangue**

A. _____

_____

B. _____

_____

C. _____

_____

10. **rapacity**

A. _____

_____

B. _____

_____

C. _____

_____

Part III.

For each of these words from "The Iks," tell something new and interesting you learned about the word from the dictionary. For example, you might have found the correct way to pronounce a word you were already familiar with from reading but not from speaking, or you might have learned that a word you thought of as entirely English came from another language.

1. **dismantle**

   _____

   _____

2. **speculative**

   _____

   _____

3. **zest**

   _____

   _____

4. **anomalous**

   _____

   _____

5. **malady**

   _____

   _____

6. **obscured**

   _____

   _____

7. **unremitting**

   _____

   _____

8. **constituency**

_____

_____

9. **harangue**

_____

_____

10. **rapacity**

_____

_____

Follow-Up Activity

Write two sentences and use at least two of the vocabulary words in each sentence. Be sure that they make sense. Read your sentences to the class.

Doing a Careful Reading of "The Iks"

Now that you know the meaning of all of the words in "The Iks," you should spend more time with the essay, focusing this time on the essay's ideas so that you not only get a better understanding of it, but you also begin forming judgments about its ideas. Use the "Steps for a Thoughtful Reading of an Essay" (introduced in Part 2) to help you with this part of the writing process. Here are the steps:

1. **Read the title again.**
   - The title will tell you something about the reading's main topic.
   - It may also tell you something about Thomas's opinion on the topic.
   - Think about what you already know about the topic and what more you want to know.

2. **Learn about the author.**
   - Read the biographical information about Lewis Thomas at the top of the selection.
   - As you go through the remaining steps below, take note of how Thomas's life or work might connect with his topic.

3. **Read through the selection once quickly.**
   - Read quickly through "The Iks" again so that you get a general fresh impression of what it is about and what Thomas's attitude is toward the topic.
   - Find and mark the things—people, places, experiences, concepts, for example—that he brings up to develop and support his opinion about the topic.

4. **Read again to identify the thesis.**
   - Now read Thomas's essay a second time, but more slowly and carefully, and *with a pen or highlighter in your hand.*
   - Find the thesis and underline it or write it in the margin. Remember, the thesis states the author's overall opinion on the topic of the reading. Often, the thesis is contained in a single sentence, but, in some cases, it takes several sentences to make the main argument of the reading selection clear. There are times, too,

when the author does not state his or her thesis explicitly, but, if you read the selection carefully, you should be able to state it and then write it in the margin.

- To help, ask yourself, "What does Thomas seem to want readers to think about his topic?"

5. **Read slowly and methodically through the rest of the reading.**

- Examine each body paragraph one at a time, and list or underline the kinds of evidence that Thomas uses to support his thesis

- Look in each body paragraph for a *topic sentence*—a sentence that both presents an idea and tells how it gives support to the author's overall opinion.

- As you read and study the selection, *be sure to write down any thoughts you have* about the author's opinion and his supporting evidence.

- It is your job to evaluate this evidence for its logic and validity, so be sure to *make notes in the margins* as you read.

- *Mark the points* that you found interesting or convincing, and write a few words explaining your thoughts.

- Note, too, any weaknesses you find.

- When you look back at the notes you made in the margins, you should have a general idea of how convincing you found "The Iks" and what you found to be its strengths and weaknesses.

6. **Read again for review.**

- Once you have completed steps 1-5 and have thought carefully about Thomas's ideas, read it once more, looking for places where you don't quite understand what is being said.

- Underline any terms that you aren't familiar with, and look them up in a dictionary.

- Mark any places that don't fit with your understanding of "The Iks" as a whole. Decide whether this is something that Thomas should have revised, or whether it is something that you need to read again because you don't understand it. You may find that you need to go back to Step 4 and begin working through the reading selection again.

- Once you are certain that you understand the entire reading, you are prepared to discuss, summarize, and/or respond to the writing topic that follows "The Iks."

Follow-Up Activity

Before taking this class, how many times did you usually read an essay such as "The Iks" before you felt you understood it entirely? Go back over the six steps for a careful reading listed above and count how many times you are directed to read through "The Iks." Compare the two numbers and, if they do not match, evaluate your reading strategy before taking this class against the one you are using now. Explain your conclusions to the class.

Questions to Review Your Understanding of "The Iks"

Working with a partner, write your answers to the following questions. Then, share your answers with the class.

Paragraph 1

What two bad things does the author say happened to the Iks? Do you agree that these things should both be called "bad"? Explain.

Paragraph 2

What kind of people did the Iks turn into as a result of the bad things that happened to them? When the rest of us have similarly bad experiences, what, according to the anthropologist, will happen to us?

Paragraphs 3–5

To agree that we all have the potential to turn into Iks, what assumptions about human nature must we make?

Paragraphs 6–7

Why does Thomas say the Iks are not representative of ordinary human nature?

Paragraphs 7–8

What is Thomas's theory about the Iks? Does his explanation seem plausible to you? Why or why not?

Paragraph 9
In what ways are cities and nations like the Iks?

Paragraph 10
What do you think Thomas means when he concludes that we must "learn to stay human when assembled in masses"? Do you agree?

Responding to the Writing Topic

You should now have a good understanding of the ideas and overall message of "The Iks." Now is a good time in the writing process to look again at the writing topic and begin to think about how you will respond. Remember that the essay you write must respond to all parts of the writing topic. Here is the topic again:

Writing Topic

According to Thomas, why can the behavior of individual Iks be compared to the behavior of "groups of one size or another, ranging from committees to nations"? What do you think of his argument? Support your answer with examples from your own experience, your observation of others, or your readings.

Examine all parts of the writing topic:

- You are first asked a question about a specific aspect of "The Iks," a question that uses the word "**why**." It asks you to explain **why** Thomas believes that the behavior of the Iks is similar to the behavior of groups, including political ones. Why does he make that claim, and how does he support his argument? Your essay will have to answer this first part of the writing topic.

  You may remember from Assignment 4 that your response to this part of the writing topic can be called the *directed summary*, and you will present it in the introductory paragraph of your essay.

- The second question in the writing topic asks you to state whether you think that Thomas's claim that these two things—Iks and various kinds of groups—holds true. If you annotated "The Iks" carefully, you should have identified the characteristics of the Iks. Think about the various kinds of groups you have belonged to or observed. Do most of them act in ways similar to the Iks, as Thomas claims? Your answer to this question will become the thesis of your essay because it will state your overarching view on the topic.

  Your thesis *statement* will follow your directed summary and will close your introductory paragraph.

- The third part of the writing topic tells you to support your opinion—your thesis—with clear examples taken from your own experiences. The following activity will help you begin to find some of those examples. Be sure to keep notes on your ideas so that you can turn back to them later.

Follow-Up Activity

1. List ten groups that you have been a part of or have observed—for example, college or professional football teams, Republicans and Democrats during an election year, sororities and fraternities, or perhaps groups formed as part of a church or religious institution.

2. Under each of the ten groups you listed, give five words or phrases that describe the group's actions. Try to choose five words or phrases that capture how each group behaves or what its members try to accomplish.

3. From your list of ten and based on each group's actions and accomplishments, choose the group you would most want to be a part of, and tell why.

4. From your list of ten and based on each group's actions and accomplishments, choose the group you would least want to be a part of, and tell why.

5. Partner with a classmate and discuss your lists and opinions.

Strategies to Help You Analyze a Reading Selection and Develop Your Ideas for Writing a Response

All of the activities you have done so far will contribute to the essay you ultimately write, but a deeper analysis of Thomas's ideas is an important part of the process. You want to be sure to avoid misrepresenting any author's ideas or views.

It is especially important that you begin with an open mind and fully explore all of the aspects of an author's ideas. If you do not spend time with them, you might represent them unfairly or less seriously than the ideas deserve. To avoid these mistakes, use the strategies for analysis that you learned in Assignment 4. Take your time with them and, keeping an open mind, use them to look more deeply at Thomas's argument and evidence.

Remember the strategies for analyzing a reading selection: *questioning*, *freewriting*, and *listing*. This time, as you use the various subparts under each, see if you can commit them to memory so that you can use them any time you engage with reading material. Each time you use them, you will notice that one strategy may work better for a particular reading selection than the others. If you memorize them, you will be able to decide which strategy or strategies might work best for the writing assignment you are completing. For now, though, because they are new to you, go through them all to analyze "The Iks."

Questioning

- questions about the highlighting you did:
  Why did I underline this part of the reading?

  How is this information important to Thomas's point?

  What is the relationship between this information and the question I am being asked to write about?

- questions about Thomas's ideas:
  What things in this essay do not make sense to me?

  Where do I think the author should have explained further?

  How do the examples in the essay relate to the author's point?

- questions about "The Iks" that seem important:

What are some of the things that Thomas says that I am happy to hear someone say?

What things that the author says seem true to me?

What things that the author says seem wrong to me?

What thing that the author says is most important to me?

What idea in this essay is completely new to me?

Freewriting

If you still feel that you have little to say to respond to Thomas's essay and topic, try some freewriting.

- Pick one or more of your answers to the questions you have already answered, and just begin to write about it.
- While you are doing this writing, do not stop; do not censor yourself; just let the words come.
- Do this for about five or ten minutes without thinking about spelling, grammar, word choice, or even the sense of what you are saying.
- When you have completed this activity, you will want to take a break.
- After your brief break, come back and read what you have written. Most of what you now have down on paper will not end up in your essay, but, as you read through your freewriting, you will find one or more sentences or ideas that seem interesting, important, or even compelling to you. Highlight these points and ideas.

Listing

With this strategy, you simply list all of the thoughts and reactions you have noted so far. By looking down your list, you may see a pattern of ideas develop, one that you can use to develop an essay of your own.

- List all of the annotations you made for "The Iks."
- List the main ideas you can see in your answers to the questioning phase above.
- List any main ideas that developed from your responses to the follow-up activities above.

- Be sure to list all the items from your freewriting that you thought were interesting. As you make this list, other ideas may come into your head. Put them on your list as well.

Study your list. Connect with some kind of mark all the ideas that seem related to each other. When you are done, one related group of ideas will probably be longer than the others. This group should give you a good start on what you want to say in your own essay in response to Thomas's ideas.

Shaping Your Ideas into a Rough Draft

Now that you have done extensive prewriting, you are prepared to plan the rough draft of your essay. Although you may already have written out parts of your draft as you worked on some of the activities above, it is time now to think about each part of your essay and how you will compose it. Turn back to Part 2 and examine "A Suggested Structure for an Essay That Responds to Another Writer's Essay." Also, look again at the writing topic for "The Iks." Notice that it asks you to do three things:

1) Write a summary that tells **why** Thomas believes that the behavior of individual Iks can be compared to the behavior of people in groups.

Remember that you have already worked on this in earlier activities. Look back now to the work you did. You may be able to use some of it below, when you write your essay's *directed summary*.

2) Take a position on this idea; do you agree with Thomas?

This is your thesis statement, and it will unify your essay, so it's important that you write it out clearly. Turn back to the review questions you answered and the follow-up activities you did. What were your thoughts and ideas? You will use them below when you write a thesis statement. Remember that you can always revise it as you work on your rough draft.

3) Support and develop your position using specific evidence taken from your own experiences and readings.

Your response to this part of the writing topic will make up nearly your entire essay. The explanations and support you offer will make up your essay's body paragraphs. Remember some of the thinking you did about groups you've belonged to or observed. You will be able to use some of this as evidence to support your thesis. Remember it when you begin working on body paragraphs.

Drafting Your Directed Summary

Here are some questions that will help you answer the first part of the writing topic. Answer each one as thoroughly and carefully as you can; then, use your answers and those you wrote in earlier activities to draft a directed summary that answers the first question:

> According to Thomas, **why** can the behavior of individual Iks **be compared to** the behavior of "groups of one size or another, ranging from committees to nations"?

Notice that this question does *not* ask you to summarize the entire essay. Rather, it asks you to explain one aspect of Thomas's essay. The important action words are bolded. Notice that the first question asks you to **explain why** Thomas finds similarities between the Iks and groups of various sizes. How do Iks behave, and why does Thomas find the same kind of behavior when people are in groups, including large groups such as nations?

Here are some questions that will help you plan your directed summary in response to the first question.

1. Why does Thomas say the Iks have a "mean society"?

2. Why does he think the Iks act in the way that they do?

3. In what ways do groups exhibit behavior similar to the Iks, according to Thomas?

4. Why does he think groups act the way they do?

Follow-Up Activity

1. After completing the questions above, share your answers with the class. Discuss the important points from "The Iks" that should be included in the directed summary.
2. Draft your directed summary.
3. Form small groups, and take turns in each group reading your summaries aloud. Discuss the strengths and weaknesses of each.

Developing Your Thesis Statement

The second question in the writing topic asks you to evaluate Thomas's point of view regarding the behavior patterns shared by the Iks and groups of various sizes. Do groups frequently exhibit the kinds of behavior shown by the Iks? You are asked: "What do you think of his argument?" How will you respond to this question? Your answer will be the *thesis* of your essay.

Think of your thesis as composed of three parts:

- the subject being considered
- Thomas's claim about the subject
- your opinion about the subject

Fill in your answer on the line below to form your thesis statement.

The subject/Thomas's idea about the subject AND your opinion about the subject

_____

_____

_____

_____

_____

_____

After you have finished writing your sentence, review your statement to see that it contains the following elements:

- Thomas's point of view on the subject
- your point of view on the subject

If either of these elements is missing, rewrite your thesis statement so that both are included.

Up to this point, you have been planning the draft of your introductory paragraph. Now that you have drafted your thesis statement, you can begin planning your body paragraphs. They will have to explain your ideas and give support to your thesis statement.

Developing Body Paragraphs for an Essay That Presents a Thesis

Reminders:

Body paragraphs make up the largest part of an essay.

- The job of each body paragraph is to develop one point that supports the thesis statement.
- Taken together, these points constitute the argument of the essay.
- Writing a good body paragraph can be easy once you understand the criteria that the body paragraph must fulfill.

Here is a review of the three most important criteria for paragraphs in an argumentative essay:

1. **an appropriate or suitable topic**—one that supports the thesis statement

2. **evidence**—for instance, a concrete fact, example, or quotation—that demonstrates the point of the paragraph

3. **a link to the thesis**—sentences that show how and why the paragraph, including the evidence, relates to the thesis

A Basic Outline Form for an Essay That Presents a Thesis

All of the work you have done so far—reading and carefully annotating "The Iks," analyzing its ideas, writing a directed summary in response to the first question in the writing topic, thinking about your own experiences and deciding on your thesis statement, and drafting your essay's introduction—should be gathered together now into a shape that will become your essay, your response to the writing topic for "The Iks."

- Remember that you should follow the basic structure of an academic essay.
- To refresh your memory, turn back to Part 2 and review the diagram of the academic essay format.
- As you begin filling in this diagram form, you should be able to turn back to material you have already drafted as you worked through the exercises in this unit.
- Fill in the diagram form as fully as you can. A good plan will help you draft an essay that is clear and coherent.

I. Introductory Paragraph:

A. one or two opening sentences that give the reading selection's title, author, and main topic:

_____

_____

_____

B. the main points that will be included in the directed summary:

1.

2.

3.

4.

C. your thesis statement: Be sure that it presents a clear position in response to the writing topic. State your thesis in your own words.

_____

_____

_____

II. **Body Paragraphs: For each body paragraph you will include in your essay, plan the following parts:**
Write down the main point for the paragraph.

_____

_____

_____

List the evidence you will use to support your main point (fact, example, etc.).

_____

_____

_____

_____

_____

_____

Tell how the evidence and your ideas link to the thesis statement.

_____

_____

_____

_____

_____

(Repeat this part of the outline as often as necessary to plan all of your body paragraphs.)

III. **Conclusion: What are some general remarks you can make to close your essay? Perhaps you will remind your readers of the main argument of your paper, for example.**

_____

_____

_____

Drafting Your Essay

Now that you have a basic plan for the structure of your essay and a map of its various parts, you are ready to begin drafting.

- Look back to Part 2 and review the diagram of the thesis-centered essay. It will help you to keep a coherent structure in mind as you put together the sections of your outline.

- If your thinking changes as you draft, return to your outline and make necessary adjustments. Every time you decide to revise your outline and essay, remember that this is a good sign, a sign that your thinking is developing and becoming more thoughtful and convincing.

- Don't stop thinking. Allow yourself to pursue lines of thought that sometimes develop during the drafting stage. Keep turning back to all of the activities in this unit as you draft your essay. Try to recall some of your reactions, thoughts, and ideas as you worked on these activities. This may help you to strengthen, expand on, or more fully develop your essay's argument.

Follow-Up Activity

Your draft will always benefit from careful rereadings. Even better is to let others hear or read your draft and give you their feedback. Sometimes, a classmate or family member can spot places in your draft where you aren't clear, or where you have neglected to fix a grammar error.

1. Working with a partner or small group, have a classmate read your draft out loud slowly. Stop the person whenever anyone hears a problem or an error. As you listen, make notes on the changes you want to make. Then, discuss the draft with your partner or group. Give everyone a chance to hear his or her draft read out loud.

2. Read a classmate's rough draft. Then, choose the paragraph or group of sentences that, in your opinion, are the strongest part of the essay. Read the sentences out loud to the writer of the draft, and explain why you chose them.

3. Working with a partner, each of you read aloud one of the two student essays below. As one person reads it, the second one should mark places where revision is necessary or where it would help improve the essay. After you finish reading, discuss your suggestions for revising the essay.

Student Essay 1

THE IKS

In the essay the "Iks" by Lewis Thomas, the author describes a society that had got their homes taken away by the government. The Iks were a tribe of selfish people, who didn't care for anybody but for themselves. They left the elderly to starve and die, in the middle of nowhere, and they did not care about their children. Anthropologists were sent to observe the Iks behavior after they were removed from their home. Knowing they were being watched, it caused them to act differently. Thomas believed that nations behave like the Iks quoting, "groups of one size or another, ranging from committees to nations," meaning that cities and nations all over the world act like Iks because of the selfish ways they obtain. If people were to look the way each nation treats each other is the same way, the Iks treat one another. Thomas implies that many nations' and cities' behavior can be compared to the Iks; this is true due to all the discrimination, racism, and cruelty people present to each other in various ways.

Discrimination is an act or instance, when distinctions are made between 'two groups. Thomas suggests that cities and nations behave like the Iks because of all the selfish things nations do to each other. In the United States there is major historical events of discrimination, showing how the United States behaved like the !ks. The trail of tears was one of America's worst examples of discrimination. In the 1800's, President Andrew Jackson passed the Indian removal act of 1830, making all Indian nations move out to the city of Oklahoma, where all Indian tribes were kept. This example is very accurate to Thomas' essay because it proves how nations discriminate against others even if they live on the same land.

Racism to this day continues to be a major act of discrimination all over the world. Edward Said's Essay "Clashing Civilizations" explains how racial discrimination is expressed. Since the air plane crash of 9111, Americans come together in memory of the tragical event that took place. Said quotes, "What has persisted, often insidiously and implicitly, in discussion since the terrible events of September 11." Said's meaning to this quote is that since the United States knows that Osama Binladin was responsible for this horrible event, and just because his ethnicity is Muslim, U.S. citizens believe that all Muslim nations are bad just because of one man's actions. Not all Muslims are bad as there are innocent men, women and children just like in every other country. Even in the United States, many ethnic groups discriminate each other based on the color of their skin. White men come together and formed the KKK, discriminating against African Americans because of their skin color.

In all these Major events, evidence of cruelty is the reason why people feel depressed and makes nations behave differently. When Anthropologist were observing the !ks, the tribe acted differently, and became angry towards the outsiders. In my opinion that would be known as cruelty. In World War 2, Adolf Hitler wanted to abolish the Jewish nation by sending them to concentration camps where they were tortured, burned, and shot. All these cruel horrific crimes were very shocking to many, but the Nazis didn't care about anybody but for Germans. The whole point ofa World War, is the battle of nations fighting for territory, land, or supplies for their country.

In conclusion, Thomas's argument about nations and cities behaving like the !ks is correct. The discrimination, racism, and cruelty happening around the world prove his point. Historical events in the United States prove that nations are selfish and only care about what benefits them and people only come together, to battle other nations and prove whose better than the other. In addition, internal discrimination takes place when citizens form ethnic groups and discriminate against each other, and cause racism in the nation. All these events are very cruel and still persist today, as if nothing has really changed.

Student Essay 2

THE "IKS"

Essay

In "The Iks", Lewis Thomas compares the behavior of the Iks with nations and committees. The behaviors ofIks are demeaning and are known as " brutish creatures" (Lewis Thomas "The Iks"). The Iks are known to defecate on "each other's doorstep." Thomas uses cities and nation as his examples for comparing the Iks. Thomas compares them to nations because the individual Iks are their own country. Fending off for themself and telling others that he is their own man. Thomas'

(Continues)

explanation of the Iks being their own group is because they "built a new defense for himself" (Lewis Thomas "The Iks"). Since the governmnent of Uganda took away their land and life as nomads. With their main resource gone, Iks started to behave irregularly. An anthropologist, who had stayed and studied the Iks was treated in a ill-mannered fashion. For two years, he was constantly harassed and shamed by the Iks, in the end he wrote a book on how he despised the Iks. According to Thomas, nations resemble the Iks since they usually help themselves and do not bother to help others. He believes that Iks are like this because of their own egoism. I do not agree with Thomas' conclusion of nations and cities becoming like the Iks, because the country of Taiwan, United States of America, and Thomas' example do not resemble the Iks at all.

The government and cities of Taiwan has always helped their own people and tried do their very best when the inhabitants were in dire need. Taiwan was in deep trouble when the ex-president, Chen Shui-bian, was in presidency. He was well known for scandals that caused Taiwan's system to be in chaos. He and his wife, Wu Shu-chen, have been stealing money from the government spending. Also, stealing money that was to be given to the needy. Each city in Taiwan detested the president, because he had claim he did take the money. These two people were very corrupted and the citizens had to do something about them. During the year 2008, many citizens and some of the government officials who despised Chen, voted for the other president, Ma Ying-jeou. Most citizens admired Ma because he was true to his country. Also, he campaigned his own opinions to help Taiwan's economy and government. While, Chen tried to sabotage Ma's rating of the votes. The behaviors of the citizens has redefined Taiwan's system. Since the inauguration of Ma, the economy of Taiwan has been growing rapidly. The citizens has acted in unification to rid the illness causing Taiwan's problems. Taiwan as a nation has proven Thomas's conclusion to be incorrect. Like Taiwan, United States of America has been helpful to other nations.

Their is no relation between the Iks and America, because America helps other nation's problems while trying to fix their own problems. United States has been known for helping other nations who can not defend for themselves. America has also forgiven the debts of other countries and lent aid to nations that are in need of military support and funding: America's troops are spread out in different countries to take care and help out. Thomas believes that "their is no such thing as affection between nations" (Lewis Thomas "The Iks"). America has shown affection towards nations, such as Iraq, Japan, and third world countries. Each city in America are unique in their own ways. All cities has their own governor. The citizens of each city, voices their own opinions to the governor in order to get an idea across. America will never come close to becoming like the Iks. The information Thomas gives, reveal that the Iks does not have a base system anymore.

The Iks has been cornered off by the government of Uganda. Their hunting rights has been revoked in front of their very own eyes. Also, they are made to convert to farming with an area to poor to grow crops. Thomas's theory of "the Iks have gone crazy" (Lewis Thomas "The Iks") is completely true. Which tribe would not have gone crazy, if their main export is hunting and it has been taking right out of their hands. Also, to be given farming supplies to farm, where the idea of farming is new to them. The Iles should not be distinguished between nations because the Iks are just not adapting to what they have right now. The tribe is showing survival of the fittest instead of staying as a group and trying to figure out things to benefit each other. If the Iks had put their heads together and think, they would not be known as "brutish creatures who are heartless" (Lewis Thomas "The Iks").

The whole idea of Thomas's statement of Iks being just like nations, should be revoked. The Iks are not nations nor cities, they are a tribe that does not know what to do when things are taken away from them. The example of Taiwan has proven cities to be helpful towards their citizens and not to be greedy. Nations, such as America, are helpful towards other nations and are not irresponsible. I believe Iks are their own group and should not be compared to committees, cities, nor nations. People try to help each other out unlike the Iks, who only help themselves.

Supplemental Reading

A World Not Neatly Divided

Essay

AMARTYA SEN

> *Amartya Sen is an economist presently teaching at Harvard. Many of his books and articles focus on globalization and gender inequality.*

When people talk about clashing civilizations, as so many politicians and academics do now, they can sometimes miss the central issue. The inadequacy of this thesis begins well before we get to the question of whether civilizations must clash. The basic weakness of the theory lies in its program of categorizing people of the world according to a unique, allegedly commanding system of classification. This is problematic because civilizational categories are crude and inconsistent and also because there are other ways of seeing people (linked to politics, language, literature, class, occupation, or other affiliations).

The befuddling influence of a singular classification also traps those who dispute the thesis of a clash: To talk about "the Islamic world" or "the Western world" is already to adopt an impoverished vision of humanity as unalterably divided. In fact, civilizations are hard to partition in this way, given the diversities within each society as well as the linkages among different countries and cultures. For example, describing India as a "Hindu civilization" misses the fact that India has more Muslims than any other country except Indonesia and possibly Pakistan. It is futile to try to understand Indian art, literature, music, food, or politics without seeing the extensive interactions across barriers of religious communities. These include Hindus and Muslims, Buddhists, Jains, Sikhs, Parsees, Christians (who have been in India since at least the fourth century, well before England's conversion to Christianity), Jews (present since the fall of Jerusalem), and even atheists and agnostics. Sanskrit has a larger atheistic literature than exists in any other classical language. Speaking of India as a Hindu civilization may be comforting to the Hindu fundamentalist, but it is an odd reading of India.

A similar coarseness can be seen in other categories invoked, like "the Islamic world." Consider Akbar and Aurangzeb, two Muslim emperors of the Mogul dynasty in India. Aurangzeb tried hard to convert Hindus into Muslims and instituted various policies in that direction, of which taxing the non-Muslims was only one example. In contrast, Akbar reveled in his multiethnic court and pluralist laws, and issued official proclamations insisting that no one "should be interfered with on account of religion" and that "anyone is to be allowed to go over to a religion that pleases him."

If a homogeneous view of Islam were to be taken, then only one of these emperors could count as a true Muslim. The Islamic fundamentalist would have no time for Akbar; Prime Minister Tony Blair, given his insistence that tolerance is a defining characteristic of Islam, would have to consider excommunicating Aurangzeb. I expect both Akbar and Aurangzeb would protest, and so would I. A similar crudity is present in the characterization of what is called "Western civilization." Tolerance and individual freedom have certainly been present in European history. But there is no dearth of diversity here, either. When Akbar was making his pronouncements on religious tolerance in Agra, in the 1590s, the Inquisitions were still going on; in 1600, Giordano Bruno was burned at the stake, for heresy, in Campo dei Fiori in Rome.

Dividing the world into discrete civilizations is not just crude. It propels us into the absurd belief that this partitioning is natural and necessary and must overwhelm all other ways of identifying people. That imperious view goes not only against the sentiment that "we human beings are all much the same," but also against the more plausible understanding that we are diversely different. For example, Bangladesh's split from Pakistan was not connected with religion, but with language and politics.

Each of us has many features in our self-conception. Our religion, important as it may be, cannot be an all-engulfing identity. Even a shared poverty can be a source of solidarity across the borders. The kind of division highlighted by, say, the so-called "antiglobalization" protesters—whose movement is, incidentally, one of the most globalized in the world—tries to unite the underdogs of the world economy and goes firmly against religious, national, or "civilizational" lines of division.

The main hope of harmony lies not in any imagined uniformity, but in the plurality of our identities, which cut across each other and work against sharp divisions into impenetrable civilizational camps. Political leaders who think and act in terms of sectioning off humanity into various "worlds" stand to make the world more flammable—even when their intentions are very different. They also end up, in the case

(Continues)

of civilizations defined by religion, lending authority to religious leaders seen as spokesmen for their "worlds." In the process, other voices are muffled and other concerns silenced. The robbing of our plural identities not only reduces us; it impoverishes the world.

Discussion Questions

1. Why, according to Sen, is it wrong to classify the people of the world into clashing civilizations?

2. How does his example of Akbar and Aurangzeb illustrate his point about the failure of civilization categories?

3. What change in conception about the world and its people does Sen propose?

From *New York Times*, November 23, 2001 by Amartya Sen. Copyright © 2001 by Amartya Sen. Reprinted by permission of the author.

from *The Cosmic Connection*

Carl Sagan

Carl Sagan (1934–1996) was an American astronomer, an astrochemist, and a successful writer. He popularized astronomy and astrophysics, and promoted the search for extraterrestrial intelligence. He was a professor at Cornell University and a leading promoter of the space program. Sagan contributed to most of the unmanned space missions that explored the solar system, and he conceived the idea of adding a universal message on spacecraft charted to leave the solar system that might be understood by any extraterrestrial intelligence.

In our earliest history, so far as we can tell, individuals held an allegiance toward their immediate tribal group, which may have numbered no more than ten or twenty individuals, all of whom were related by blood. As time went on, the need for cooperative behavior—in the hunting of large animals or large herds, in agriculture, and in the development of cities—forced human beings into larger and larger groups. The group that was identified with, the tribal unit, enlarged at each stage of this evolution. Today, a particular instant in the 4.5-billion-year history of Earth and in the several-million-year history of mankind, most human beings owe their primary allegiance to the nation-state (although some of the most dangerous political problems still arise from tribal conflicts involving smaller population units).

Many visionary leaders have imagined a time when the allegiance of an individual human being is not to his or her particular nation-state, religion, race, or economic group, but to mankind as a whole; when the benefit to a human being of another sex, race, religion, or political persuasion ten thousand miles away is as precious to us as to our neighbor or our brother. The trend is in this direction, but it is agonizingly slow. There is a serious question whether such a global self-identification of mankind can be achieved before we destroy ourselves with the technological forces our intelligence has unleashed.

There is no doubt that our instinctual apparatus has changed little from the hunter-gatherer days of several hundred thousand years ago. Our society has changed enormously from those times, and the greatest problems of survival in the contemporary world can be understood in terms of this conflict—between what we feel we must do because of our

(Continues)

primeval instincts and what we know we must do because of our learned knowledge.

If we survive these perilous times, it is clear that even an identification with all of mankind is not the ultimate desirable identification. If we have a profound respect for other human beings as co-equal recipients of this precious patrimony of 4.5 billion years of evolution, why should the identification not apply also to all the other organisms on Earth, which are equally the product of 4.5 billion years of evolution? We care for a small fraction of the organisms on Earth—dogs, cats, and cows, for example—because they are useful or because they flatter us. But spiders and salamanders, salmon and sunflowers are equally our brothers and sisters.

I believe that the difficulty we all experience in extending our identification horizons in this way is itself genetic. Ants of one tribe will fight to the death intrusions by ants of another. Human history is filled with monstrous cases of small differences—in skin pigmentation, in religious beliefs, or even manner of dress and hair style—being the cause of harassment, enslavement, and murder.

A being quite like us, but with a small physiological difference—a third eye, say, or blue hair covering the nose and forehead—somehow evokes feelings of revulsion. Such feelings may have had adaptive value at one time in defending our small tribe against the beasts and neighbors. But in our times, such feelings are obsolete and dangerous.

The time has come for a respect, a reverence, not just for all human beings, but for all life forms—as we would have respect for a masterpiece of sculpture or an exquisitely tooled machine. This, of course, does not mean that we should abandon the imperatives for our own survival. Respect for the tetanus bacillus does not extend to volunteering our body as a culture medium. But at the same time, we can recall that here is an organism with a biochemistry that tracks back deep into our planet's past. The tetanus bacillus is poisoned by molecular oxygen, which we breathe so freeely. The tetanus bacillus, but not we, would be at home in the hydrogen-rich oxygen-free atmosphere of primitive Earth.

A reverence for all life is implemented in a few of the religions of the planet Earth—for example, among the Jains of India. And something like this idea is responsible for vegetarianism, at least in the minds of many practitioners of the dietary constraint. But why is it better to kill plants than animals?

Human beings can survive only by killing other organisms. But we can make ecological compensation by also growing other organisms; by encouraging the forest; by preventing the wholesale slaughter of organisms such as seals and whales, imagined to have industrial or commercial value; by outlawing gratuitous hunting; and by making the environment of Earth more livable—for all its inhabitants.

There may be a time when contact will be made with another intelligence on a planet of some far-distant star, beings with billions of years of quite independent evolution, beings with no prospect of looking very much like us—although they may think very much like us. It is important that we extend our identification horizons, not just down to the simplest and most humble forms of life on our own planet, but also up to the exotic and advanced forms of life that may inhabit, with us, our vast galaxy of stars.

Discussion Questions

1. Explain the evolutionary trend that Sagan sees toward global self-identification. Do you think we will ever reach this state? Why or why not?

2. What does Sagan believe to be the greatest threat to the survival of our world? What do you think is the biggest danger facing the world as we know it?

3. Give an example of an organism Sagan would believe it is necessary to kill. How does he justify killing such a life form? Do you support his position? What does Sagan think humans must do to compensate for killing these organisms? What other compensatory actions can you suggest?

4. Compare Sagan's ideas to Thomas's. Considering such anomalies as the Iks and the examples of political situations pointed out by Sen, whose exploration of group-think makes the most sense to you? Explain your choice.

I Believe in Empathy

Azar Nafisi

Azar Nafisi, who was born in Iran and became an American citizen in 2008, has published both scholarly and popular works. Her memoir Reading Lolita in Tehran: A Memoir in Books *(2003) was a New York Times bestseller that has been translated into more than thirty languages. Nafisi is a visiting fellow at Johns Hopkins University's School of Advanced International Studies.*

I believe in empathy. I believe in the kind of empathy that is created through imagination and through intimate, personal relationships. I am a writer and a teacher, so much of my time is spent interpreting stories and connecting to other individuals. It is the urge to know more about ourselves and others that creates empathy. Through imagination and our desire for rapport, we transcend our limitations, freshen our eyes, and are able to look at ourselves and the world through a new and alternative lens.

Whenever I think of the word "empathy," I think of a small boy named Huckleberry Finn contemplating his friend and runaway slave, Jim. Huck asks himself whether he should give Jim up or not. Huck has been told in Sunday school that people who let slaves go free go to "everlasting fire" (Twain 295). But then, Huck says he imagines himself and Jim in "the day and in the night-time, sometimes" moonlight, sometimes storms, and we a-floating along, talking and singing and laughing" (Twain 296). Huck remembers Jim and their friendship and warmth. He imagines Jim not as a slave but as a human being, and he decides that, "All right, then, I'll go to hell" (Twain 297).

What Huck rejects is not religion but an attitude of self-righteousness and inflexibility. I remember this particular scene out of Huckleberry Finn so vividly today because I associate it with a difficult time in my own life. In the early 1980s, when I taught at the University of Tehran, I, like many others, was expelled. I was very surprised to discover that my staunchest allies were two students who were very active at the university's powerful Muslim Students' Association. These young men and I had engaged in very passionate and heated arguments. I had fiercely opposed their ideological stances. But that didn't stop them from defending me. When I ran into one of them after my expulsion, I thanked him for his support. "We are not as rigid as you imagine us to be, Professor Nafisi," he responded. "Remember your own lectures on Huck Finn? Let's just say, he is not the only one who can risk going to hell!"

This experience in my life reinforces my belief in the mysterious connections that link individuals to each other despite their vast differences. No amount of political correctness can make us empathize with a child left orphaned in Darfur or a woman taken to a football stadium in Kabul and shot to death because she is improperly dressed. Only curiosity about the fate of others, the ability to put ourselves in their shoes, and the will to enter their world through the magic of imagination create this shock of recognition. Without this empathy, there can be no genuine dialogue, and we as individuals and nations will remain isolated and alien, segregated and fragmented.

I believe that it is only through empathy that the pain experienced by an Algerian woman, a North Korean dissident, a Rwandan child, or an Iraqi prisoner becomes real to me and not just passing news. And it is at times like this when I ask myself, am I prepared—like Huck Finn—to give up Sunday school heaven for the kind of hell that Huck chose?

Work Cited

Twain, Mark. Huckleberry Finn. 1884. New York: Harper, 1918. Print.

Discussion Questions

1. Define the word "empathy." How does Azar Nafisi believe empathy is created? What personal characteristics do you think a person must have to feel empathy? Tell about a time when you had empathy for a stranger or strangers, whether human or animal, caused you to go out of your way to take action. What was the situation? What did you do? Discuss an example of someone you know personally, read about in a book, or experienced through visual media who lacked empathy. What specific behaviors were the result of this lack of empathy?

2. Identify and discuss the two examples Nafisi gives of behaviors that result from empathy. Give some examples in which empathizing with others could change or has changed the way we behave as a society or a nation.

(Continues)

3. What behaviors of the Iks could be a result of their lack of empathy? How would learning to experience empathy change their society? If you were a Peace Corps worker sent to help the Iks, where would you begin?

It Takes a Tribe

Essay

DAVID BERREBY

Independent scholar David Berrery earned his BA in English from Yale University in 1981. His science writing has appeared in many publications, including Smithsonian, the New Yorker, and the scholarly journal Nature. His 2005 book Us and Them: Understanding Your Tribal Mind (revised in 2008 as Us and Them: The Science of Identity) won the Erving Goffman Award for Outstanding Scholarship.

When the budding pundit Walter Lippmann coined the term "stereotype" back in 1922, he offered several examples from the America of his time: "Agitator." "Intellectual." "South European." "From the Back Bay." You know, he told the reader, when a glimpse and a word or two create a full mental picture of a whole group of people. As in "plutocrat." Or "foreigner." Or "Harvard man." Harvard man? We know, thanks to Lippmann, that stereotypes are part of serious problems like racism, prejudice, and injustice. What is Lippmann's alma mater doing on such a list? (He even added: "How different from the statement, 'He is a Yale man.'")

Spend time on a campus in coming weeks, though, and you'll see what he meant.

At colleges across the country, from Ivy League to less exclusive state schools, students who are mispronouncing the library's name this month will soon feel truly and deeply a part of their college. They'll be singing their school songs and cherishing the traditions (just as soon as they learn what they are). They'll talk the way "we" do. (Going to Texas A&M? Then greet people with a cheerful "howdy.") They'll learn contempt for that rival university—Oklahoma to their Texas, Sacramento State to their UC Davis, Annapolis to their West Point.

They may come to believe, too, that an essential trait separates them from the rest of humanity—the same sort of feeling most Americans have about races, ethnic groups, and religions. As the writer Christopher Buckley said recently in his college's alumni magazine: "When I run into a Yale man I somehow feel that I am with a kindred spirit. A part of that kindred-ness comes from his gentility and his not being all jumped up about it. It's a certain sweetness of character."

(Continues)

All this sentiment comes on fast (a study last year at Ivy League campuses found freshmen even more gung-ho than older students). Yet college loyalty, encouraged by alumni relations offices, can last a lifetime—as enduring as the Princeton tiger tattooed on the buttock of former Secretary of State George P. Shultz, or the Yale sweater sported by evil Mr. Burns on "The Simpsons," a number of whose writers went to Harvard.

New identities are forged within the university as well, in elite groups like Skull and Bones at Yale or the Corps of Cadets at Texas A&M or Michigamua at the University of Michigan; in sororities and fraternities; even in particular majors and particular labs. Students don't just attend a college; they join its tribes.

"What endlessly impresses me is people losing sight of how arbitrary it is," says Robert M. Sapolsky, a Stanford biologist who specializes in the links between social life and stress. "Students understand how readily they could have wound up at another school or wound up in another lab." Yet every year, he adds, "they fall for it." For most, what Professor Sapolsky calls that "nutty but palpable" onset of college tribalism is just a part of campus life. For social scientists, it's an object of research, offering clues to a fundamental and puzzling aspect of human nature: People need to belong, to feel a part of "us." Yet a sense of "us" brings with it a sense of "them."

Human beings will give a lot, including their lives, for a group they feel part of—for "us," as in "our nation" or "our religion." They will also harm those labeled "them," including taking their lives. Far as genocide and persecution seem from fraternity hazings and Cal versus Stanford, college tribes may shed light on the way the mind works with those other sorts of groups, the ones that shape and misshape the world, like nation, race, creed, caste, or culture.

After all, a college campus is full of people inventing a sense of "us" and a sense of "them." As one junior at the University of California, Los Angeles, told her school paper before a game against the University of Southern California: "School spirit is important because it gives us a sense of belonging and being a part of something bigger. Besides," she said, "USC sucks in every way."

In an e-mail interview, Professor Sapolsky writes that "Stanford students (and faculty) do tons of this, at every possible hierarchical level." For instance, he says, they see Stanford versus Harvard, and Stanford versus the University of California at Berkeley. "Then, within Stanford, all the science wonks doing tribal stuff to differentiate themselves from the fuzzies—the humanities/social science types. Then within the sciences, the life science people versus the chemistry/physics/math geeks." Within the life sciences, he adds, the two tribes are "bio majors and majors in what is called 'human biology'—former deprecated as being robotic pre-meds, incapable of thinking, just spitting out factoids; latter as fuzzies masquerading as scientists."

Recent research on students suggests these changes in perception aren't trivial. A few years ago, a team of social psychologists asked students at the University of California at Santa Barbara to rank various collections of people in terms of how well they "qualify as a group." In their answers to Lickel and his colleagues, "students at a university" ranked above "citizens of a nation." "Members of a campus committee" and "members of a university social club" ranked higher than "members of a union" or "members of a political party," romantic couples, or office colleagues working together on a project. For that matter, "students at a university" and "members of a campus committee" ranked well above blacks and Jews in the students' estimation of what qualifies as a group (227).

Much of this thinking, researchers have found, is subconscious. We may think we care about our college ties for good and sensible reasons—wonderful classes! dorm-room heart-to-hearts! job connections!—when the deeper causes are influences we didn't notice.

Some 20 years ago, researchers asked students at Rutgers to describe themselves using only words from a set of cards prepared in advance. Some cards contained words associated with Rutgers, like "scarlet," the school color, and "knight," the name of its athletic teams. Others, like "orange," were associated with archrival Princeton. Some students took the test in a room decorated with a Rutgers pennant; others took it under a Princeton flag. A third group saw only a New York Yankees banner.

Students who saw a Princeton or Rutgers emblem were more likely to use Rutgers-related words to describe themselves. They also mentioned that they were students at Rutgers earlier than those who saw only the neutral flag. They didn't consciously decide to stand up for Rutgers. Outside their conscious minds, though, that identity was in place, ready to be released by symbols of the tribe.

More recently, three social psychologists at Harvard looked at another example of subconscious tribal beliefs. Mahzarin R. Banaji, who led the study, argues that people in similar, equivalent groups will place those groups into a hierarchy, from best to worst, even when there is no

(Continues)

rational basis for ranking them. The psychologists tested Yale sophomores, juniors, and seniors, who live and eat together in "residential colleges." Students know that these colleges are effectively all alike and that people are assigned to them at random. Still, the team found, Yalies did indeed rank them from best to worst. (In the interests of peace and comity, the colleges were kept anonymous.) Moreover, students assigned to the less prestigious units were less enthusiastic about their homes than those from the ones with a better reputation.

What this suggests, Professor Banaji says, is that taking one's place in a tribe, and accepting the tribe's place in a larger society, are mental acts that happen regardless of the group's purpose or meaning. Once people see that they've been divided into groups, they'll act accordingly, even if they know that the divisions are as meaningless as, oh, the University of Arizona versus Arizona State. "We know that human beings identify with social groups, sometimes sufficiently to kill or die on their behalf," she says. "What is not as well known is that such identity between self and group can form rapidly, often following a psychological route that is relatively subconscious. That is, like automata, we identify with the groups in which we are accidentally placed."

Not all researchers agree that people care about so-called nonsense groups with the same passion they give to religion, politics, or morals. Another theory holds that the subconscious mind can distinguish which groups matter and how much. One example comes from a much-cited experiment, performed, naturally, on college students.

In 1959, the social psychologists Elliot Aronson and Judson Mills asked undergraduate women to join a discussion group after a short initiation. For one set of participants, the initiation required reciting a few mild sexual words. The other group had to say a list of much saltier words about sex, which embarrassed them no end (remember, this was 1959). The discussion group was dull as dishwater, but the women who suffered to join rated it as much more valuable than those who had a mild initiation (and higher than a control group that didn't have to do anything).

A subconscious clue for perceiving a tribe as real and valuable, then, may be expending sweat, tears, and embarrassment to get in. The political activist Tom Hayden recently recalled just such a rite at the University of Michigan, in an article on the left-wing Web site *alternet.org*. He was complaining about the lock that Skull and Bones has on November's election [2004] (President Bush and the Democratic nominee, Senator John Kerry, are members).

"As a junior, I was tapped for the Druids," Mr. Hayden wrote about his own campus clan, "which involved a two-day ritual that included being stripped to my underpants, pelted with eggs, smeared with red dye, and tied to a campus tree. These humiliations signified my rebirth from lowly student journalist to Big Man on Campus."

As for Professor Aronson, had he not wanted tight control over the experiment, he writes in his widely used textbook, *The Social Animal*, he and Professor Mills could simply have studied an initiation outside the lab—at a campus fraternity or sorority.

That kind of lumping together—studying one group to explain another—drives scholars in other fields to distraction. To them, a pep rally is different from a political rally. Historians, trained to see big generalizations as meaningless, are often aghast at the way psychologists' theories about groups ignore the difference between, say, today's two-gendered, multiethnic, and meritocratic Harvard College and the one that gave Lippmann his degree in 1909. And anthropologists for generations have disdained psychology for ignoring cultural differences.

But one fact is clear, and college groups exemplify it well: While many creatures live in groups, humanity's are unlike anything else found in nature. Peter Richerson, a biologist at Sacramento State's rival, the University of California at Davis, likes to point out that his students, sitting quietly together on the first day of class, are an amazing exception to the general rules of animal behavior. Put chimpanzees or monkeys that don't know one another in a room, and they would be in hysterics. People team up with strangers easily.

Professor Richerson and his longtime collaborator, Robert Boyd, an anthropologist at USC's hated enemy, UCLA, argue that we will sign up for membership in tribelike groups for the same reason birds sing: It feels right because we evolved to do it. "We want to live in tribes," Professor Richerson says. Humans are "looking to be told what group they belong to, and then once they do that, they want to know, 'What are the rules?'"

The tricky part, says Professor Sapolsky of Stanford, Cal-Berkeley's bitter rival, is that humans alone among animals can think about what a tribe is and who belongs. "Humans actually think about who is an 'us' and who is a 'them' rather than just knowing it," he says. "The second it becomes a cognitive process, it is immensely subject to manipulation."

And, of course, studying the phenomenon won't make you immune, "I'm true blue," says Professor Banaji, who taught at Yale from 1986 until 2002, when she joined the Harvard faculty. "I was physically

(Continues)

unable to sit through a women's basketball game between Harvard and Yale on the Harvard side."

Work Cited

Buckley, Christopher. Interview by Warren Goldstein. "When Yale Men Meet." *Yale Alumni Magazine* May/June 2004: n. pag. Yale Alumni Publications, Inc., n.d. No access date. Web. <http://archive.yalealumnimagazine.com/issues/2004_05/presidents.html>.

Hayden, Tom. "When Bonesmen Fight." Alternet.org. Independent Media Institute, 17 May 2004. Web. No access date. <http://www.alternet.org/story/18726/when_bonesmen_fight>. Lickel, Brian, et al. "Varieties of Groups and the Perception of Group Entitativity." *Journal of Personality and Social Psychology* 78.2 (2000): 223–46. Print.Lippmann, Walter. Public Opinion. New York: Harcourt, Brace, and Company, 1922. Print.

Discussion Questions

1. What, according to David Berreby, happens to the way people think, believe, and self-identify when they become part of a group? Consider your own identity, the things you believe and think. Which ones can you recognize are a result of belonging to a particular group or groups? (Think about such identifiers as nationality, religion, and education.)

2. How does individual behavior, when individuals are grouped with strangers, differ from that of other animals? Given this aspect of human behavior, and your experience of the "us versus them" mentality that is discussed in "It Takes a Tribe," do you think it is possible to achieve world peace in the future?

3. Is Berreby's explanation of tribal mentality consistent with Thomas's? List the similarities and differences between their views. Which of these two readings was more helpful to you in examining your own habits and behaviors? Which ones helped in understanding the behavior of others? Explain.

Assignment 6

In this unit you will be writing a paper in response to the writing topic for Clyde Kluckhohn's "Mirror for Man." This unit also asks you to read and discuss three related essays, and to think about how they connect to the topic of "Mirror for Man" and its thesis statement.

Mirror for Man

CLYDE KLUCKHOHN

Clyde Kluckhohn was a Rhodes Scholar from 1928–1930 and earned his PhD from Harvard University, where he remained as a professor of social anthropology for the rest of his life. He was both an anthropologist and social theorist and is best known for his long-term study of the Navajo in the American Southwest.

One of the interesting things about human beings is that they try to understand themselves and their own behavior. While this has been particularly true of Europeans in recent times, there is no group which has not developed a scheme or schemes to explain human actions. To the insistent human query "why?" the most exciting illumination anthropology has to offer is that of the concept of culture. Its explanatory importance is comparable to categories such as evolution in biology, gravity in physics, disease in medicine.

Why do so many Chinese dislike milk and milk products? Why during World War II did Japanese soldiers die willingly in a Banzai charge that seemed senseless to Americans? Why do some nations trace descent through the father, others through the mother, still others through both parents? Not because different peoples have different instincts, not because they were destined by God or Fate to different habits, not because the weather is different in China and Japan and the United States. Sometimes shrewd common sense has an answer that is close to that of the anthropologist: "because they were brought up that

(Continues)

way." By "culture," anthropology means the total life way of a people, the social legacy individuals acquire from their group. Or culture can be regarded as that part of the environment that is the creation of human beings.

This technical term has a wider meaning than the "culture" of history and literature. A humble cooking pot is as much a cultural product as is a Beethoven sonata. In ordinary speech, "people of culture" are those who can speak languages other than their own, who are familiar with history, literature, philosophy, or the fine arts. To the anthropologist, however, to be human is to be cultured. There is culture in general, and then there are the specific cultures such as Russian, American, British, Khoikhoi, Inca. The general abstract notion serves to remind us that we cannot explain acts solely in terms of the biological properties of the people concerned, their individual past experience, and the immediate situation. The past experience of other people in the form of culture enters into almost every event. Each specific culture constitutes a kind of blueprint of all of life's activities.

A good deal of human behavior can be understood, and indeed predicted, if we know a people's design for living. Many acts are neither accidental nor due to personal peculiarities nor caused by supernatural forces nor simply mysterious. Even we Americans who pride ourselves on our individualism follow most of the time a pattern not of our own making. We brush our teeth on arising. We put on pants—not a loincloth or a grass skirt. We eat three meals a day—not four or five or two. We sleep in a bed—not in a hammock or on a sheep pelt. I do not have to know individuals and their life histories to be able to predict these and countless other regularities, including many in the thinking process of all Americans who are not incarcerated in jails or hospitals for the insane.

To the American woman a system of plural wives seems "instinctively" abhorrent. She cannot understand how any woman can fail to be jealous and uncomfortable if she must share her husband with other women. She feels it "unnatural" to accept such a situation. On the other hand, a Koryak woman of Siberia, for example, would find it hard to understand how a woman could be so selfish and so undesirous of feminine companionship in the home as to wish to restrict her husband to one mate.

Some years ago, I met in New York City a young man who did not speak a word of English and was obviously bewildered by American ways. By "blood" he was American, for his parents had gone from

Indiana to China as missionaries. Orphaned in infancy, he was reared by a Chinese family in a remote village. All who met him found him more Chinese than American. The facts of his blue eyes and light hair were less impressive than a Chinese style of gait, Chinese arm and hand movements, Chinese facial expression, and Chinese modes of thought. The biological heritage was American, but the cultural training had been Chinese. He returned to China.

Another example of another kind: I once knew a trader's wife in Arizona who took a somewhat devilish interest in producing a cultural reaction. Guests who came her way were often served delicious sandwiches filled with a meat that seemed to be neither chicken nor tuna fish yet was reminiscent of both. To queries, she gave no reply until each had eaten his or her fill. She then explained that what they had eaten was not chicken, not tuna fish, but the rich, white flesh of freshly killed rattlesnakes. The response was instantaneous, often violent vomiting. A biological process is caught in a cultural web.

All this does not mean that there is no such thing as raw human nature. The members of all human groups have about the same biological equipment. All people undergo the same poignant life experiences, such as birth, helplessness, illness, old age, and death. The biological potentialities of the species are the blocks with which cultures are built. Some patterns of every culture crystallize around focuses provided by biology: the difference between the sexes, the presence of persons of different ages, the varying physical strength and skill of individuals. The facts of nature also limit culture forms. No culture provides patterns for jumping over trees or for eating iron ore. There is thus no "either-or" between nature and that special form of nurture called culture. The two factors are interdependent. Culture arises out of human nature, and its forms are restricted both by human biology and by natural laws.

Adapted from *Mirror for Man* by Clyde Kluckhohn. Copyright © by Bruce Kluckhohn. Reprinted by permission.

Writing Topic

According to Kluckhohn, what accounts for the differences in peoples throughout the world? Do you accept his explanation? To develop your essay, be sure to support your position by using examples from your own experiences, your observations of others, and your readings.

Vocabulary and Dictionary Practice

Part I.

Look up the following words used in "Mirror for Man." For each, write the two most common definitions on the lines provided, and include what part of speech each definition is (noun, verb, adjective, etc.). Then, under each of the two definitions, write a sentence that uses the word in a way that reflects that particular definition and part of speech.

 1. query
 2. comparable
 3. descent
 4. abstract
 5. regularity
 6. incarcerate
 7. abhorrent
 8. poignant
 9. potentiality
10. interdependent

 1. **query**

first definition: _____

_____

part of speech: _____

sentence: _____

_____

second definition: _____

_____

part of speech: _____

sentence: _____

_____

2. **comparable**

first definition: _____

_____

part of speech: _____

sentence: _____

_____

second definition: _____

_____

part of speech: _____

sentence: _____

_____

3. **descent**

first definition: _____

_____

part of speech: _____

sentence: _____

_____

second definition: _____

_____

part of speech: _____

sentence: _____

_____

4. **abstract**

first definition: _____

_____

part of speech: _____

sentence: _____

_____

second definition: _____

_____

part of speech: _____

sentence: _____

_____

5. **regularities**

first definition: _____

_____

part of speech: _____

sentence: _____

_____

second definition: _____

_____

part of speech: _____

sentence: _____

_____

6. **incarcerated**

first definition: _____

_____

part of speech: _____

sentence: _____

_____

second definition: _____

_____

part of speech: _____

sentence: _____

_____

7. **abhorrent**

first definition: _____

_____

part of speech: _____

sentence: _____

_____

second definition: _____

_____

part of speech: _____

sentence: _____

_____

8. **poignant**

first definition: _____

_____

part of speech: _____

sentence: _____

_____

second definition: _____

_____

part of speech: _____

sentence: _____

_____

9. **potentialities**

first definition: _____

_____

part of speech: _____

sentence: _____

_____

second definition: _____

_____

part of speech: _____

sentence: _____

_____

10. **interdependent**

first definition: _____

_____

part of speech: _____

sentence: _____

_____

second definition: _____

_____

part of speech: _____

sentence: _____

_____

Part II.

A. Write down each sentence from Kluckhohn's essay that contains the following words.

B. Tell which of the word's various definitions best fits the sentence.

C. Paraphrase the sentence without using the vocabulary word; in other words, write the sentence using your own words.

1. **query**

   A. _____

   _____

   B. _____

   _____

   C. _____

   _____

2. **comparable**

   A. _____

   _____

   B. _____

   _____

   C. _____

   _____

3. **descent**

   A. _____

   _____

   B. _____

   _____

C. _____

_____

4. abstract

A. _____

_____

B. _____

_____

C. _____

_____

5. regularities

A. _____

_____

B. _____

_____

C. _____

_____

6. incarcerated

A. _____

_____

B. _____

_____

C. _____

_____

7. **abhorrent**

   A. _____

   _____

   B. _____

   _____

   C. _____

   _____

8. **poignant**

   A. _____

   _____

   B. _____

   _____

   C. _____

   _____

9. **potentialities**

   A. _____

   _____

   B. _____

   _____

   C. _____

   _____

10. **interdependent**

   A. _____

   _____

B. _____

_____

C. _____

_____

Part III.

For each of these words from the essay, tell something new and interesting you learned about the word from the dictionary. For example, you might have found the correct way to pronounce a word you were already familiar with from reading but not from speaking, or you might have learned that a word you thought of as entirely English came from another language.

1. **query**

_____

_____

2. **comparable**

_____

_____

3. **descent**

_____

_____

4. **abstract**

_____

_____

5. **regularities**

_____

_____

6. **incarcerated**

_____

_____

7. **abhorrent**

_____

_____

8. **poignant**

_____

_____

9. **potentialities**

_____

_____

10. **interdependent**

_____

_____

Follow-Up Activity

Write three sentences about your favorite pastime, making sure to include at least one of the vocabulary words in each sentence. Exchange papers with a partner. Look over each other's sentences and see if you can improve them. When everyone is finished, share one another's sentences by reading them aloud to the class.

Doing a Careful Reading of "Mirror for Man"

First, if time permits, begin by reading "Mirror for Man" aloud with the class. Take turns reading paragraphs. This exercise will allow you to listen to the essay as someone else speaks it, giving you a unique experience in absorbing the essay's ideas.

By now you should be aware of the importance of working systematically with a reading selection to make sure that you understand its purpose and ideas. In previous assignments, you practiced some helpful techniques for a thoughtful reading of an essay; use them again now to better understand "Mirror for Man."

The steps are reproduced here, but your goal should be to memorize them so that they become a normal part of the writing process for you.

1. **Read the title again.**
   - The title will tell you something about the reading's main topic.
   - It may also tell you something about Kluckhohn's opinion on the topic.
   - Think about what you already know about the topic and what else you want to know.
2. **Learn about the author.**
   - Read the biographical information about Kluckhohn at the top of the selection.
   - As you go through the remaining steps below, take note of how Kluckhohn's life or work might connect with his topic.
3. **Read through the selection once quickly.**
   - Read quickly through the reading again so that you get a general fresh impression of what it is about and what Kluckhohn's attitude is toward the topic.
   - Notice the things—people, places, experiences, concepts, for example—he brings up to develop and support his opinion about the topic.
4. **Read again to identify the thesis.**
   - Now read the selection a second time, but more slowly and carefully, and *with a pen or highlighter in your hand.*

- Find the thesis and underline it or write it in the margin. Remember, the thesis states Kluckhohn's overall opinion on the topic of the reading. Often, the thesis is contained in a single sentence, but, in some cases, it takes several sentences to make the main argument of the reading selection clear. There are times, too, when the author does not state his or her thesis explicitly, but, if you read the selection carefully, you should be able to state it and then write it in the margin.
- To help, ask yourself, "What does Kluckhohn seem to want readers to think about his topic?"

5. **Read slowly and methodically through the rest of the reading.**
   - Examine each body paragraph one at a time, and list or underline the kinds of evidence that Kluckhohn uses to support his thesis.
   - Look in each body paragraph for a *topic sentence*—a sentence that both presents an idea and tells how it gives support to the reading's overall opinion.
   - As you read and study the selection, *be sure to write down any thoughts you have* about Kluckhohn's opinion and supporting evidence.
   - It is your job to evaluate this evidence for its logic and validity, so be sure to *make notes in the margins* as you read.
   - *Mark the points* that you found interesting or convincing, and write a few words explaining your thoughts.
   - Note, too, any weaknesses you find.
   - When you look back at the notes you made in the margins, you should have a general idea of how convincing you found "Mirror for Man" and what you found to be its strengths and weaknesses.

6. **Read again for review.**
   - Once you have thought through the reading selection, read it once more, looking for places where you don't quite understand what is being said.
   - Underline any terms that you aren't familiar with, and look them up in a dictionary.
   - Mark any places in the reading that don't fit with your understanding of the reading as a whole. Decide whether this is something that Kluckhohn should have revised, or whether it is something that you need to read again because you don't understand it. You may find that you need to go back to Step 4 and begin working through the reading again.
   - Once you are certain that you understand the entire reading, you are prepared to discuss, summarize, and/or respond to the reading with your own essay.

Questions to Review Your Understanding of "Mirror for Man"

Answer the following questions to check your complete understanding of Kluckhohn's argument as a whole.

Paragraph 1

Explain the way Kluckhohn uses other disciplines to show the importance of the concept of culture to anthropology.

Paragraph 2

How does Kluckhohn define culture? How does culture explain the examples, such as that of the Banzai soldiers, which he cites?

Paragraph 3

Kluckhohn contrasts the anthropologist's definition of culture with the wider, more general way the word is used. Explain the difference. Give an example to illustrate each definition.

Paragraph 4

By knowing the culture, what things can Kluckhohn predict about an American male? Is he accurate? If so, in what way is his definition of culture responsible for his accuracy? If not, locate his error. Does the error point to a problem in his definition of culture?

Paragraph 5

How does culture explain Kluckhohn's example of attitudes toward plural wives?

Paragraphs 6-7

Summarize the two examples Kluckhohn gives in these paragraphs. What does each say about the relationship between culture and biology?

Paragraph 8

What similarities does Kluckhohn find in all human groups? How does nature restrict culture?

Responding to the Writing Topic

You have spent time with "Mirror for Man" and should now have a good understanding of its ideas and overall message. It is important now to look at the writing topic at the bottom of the selection because the essay you write must answer directly the questions in the writing topic. Here it is again, but this time formatted so that each part is on its own line:

Writing Topic

According to Kluckhohn, what accounts for the differences in peoples throughout the world?

Do you accept his explanation?

To develop your essay, be sure to support your position by using examples from your own experiences, your observations of others, and your readings.

Pay careful attention to all parts of the writing topic.

- You are first asked a question about a specific aspect of "Mirror for Man," a question that asks you to consider the ways that people are different in different parts of the world. When examining a writing topic, always underline the question words (who, what, why, how, when, where). In this writing topic, the first question asks *what:* what accounts for the differences in peoples? In other words, how does Kluckhohn *explain why* people of different races or from different cultures are so markedly different from one another? Note that he isn't talking about why you like Coke and your friend likes Dr. Pepper. Kluckhohn is interested in differences of a greater significance.

- The second question in the writing topic asks you to state whether you think Kluckhohn's explanation seems valid to you. Does his point of view on difference seem to explain difference reasonably well, in your opinion? What do *you* think accounts for the differences in peoples throughout the world? Your answer to this question will become the thesis of your essay because it will state your overarching view on the topic.

- The third part of the writing topic tells you to support your opinion—your thesis—with clear examples taken from your own experiences. The following activity will help you begin to find some of those examples. Be sure to keep notes on your ideas so that you can turn back to them later.

Follow-Up Activity

1. Tell the class how your family celebrates a major holiday. Include all significant details such as special foods that are prepared or special clothing that is worn. Explain to the class why your family celebrates this holiday in the way that they do.

2. Look around the classroom and notice the clothing people are wearing. Have a discussion of why people choose the clothes they wear. What determines their choices?

Strategies to Help You Analyze a Reading Selection and Develop Your Ideas for Writing a Response

Students often say that they don't know what to write *about*—that is, they think they have no ideas to put into the essay. In fact, students have many thoughtful ideas; they just need a few techniques for accessing and clarifying their ideas. Try the ones below to analyze and think about "Mirror for Man."

Questioning

You will have already taken the first step toward writing your essay when you did a careful reading of "Mirror for Man" and the writing topic that follows it. Looking back at your annotations is a good way to remind yourself about things in the essay you thought were important. Now you need to enter the *question phase* of your prewriting. At this point, you can ask yourself several kinds of questions:

- questions focused on your annotations, such as:

  Why did I highlight/underline this part of the essay?

  How is this information important to the author's point?

  What is the relationship between this information and the question I am being asked to write about?

- questions about your comprehension of the reading, such as:

  What things in this essay do not make sense to me?

  Where do I think the author needed to explain further?

  How do the examples in the essay relate to the author's point?

- questions about the author's ideas, such as:

  What idea in this essay is completely new to me?

What are some of the things that the author says that I am happy to hear someone say?

What things that the author says seem true to me?

What things that the author says seem wrong to me?

What thing that the author says is most important to me?

What idea in this essay is completely new to me?

The answers to these questions will help you understand your own thoughts about the topic of the reading and help you see how you want to respond to the writing topic.

Freewriting

A further step in the prewriting process that you may want to take is *freewriting*. After having answered for yourself a number of the questions about the reading and topic, you still may be having trouble expanding on your initial reaction to the author's position on the topic. Pick one or more of your answers to the questions you have already answered, and just begin to write about it. While you are doing this writing, do not stop or censor yourself; just let the words come. Do this for about five or ten minutes without thinking about spelling, grammar, word choice, or even the sense of what you are saying. When you have completed this activity, you will want to take a break.

After your brief break, come back and read what you have written. Most of what you now have down on paper will not end up in your essay, but, as you read through your freewriting, you will find one or more sentences or ideas that seem interesting, important, or even compelling to you. Highlight these points and ideas.

Listing

Next, you may decide to make a list of your highlightings from all your freewritings. *Listing* is another technique for finding the ideas you want to write about. Be sure to list all the items from your freewriting that you thought were interesting. As you make this list, other ideas may come into your head. Put them on your list as well.

Study your list. Connect with some kind of mark all the ideas that seem related to each other. When you are done, one related group of ideas will probably be longer than the others. This group should provide insight into a topic for your paper.

Shaping Your Ideas into a Rough Draft

At this stage of the writing process, you are ready to begin planning your essay draft. It is important to understand the conventional structure of an academic essay because it will guide you when you are ready to put your ideas in writing. Go back to the writing topic for this assignment and reread it. Notice that it asks you to do three things:

1. **Summarize a topic** idea that Kluckhohn develops in his essay.

2. **Present your position** on this topic idea.

3. **Support and develop your position** using specific evidence taken from your own experiences and readings.

The first part of the writing topic for "Mirror for Man" asks:

"According to Kluckhohn, ***what accounts for*** the differences in peoples throughout the world?"

We have bolded the important action words to help you focus your response correctly. You should not summarize Kluckhohn's entire essay, only one particular aspect of it. This question is asking you to explain "what accounts for the differences in peoples." In other words, how does Kluckhohn reason out, reconcile, or think through an explanation for the differences among large groups of people in the world? Obviously, the idea of *differences* here means something other than, for example, one person can sing while another one cannot. What kinds of differences do you think Kluckhohn is interested in exploring?

Here are some questions that will help you answer the first part of the writing topic. Answer each one as thoroughly and carefully as you can; then, use your answers to draft an introductory paragraph that answers the first question.

1. Explain the difference Kluckhohn establishes between "culture in general" and "specific cultures." Is a "humble cooking pot" an artifact of culture in general or of a specific culture?

2. List all of the differences that Kluckhohn refers to in his essay. For each one, tell whether it is an example of "culture in general" or "specific culture."

3. What does Kluckhohn mean by "the social legacy individuals acquire from their group"? What are some of the things people do as a result of their "social legacy"?

4. Can biological processes be influenced by culture? To what extent?

5. Explain the distinction Kluckhohn makes between nature and culture.

Follow-Up Activity

Working with a partner or a small group, take turns reading your answers to the above questions and getting feedback from your partner or group members. For each answer, ask your partner or group:

1. How clearly written was my answer?
2. Did it thoroughly answer the question, or could more have been added to make it clear?
3. What suggestions can you make to help me improve my work?
4. Give everyone a chance to give and to receive feedback.

Drafting Your Directed Summary

- Begin drafting the directed summary by reviewing the writing topic for "Mirror for Man," paying particular attention to the first question asked. The answer you give to this question is called a *directed summary* because it summarizes only the parts of Kluckhohn's essay that answer this first question.

- As you learned in Part 2, the question that calls for a directed summary often opens with a question word such as *what, how,* or *why*. In Kluckhohn's essay, the first question asks "***what accounts for*** the differences in peoples throughout the world?" You will have to go back to his essay to find his explanation. It will not be enough simply to tell what these differences are; you will also have to summarize *how* Kluckhohn accounts for them.

- You might find it helpful to turn back to "Mirror for Man" and mark the sentences that respond directly to the directed summary question. When writing your directed summary, be very careful to use your own words to *paraphrase* his ideas, as you learned to do in Part 2.

- You should avoid including any of the following in a *directed summary*:
    1. a summary of the entire essay rather than a summary that pays attention only to what is asked for in the first question of the writing topic
    2. minor details or points that are irrelevant to the question
    3. your own opinion or ideas
    4. examples of your own, and, unless particularly helpful, those of the author

Once you have written a directed summary, you will be ready to draft your essay's introductory paragraph. These steps will help guide you:

- Introduce Kluckhohn's essay by giving its title and the full name of its author.
- Follow these opening sentences with the directed summary.
- Last, present your thesis statement, or the answer to the second question in the writing topic. To develop your thesis statement, use the guides in the following section.

Follow-Up Activity

1. After the class as a whole has discussed the important points from "Mirror for Man" that need to be included in the directed summary, form small groups. Have each member of the group read his or her summary aloud. Then, discuss the correctness and completeness of each summary.

2. Discuss with the class the differences among these terms:
   people
   peoples
   people's
   peoples'

Developing Your Thesis Statement

As you know by now, your answer to the second question will be the *thesis* of your essay. The rest of your essay will be built around your answer to the second question in the writing topic, "Do you accept his explanation?" because this question is directing you to explain your own understanding of why there are differences among peoples of the world. Do you think the differences in the customs and behaviors of people are a result of their different cultures, as Kluckhohn does? However you decide to respond, you will have to state your position clearly and support it with explanation and evidence. Begin by taking special notice of the important words.

Do you **accept** his **explanation**?

As you consider your response, go back through "Mirror for Man" and look at Kluckhohn's evidence ("We put on pants—not a loincloth or a grass skirt") and go back over his attempt to account for these differences. Does his reasoning seem sound to you? Or do you have a different viewpoint that accounts for differences among peoples? Look through the activities and exercises you've done in this unit; they will help you to develop your thoughts and insights.

To help focus your thoughts, ask yourself the following questions;

• What is the subject of Kluckhohn's argument?

Notice that, although we can say that "differences among peoples" is the topic idea of Kluckhohn's essay, in fact it is the impact of culture on human behavior that is the actual subject of his argument.

- Based on his own experiences, what is his opinion about the subject?

Kluckhohn, an expert in anthropology, argues that differing cultural practices account for the differences among peoples in the world. Notice that he lived and studied more than fifty years ago. Is there a more modern understanding of difference, or do Kluckhohn's ideas still hold true? What explanation do you have for the differences among peoples of the world?

- Do I think that his understanding of the way societies' cultures account for human differences makes sense?

What alternative explanations might there be to account for differences among peoples in the world? Perhaps family traditions? Could it be gene pools? Could difference be the result of random developments that are unexplainable? Is human nature universal, or do some people's basic nature differ from other people's? You will have to think carefully and sort through your own experiences and knowledge to determine the position you want to take.

Now, use these answers to help write your own thesis. Your thesis will need to include:

- the subject being considered
- the author's opinion about the subject
- your opinion about the subject

Fill in your answers on the line below to form your thesis statement.

subject/author's idea about the subject   your opinion about the subject

_____

_____

_____

_____

After you have finished writing your sentence, review your statement to see that it contains the following elements:

- Kluckhohn's point of view on the subject
- your point of view on the subject

If either of these elements is missing, rewrite your thesis statement so that both are included.

Developing Body Paragraphs for an Essay That Presents a Thesis

Body paragraphs make up the largest part of an essay.

- The job of each body paragraph is to develop one point that supports the thesis statement.
- Taken together, these points build the argument of the essay.
- Writing an effective body paragraph can be easy once you understand the criteria that the body paragraph must fulfill.

Here are the three most important criteria for paragraphs in an argumentative essay:

Body Paragraphs Need:

1. an appropriate or suitable topic
2. evidence (fact, example, and/or quotation)
3. a link to the thesis

An appropriate or suitable topic

First, write a topic sentence that states the point you wish to make in this paragraph. The point must be on topic; that is, it must state an idea that is relevant to the claim you make in your thesis.

Evidence

The major part of the paragraph will be devoted to evidence. In your essays, that evidence will most often be an example, but specific facts, paraphrases, and quotations can also support the topic sentence of your paragraph. You must be careful to choose a clear example, one that clearly demonstrates the point of the paragraph. Then, you must explain the example with details.

A link to the thesis

After you have given all the evidence and supplied all the details that support the topic sentence of the paragraph, you must show the way this evidence links back to the thesis of your essay. It is not enough to just provide an example. You have to tell the reader the reason this particular example connects to the main argument of your essay.

A Basic Outline Form for an Essay That Presents a Thesis

All of the work you have done so far—reading and carefully annotating "Mirror for Man," analyzing its ideas, writing a directed summary in response to the first question in the writing topic, thinking about your own experiences and deciding on your thesis statement, and drafting your essay's introduction—should be gathered together now into a shape that will become your essay, your response to the writing topic at the bottom of "Mirror for Man."

- Remember that you should follow the basic structure of an academic essay.
- To refresh your memory, turn back to Part 2 and review the diagram of the academic essay format.
- As you begin filling in this diagram form, you should be able to turn back to material you have already drafted as you worked through the exercises in this unit.
- Fill in the diagram form as fully as you can. A good plan will help you draft an essay that is clear and coherent.

I. Introductory Paragraph:

A. one or two opening sentences that give the reading selection's title, author, and main topic:

_____

_____

_____

B. the main points that will be included in the directed summary:

1.

2.

3.

4.

C. your thesis statement: Be sure that it presents a clear position in response to the writing topic. State your thesis in your own words.

_____

_____

_____

II. **Body Paragraphs: For each body paragraph you will include in your essay, plan the following parts:**

Write down the main point for the paragraph.

_____

_____

_____

List the evidence you will use to support your main point (fact, example, etc.).

_____

_____

_____

_____

_____

_____

Tell how the evidence and your ideas link to the thesis statement.

_____

_____

_____

_____

_____

_____

(Repeat this part of the outline as often as necessary to plan all of your body paragraphs.)

III. Conclusion: What are some general remarks you can make to close your essay? Perhaps you will remind your readers of the main argument of your paper, for example.

_____

_____

_____

Drafting Your Essay

Now that you have a basic plan for the structure of your essay and a map of its various parts, you are ready to begin drafting.

- Turn back to the helpful guidelines in Part 2 before you begin. These guidelines will help you to evaluate the parts of your draft and your essay as a whole.

- If your thinking changes as you draft, return to your outline and make necessary adjustments. Every time you decide to revise your outline and essay, remember that this is a good sign, a sign that your thinking is developing and becoming more thoughtful and convincing.

- Keep turning back to all of the activities in this unit as you draft your essay. Try to recall some of your reactions, thoughts, and ideas as you worked on these activities. This may help you to strengthen, expand on, or more fully develop your essay's argument.

Follow-Up Activity

Your draft will always benefit from careful rereadings. Even better is to let others hear or read your draft and give you their feedback. Sometimes, a classmate or family member can spot places in your draft where you aren't clear, or where you have neglected to fix a grammar error.

1. Read a classmate's rough draft. Then, choose the paragraph or group of sentences that, in your opinion, are the strongest part of the essay. Read the sentences out loud to the writer of the draft and explain why you chose them.

2. Using three different colors of ink or pencil, exchange drafts with a classmate, read the draft, and then do the following:

   Put a bracket in the margin around the directed summary.

   Underline the thesis statement.

   In each body paragraph, and using three different colors, underline the three elements required: the appropriate topic, the evidence, and the link to the thesis.

   Return the draft to its writer and discuss your markings. Be sure to mention any questions, concerns, or suggestions you have for improving the draft.

Supplemental Reading

Read the following essays, and practice the strategies of annotating, questioning, listing, and freewriting so that you comprehend the arguments and explanations of each. Then, consider them in terms of Kluckhohn's ideas. This activity will help you to work through your own ideas and write a thesis statement that you can support with compelling explanations and evidence. Some of that evidence may come from the essays here.

Body Ritual among the Nacirema

Essay

HORACE MINER

Horace Miner was an anthropologist, and this essay originally appeared in the journal American Anthropologist *in June 1956.*

The anthropologist has become so familiar with the diversity of ways in which different peoples behave in similar situations that he is not apt to be surprised by even the most exotic customs. In fact, if all of the logically possible combinations of behavior have not been found somewhere in the world, he is apt to suspect that they must be present in some yet undescribed tribe. In this light, the magical beliefs and practices of the Nacirema present such unusual aspects that it seems desirable to describe them as an example of the extremes to which human behavior can go.

Professor Linton first brought the ritual of the Nacirema to the attention of anthropologists twenty years ago, but the culture of this people is still very poorly understood. They are a North American group living in the territory between the Canadian Cree, the Yaqui and Tarahumare of Mexico, and the Carib and Arawak of the Antilles. Little is known of their origin, although tradition states that they came from the east. According to Nacirema mythology, their nation was originated by a culture hero, Notgnishaw, who is otherwise known for two great feats of strength—the throwing of a piece of wampum across the river Pa-To-Mac and the chopping down of a cherry tree in which the Spirit of Truth resided.

Nacirema culture is characterized by a highly developed market economy which has evolved in a rich natural habitat. While much of the people's time is devoted to economic pursuits, a large part of the fruits of these labors and a considerable portion of the day are spent in ritual activity. The focus of this activity is the human body, the appearance and health of which loom as a dominant concern in the ethos of the people. While such a concern is certainly not unusual, its ceremonial aspects and associated philosophy are unique.

The fundamental belief underlying the whole system appears to be that the human body is ugly and that its natural tendency is to debility and disease. Incarcerated in such a body, man's only hope is to avert these characteristics through the use of the powerful influences of ritual and ceremony. Every household has one or more shrines devoted to this purpose. The more powerful individuals in the society have several shrines in their houses and, in fact, the opulence of a house is often referred to in terms of the number of such ritual centers it possesses. Most houses are of wattle and daub construction, but the shrine rooms of the more wealthy are walled with stone. Poorer families imitate the rich by applying pottery plaques to their shrine walls.

While each family has at least one such shrine, the rituals associated with it are not family ceremonies but are private and secret. The rites are normally only discussed with children, and then only during the period when they are being initiated into these mysteries. I was able, however, to establish sufficient rapport with the natives to examine these shrines and to have the rituals described to me.

The focal point of the shrine is a box or chest which is built into the wall. In this chest are kept the many charms and magical potions without which no native believes he could live. These preparations are secured from a variety of specialized practitioners. The most powerful of these are the medicine men, whose assistance must be rewarded with substantial gifts. However, the medicine men do not provide the curative potions for their clients, but decide what the ingredients should be and then write them down in an ancient and secret language. This writing is understood only by the medicine men and by the herbalists who, for another gift, provide the required charm.

The charm is not disposed of after it has served its purpose, but is placed in the charm-box of the household shrine. As these magical materials are specific for certain ills, and the real or imagined maladies of the people are many, the charm-box is usually full to overflowing. The magical packets are so numerous that people forget what their purposes were and fear to use them again. While the natives are very vague on this point, we can only assume that the idea in retaining all the old magical materials is that their presence in the charm-box, before which the body rituals are conducted, will in some way protect the worshipper.

(Continues)

Beneath the charm-box is a small font. Each day every member of the family, in succession, enters the shrine room, bows his head before the charm-box, mingles different sorts of holy water in the font, and proceeds with a brief rite of ablution. The holy waters are secured from the Water Temple of the community, where the priests conduct elaborate ceremonies to make the liquid ritually pure.

In the hierarchy of magical practitioners, and below the medicine men in prestige, are specialists whose designation is best translated "holy-mouth-men." The Nacirema have an almost pathological horror and fascination with the mouth, the condition of which is believed to have a supernatural influence on all social relationships. Were it not for the rituals of the mouth, they believe that their teeth would fall out, their gums bleed, their jaws shrink, their friends desert them, and their lovers reject them. (They also believe that a strong relationship exists between oral and moral characteristics. For example, there is a ritual ablution of the mouth for children which is supposed to improve their moral fiber.)

The daily body ritual performed by everyone includes a mouth-rite. Despite the fact that these people are so punctilious about care of the mouth, this rite involves a practice which strikes the uninitiated stranger as revolting. It was reported to me that the ritual consists of inserting a small bundle of hog hairs into the mouth, along with certain magical powders, and then moving the bundle in a highly formalized series of gestures.

In addition to the private mouth-rite, the people seek out a holy-mouth-man once or twice a year. These practitioners have an impressive set of paraphernalia, consisting of a variety of augers, awls, probes, and prods. The use of these objects in the exorcism of the evils of the mouth involves almost unbelievable ritual torture of the client. The holy-mouth-man opens the client's mouth and, using the above-mentioned tools, enlarges any holes which decay may have created in the teeth. Magical materials are put into these holes. If there are no naturally occurring holes in the teeth, large sections of one or more teeth are gouged out so that the supernatural substance can be applied. In the client's view, the purpose of these ministrations is to arrest decay and to draw friends. The extremely sacred and traditional character of the rite is evident in the fact that the natives return to the holy-mouth-men year after year, despite the fact that their teeth continue to decay.

It is to be hoped that, when a thorough study of the Nacirema is made, there will be a careful inquiry into the personality structure of these people. One has but to watch the gleam in the eye of a holy-mouth-man, as he jabs an awl into an exposed nerve, to suspect that a certain amount of sadism is involved. If this can be established, a very interesting pattern emerges, for most of the population shows definite masochistic tendencies. It was to these that Professor Linton referred in discussing a distinctive part of the daily body ritual which is performed only by men. This part of the rite involves scraping and lacerating the surface of the face with a sharp instrument. Special women's rites are performed only four times during each lunar month, but what they lack in frequency is made up in barbarity. As part of this ceremony, women bake their heads in small ovens for about an hour. The theoretically interesting point is that what seems to be a preponderantly masochistic people have developed sadistic specialists.

The medicine men have an imposing temple, or *latipso*, in every community of any size. The more elaborate ceremonies required to treat very sick patients can only be performed at this temple. These ceremonies involve not only the thaumaturge but a permanent group of vestal maidens who move sedately about the temple chambers in distinctive costume and headdress. The *latipso* ceremonies are so harsh that it is phenomenal that a fair proportion of the really sick natives who enter the temple ever recover. Small children whose indoctrination is still incomplete have been known to resist attempts to take them to the temple because "that is where you go to die." Despite this fact, sick adults are not only willing but eager to undergo the protracted ritual purification, if they can afford to do so. No matter how ill the supplicant or how grave the emergency, the guardians of many temples will not admit a client if he cannot give a rich gift to the custodian. Even after one has gained admission and survived the ceremonies, the guardians will not permit the neophyte to leave until he makes still another gift.

The supplicant entering the temple is first stripped of all his or her clothes. In everyday life the Nacirema avoids exposure of his body and its natural functions. Bathing and excretory acts are performed only in the secrecy of the household shrine, where they are ritualized as part of the body-rites. Psychological shock results from the fact that body secrecy is suddenly lost upon entry into the *latipso*. A man, whose own wife has never seen him in an excretory act, suddenly finds himself naked and assisted by a vestal maiden while he performs his natural functions into a sacred vessel. This sort of ceremonial treatment is necessitated by the fact that the excreta are used by a diviner to ascertain the course and nature of the client's sickness. Female clients, on

(Continues)

the other hand, find their naked bodies are subjected to the scrutiny, manipulation, and prodding of the medicine men.

Few supplicants in the temple are well enough to do anything but lie on their hard beds. The daily ceremonies, like the rites of the holy-mouth-men, involve discomfort and torture. With ritual precision, the vestals awaken their miserable charges each dawn and roll them about on their beds of pain while performing ablutions, in the formal movements of which the maidens are highly trained. At other times they insert magic wands in the supplicant's mouth or force him to eat substances which are supposed to be healing. From time to time the medicine men come to their clients and jab magically treated needles into their flesh. The fact that these temple ceremonies may not cure, and may even kill the neophyte, in no way decreases the people's faith in the medicine men.

There remains one other kind of practitioner, known as a "listener." This witch-doctor has the power to exorcise the devils that lodge in the heads of people who have been bewitched. The Nacirema believe that parents bewitch their own children. Mothers are particularly suspected of putting a curse on children while teaching them the secret body rituals. The counter-magic of the witch-doctor is unusual in its lack of ritual. The patient simply tells the "listener" all his troubles and fears, beginning with the earliest difficulties he can remember. The memory displayed by the Nacirema in these exorcism sessions is truly remarkable. It is not uncommon for the patient to bemoan the rejection he felt upon being weaned as a babe, and a few individuals even see their troubles going back to the traumatic effects of their own birth.

In conclusion, mention must be made of certain practices which have their base in native esthetics but which depend upon the pervasive aversion to the natural body and its functions. There are ritual fasts to make fat people thin and ceremonial feasts to make thin people fat. Still other rites are used to make women's breasts large if they are small, and smaller if they are large. General dissatisfaction with breast shape is symbolized in the fact that the ideal form is virtually outside the range of human variation. A few women afflicted with almost inhuman hyper-mammary development are so idolized that they make a handsome living by simply going from village to village and permitting the natives to stare at them for a fee.

Reference has already been made to the fact that excretory functions are ritualized, routinized, and relegated to secrecy. Natural reproductive functions are similarly distorted. Intercourse is taboo as a topic and scheduled as an act. Efforts are made to avoid pregnancy by the use of magical materials or by limiting intercourse to certain phases of the moon. Conception is actually very infrequent. When pregnant, women dress so as to hide their condition. Parturition takes place in secret, without friends or relatives to assist, and the majority of women do not nurse their infants.

Our review of the ritual life of the Nacirema has certainly shown them to be a magic-ridden people. It is hard to understand how they have managed to exist so long under the burdens which they have imposed upon themselves. But even such exotic customs as these take on real meaning when they are viewed with the insight provided by Malinowski when he wrote:

"Looking from far and above, from our high places of safety in the developed civilization, it is easy to see all the crudity and irrelevance of magic. But without its power and guidance early man could not have mastered his practical difficulties as he has done, nor could man have advanced to the higher stages of civilization."

Discussion Questions

1. This essay is a piece of social satire that is meant to amuse readers (note the backward spelling of "Nacirema," for example), but do you think the writer has a serious purpose that is served by the satire? How does satire help him accomplish this purpose?

2. What is the essay's point of view, i.e., whose perspective does it present? Explain.

3. What are the "shrines" that are used to help the Nacirema avert their "natural tendency . . . to debility and disease" described in paragraph 4? What is the focal point of the shrine described in paragraph 6?

4. What is another name for the "holy-mouth-men" mentioned in paragraph 9?

5. Torture, exorcism, and magic are terms used to describe the ritual practices of the Nacirema. What kinds of cultures are usually associated with these practices? Why does Miner use these terms here?

6. What is our common term for the temple, or "latipso," described in paragraphs 13-15? Identify some of the unexpected terms he uses to describe this "temple" and explore their effect on the reader.

(Continues)

7. What is the tone of the essay, and what effect does the tone have on its readers? Do you think you respond differently to the essay than an anthropologist would? Explain.

8. How does Miner's choice of subject—our concerns with appearance and health—and the social customs we use to address those concerns connect with Kluckhohn's idea that "biological process[es] . . . [are always] caught in a cultural web"?

DNA as Destiny

DAVID EWING DUNCAN

> *David Ewing Duncan is the Founding Director of the Center of Life Science Policy at the University of California, Berkeley. He is an author, journalist, and film producer, and a writer for the* New York Times, Fortune, Wired, *and* National Geographic. *His most recent book is titled* When I'm 164: The New Science of Radical Life Extension, and What Happens If It Succeeds *(2012).*

I feel naked. Exposed. As if my skin, bone, muscle tissue, cells, have all been peeled back, down to a tidy swirl of DNA. It's the basic stuff of life, the billions of nucleotides that keep me breathing, walking, craving, and just being. Eight hours ago, I gave a few cells, swabbed from inside my cheek, to a team of geneticists. They've spent the day extracting DNA and checking it for dozens of hidden diseases. Eventually, I will be tested for hundreds more. They include, as I will discover, a nucleic time bomb ticking inside my chromosomes that might one day kill me.

For now I remain blissfully ignorant, awaiting the results in an office at Sequenom, one of scores of biotech startups incubating in the canyons north of San Diego. I'm waiting to find out if I have a genetic proclivity for cancer, cardiac disease, deafness, Alzheimer's, or schizophrenia.

This, I'm told, is the first time a healthy human has ever been screened for the full gamut of genetic disease markers. Everyone has errors in his or her DNA, glitches that may trigger a heart spasm or cause a brain tumor. I'm here to learn mine.

Waiting, I wonder if I carry some sort of Pandora gene, a hereditary predisposition to peek into places I shouldn't. Morbid curiosity is an occupational hazard for a writer, I suppose, but I've never been bothered by it before. Yet now I find myself growing nervous and slightly flushed. I can feel my pulse rising, a cardiovascular response that I will soon discover has, for me, dire implications.

In the coming days, I'll seek a second opinion, of sorts. Curious about where my genes come from, I'll travel to Oxford and visit an "ancestral geneticist" who has agreed to examine my DNA for links back to progenitors whose mutations have been passed on to me. He will reveal the seeds of my individuality and the roots of the diseases that may kill me—and my children.

(Continues)

For now, I wait in an office at Sequenom, a sneak preview of a trip to the DNA doctor, circa 2008. The personalized medicine being pioneered here and elsewhere prefigures a day when everyone's genome will be deposited on a chip or stored on a gene card tucked into a wallet. Physicians will forecast illnesses and prescribe preventive drugs custom-fitted to a patient's DNA, rather than the one-size-fits-all pharmaceuticals that people take today. Gene cards might also be used to find that best-suited career, or a DNA-compatible mate, or, more darkly, to deny someone jobs, dates, and meds because their nucleotides don't measure up. It's a scenario Andrew Niccol imagined in his 1997 film, *Gattaca*, where embryos in a not-too-distant future are bio-engineered for perfection and where genism—discrimination based on one's DNA—condemns the lesser-gened to scrubbing toilets.

The *Gattaca*-like engineering of defect-free embryos is at least twenty or thirty years away, but Sequenom and others plan to take DNA testing to the masses in just a year or two. The prize: a projected $5 billion market for personalized medicine by 2006 and billions, possibly hundreds of billions, more for those companies that can translate the errors in my genome and yours into custom pharmaceuticals.

Sitting across from me is the man responsible for my gene scan: Andi Braun, chief medical officer at Sequenom. Tall and sinewy, with a long neck, glasses, and short gray hair, Braun, forty-six, is both jovial and German. Genetic tests are already publicly available for Huntington's disease and cystic fibrosis, but Braun points out that these illnesses are relatively rare. "We are targeting diseases that impact millions," he says in a deep Bavarian accent, envisioning a day when genetic kits that can assay the whole range of human misery will be available at Wal-Mart, as easy to use as a home pregnancy test.

But a kit won't tell me if I'll definitely get a disease, just if I have a bum gene. What Sequenom and others are working toward is pinning down the probability that, for example, a colon cancer gene will actually trigger a tumor. To know this, Braun must analyze the DNA of thousands of people and tally how many have the colon cancer gene, how many actually get the disease, and how many don't. Once these data are gathered and crunched, Braun will be able to tell you, for instance, that if you have the defective DNA, you have a 40 percent chance, or maybe a 75 percent chance, of getting the disease by age fifty, or ninety. Environmental factors such as eating right—or wrong—and smoking also weigh in. "It's a little like predicting the weather," says Charles Cantor, the company's cofounder and chief scientific officer.

The sun sets outside Braun's office as my results arrive, splayed across his computer screen like tarot cards. I'm trying to maintain a steely, reportorial façade, but my heart continues to race.

Names of SNPs [pronounced "snips," the tiny genetic variations that account for nearly all differences in humans] pop up on the screen: connexin 26, implicated in hearing loss; factor V leiden, which causes blood clots; and alpha-1 antitrypsin deficiency, linked to lung and liver disease. Beside each SNP are codes that mean nothing to me: 13q11-q12, 1q23, 14q32.1. Braun explains that these are addresses on the human genome, the PO box numbers of life. For instance, 1q23 is the address for a mutant gene that causes vessels to shrink and impede the flow of blood—it's on chromosome 1. Thankfully, my result is negative. "So, David, you will not get the varicose veins. That's good, ja?" says Braun. One gene down, dozens to go.

Next up is the hemochromatosis gene. This causes one's blood to retain too much iron, which can damage the liver. As Braun explains it, somewhere in the past, an isolated human community lived in an area where the food was poor in iron. Those who developed a mutation that stores high levels of iron survived, and those who didn't became anemic and died, failing to reproduce. However, in these iron-rich times, hemochromatosis is a liability. Today's treatment? Regular bleeding. "You tested negative for this mutation," says Braun. "You do not have to be bled." I'm also clean for cystic fibrosis and for a SNP connected to lung cancer.

Then comes the bad news. A line of results on Braun's monitor shows up red and is marked "MT," for mutant type. My body's programming code is faulty. There's a glitch in my system. Named ACE (for angiotensin-I converting enzyme), this SNP means my body makes an enzyme that keeps my blood pressure spiked. In plain English, I'm a heart attack risk.

By the time I get home, I realize that all I've really learned is, I might get heart disease, and I could get diabetes. And I should avoid smoking and unsafe sex—as if I didn't already know this. Obviously, I'll now watch my blood pressure, exercise more, and lay off the Cap'n Crunch. But beyond this, I have no idea what to make of the message Andi Braun has divined from a trace of my spit.

After probing my genetic future, I jet to England to investigate my DNA past. Who are these people who have bequeathed me this tainted bloodline? From my grandfather Duncan, an avid genealogist, I already know that my paternal ancestors came from Perth, in south-central

(Continues)

Scotland. We can trace the name back to an Anglican priest murdered in Glasgow in 1680 by a mob of Puritans. His six sons escaped and settled in Shippensburg, Pennsylvania, where their descendants lived until my great-great-grandfather moved west to Kansas City in the 1860s.

In an Oxford restaurant, over a lean steak and a heart-healthy merlot, I talk with geneticist Bryan Sykes, a linebacker-sized fifty-five-year-old with a baby face and an impish smile. He's a molecular biologist at the university's Institute of Molecular Medicine and the author of the bestselling *Seven Daughters of Eve*. Sykes first made headlines in 1994 when he used DNA to directly link a 5,000-year-old body discovered frozen and intact in an Austrian glacier to a twentieth-century Dorset woman named Marie Mosley. This stunning genetic connection between housewife and hunter-gatherer launched Sykes's career as a globe-trotting genetic gumshoe. In 1995, he confirmed that bones dug up near Ekaterinburg, Russia, were the remains of Czar Nicholas II and his family by comparing the body's DNA with that of the czar's living relatives, including Britain's Prince Philip. Sykes debunked explorer Thor Heyerdahl's *Kon-Tiki* theory by tracing Polynesian genes to Asia, not the Americas, and similarly put the lie to the *Clan of the Cave Bear* hypothesis, which held that the Neanderthal interbred with our ancestors, the Cro-Magnon, when the two subspecies coexisted in Europe 15,000 years ago.

Sykes explains to me that a bit of DNA called mtDNA is key to his investigations. A circular band of genes residing separately from the twenty-three chromosomes of the double helix, mtDNA is passed down solely through the maternal line. Sykes used mtDNA to discover something astounding: Nearly every European can be traced back to just seven women living 10,000 to 45,000 years ago. In his book, Sykes gives these seven ancestors hokey names and tells us where they most likely lived: Ursula, in Greece (circa 43,000 BC) and Velda, in northern Spain (circa 15,000 BC), to name two of the "seven daughters of Eve." (Eve was the ur-mother who lived 150,000 years ago in Africa.)

Sykes has taken swab samples from the cheeks of more than 10,000 people, charging $220 to individually determine a person's mtDNA type. "It's not serious genetics," Sykes admits, "but people like to know their roots. It makes genetics less scary and shows us that, through our genes, we are all very closely related." He recently expanded his tests to include non-Europeans. The Asian daughters of Eve are named Emiko, Nene, and Yumio, and their African sisters are Lamia, Latifa, and Ulla, among others.

Before heading to England, I had mailed Sykes a swab of my cheek cells. Over our desserts in Oxford he finally offers up the results. "You are descended from Helena," he pronounces. "She's the most common daughter of Eve, accounting for some 40 percent of Europeans." He hands me a colorful certificate, signed by him, that heralds my many-times-great-grandma and tells me that she lived 20,000 years ago in Dordogne Valley of France. More interesting is the string of genetic letters from my mtDNA readout that indicate I'm mostly Celtic, which makes sense. But other bits of code reveal traces of Southeast Asian DNA, and even a smidgen of Native American and African.

This doesn't quite have the impact of discovering that I'm likely to die of a heart attack. Nor am I surprised about the African and Indian DNA, since my mother's family has lived in the American South since the seventeenth century. But Southeast Asian? Sykes laughs. "We are all mutts," he says. "There is no ethnic purity. Somewhere over the years, one of the thousands of ancestors who contributed to your DNA had a child with someone from Southeast Asia." He tells me a story about a blond, blue-eyed surfer from Southern California who went to Hawaii to apply for monies awarded only to those who could prove native Hawaiian descent. The grant-givers laughed—until his DNA turned up traces of Hawaiian.

Discussion Questions

1. What are SNPs?
2. Explain how our genes make each of us a unique individual and connect us to those who come before and after us.
3. In your own words, what does an "ancestral geneticist" do?
4. Explain Bryan Sykes's discovery of the "seven daughters of Eve." Do you think this discovery is important? Explain.
5. Why does Sykes say that, "through our genes, we are all very closely related"? Do you agree? Why or why not?
6. Does Sykes's theory about human individuality and human connect-edness have anything in common with Kluckhohn's idea of "culture in general" and "specific culture"?

A Bamboo Grows in China: A Chinese-American Novelist Discovers Just How Deep Her Roots Go

By Lisa See

Lisa See is a New York Times *bestselling author and a public speaker. She is active in the Chinese-American community, and has developed many cultural events to promote an understanding and celebration of Chinese-American experience. Her focus on bi-racial, bi-cultural family interaction has given her broad-ranging interests. For example, for Los Angeles Opera, she wrote the libretto for* On Gold Mountain *(2000), for the Autry Museum, she curated an exhibition titled* On Gold Mountain: A Chinese American Experience *(2000), and for the Chinese American Museum in Los Angeles, she helped develop and curate an exhibition by artist Tyrus Wong (2003). See's most recent novel,* The Tea Girl of Hummingbird Lane *(2017), was published by Scribner.*

When I was a young girl, I lived with my mother in Topanga Canyon, but I spent a lot of time with my father's side of the family in Los Angeles's Chinatown, where my grandparents and aunts and uncles had particular types of gardens—filled with bamboo, Bodhi trees, and cymbidiums. These lush spots were also dotted with broken motors, empty 5-gallon soy sauce containers, and snaking piles of used electrical conduit picked up from the side of the road. I found it all beautiful, romantic, and fun, and I thought all people lived like that. Then I went to kindergarten and saw lawns and roses. I thought those people were weird. When I got a little older, I realized, no, those people weren't strange. It was my family that was odd.

I felt that way until 1988, when I took my first trip to Guangzhou, China, by way of Hong Kong, on the train. As we crossed the border, the houses of the poorest of the poor were nestled right up against the train tracks. Looking down into the little courtyards, I saw the gardens of my youth—bamboo, cymbidiums, and all kinds of junk: scrap metal, broken earthenware jugs, bicycle parts. In that instant, I realized that as long as my family had been in America—more than a hundred years at that point—and as much as we'd been educated, and as much as we did or didn't look Chinese or had the ability to speak the language anymore, we were still South China peasants at heart. We had the same visual aesthetic, but we also knew we had to be frugal and keep everything, just in case.

That realization sent me back to China a year later to search for my roots. I went to my great-great-grandfather's home village of Dimtao, between Guangzhou and Foshan, where the family house still stands and I'm still related to everyone. Since then, my books have either taken place in China or have touched on the Chinese-American experience, which is infused with Chinese traditions and culture. Going to China to do research—whether in big cities like Shanghai and Beijing or in remote villages where I've been told I was one of the first foreigners ever to visit—has given me a chance to look at what I know and don't know about myself, my family, and my culture.

I love China, and I've seen it evolve and transform. In the early days, I witnessed geometric changes as the country leapt decades, and sometimes centuries, in a matter of months. On that first trip to China nearly 30 years ago, I saw only a handful of trucks, buses, and cars. Most people, dressed in either their blue Mao suits or old People's Liberation Army uniforms, still pedaled along in great tides of bicycles. One year later, when I returned to Guangzhou, it took 20 minutes just to exit the train station parking lot because there was such a traffic jam.

These days, it seems everyone wants to venture to China. I hope visitors experience what I've experienced: the richness of a culture more than 5,000 years old, some of the world's most modern cities, impressive ancient sites like the Great Wall near Beijing and the terra-cotta warriors in Xi'an, the great diversity of its ethnic minorities, and the breathtaking beauty of its natural landscapes. The Chinese have long called their country the Middle Kingdom, for they believe that they are living in the center of the universe. For me, China is at the center of my soul.

Discussion Questions

1. Describe the garden of Lisa See's grandparents. How does it differ from the yards in the community where she lives? Which type of yard do you think she preferrs? Describe the kind of garden that makes you feel most comfortable.

2. How does See's ancestral culture and socioeconomic heritage influence her life? Explain the way your cultural, ethnic, or socioeconomic background has influenced some of the choices you have made in life. If they have had no impact, explain the reason you might find them inconsequential.

(Continues)

3. How could Kluckhohn have used See's grandparents, her neighbors, an English garden, or the book *A Tree Grows in Brooklyn* as examples in his discussion of culture?

Assignment 7

Read the following essay and the writing topic that follows it. Then, use the exercises and activities that follow to move through the writing process and develop your own essay in response to the argument Tan presents in "Mother Tongue."

Mother Tongue

Amy Tan

Amy Tan is an American writer whose novels examine family relation-ships, especially those of mothers and daughters. She has written several bestselling novels, such as The Joy Luck Club *and* The Kitchen God's Wife. *Tan has a BA and MA from San Jose State University.*

I am not a scholar of English or literature. I cannot give you much more than personal opinions on the English language and its variations in this country or others. I am a writer. And by that definition, I am someone who has always loved language. I am fascinated by language in daily life. I spend a great deal of time thinking about the power of language—the way it can evoke an emotion, a visual image, a complex idea, or a simple truth. Language is the tool of my trade. And I use them all—all the Englishes I grew up with.

Recently, I was made keenly aware of the different Englishes I do use. I was giving a talk to a large group of people, the same talk I had already given to a half a dozen other groups. The nature of the talk was about my writing, my life, and my book, *The Joy Luck Club*. The talk was going along well enough, until I remembered one major dif-ference that made the whole talk sound wrong. My mother was in the room. And it was perhaps the first time she had heard me give a lengthy speech, using the kind of English I have never used with her. I was say-ing things like, "The intersection of memory upon imagination" and "There is an aspect of my fiction that relates to thus-and-thus"—a speech filled with carefully wrought grammatical phrases, burdened, it suddenly seemed to me, with nominalized forms, past perfect tenses,

(Continues)

conditional phrases, all the forms of standard English that I had learned in school and through books, the forms of English I did not use at home with my mother.

Just last week, I was walking down the street with my mother, and I again found myself conscious of the English I was using, the English I do use with her. We were talking about the price of new and used furniture and I heard myself saying this: "Not waste money that way." My husband was with us as well, and he didn't notice any switch in my English. And then I realized why. It's because over the twenty years we've been together, I've often used that same kind of English with him, and sometimes he even uses it with me. It has become our language of intimacy, a different sort of English that relates to family talk, the language I grew up with.

So you'll have some idea of what this family talk I heard sounds like, I'll quote what my mother said during a recent conversation which I videotaped and then transcribed. During this conversation, my mother was talking about a political gangster in Shanghai who had the same last name as her family's, Du, and how the gangster in his early years wanted to be adopted by her family, which was rich by comparison. Later, the gangster became more powerful, far richer than my mother's family, and one day showed up at my mother's wedding to pay his respects. Here's what she said in part:

> "Du Yusong having business like fruit stand. Like off the street kind. He is Du like Du Zong—but not Tsung-ming Island people. The local people call putong, the river east side, he belong to that side local people. That man want to ask Du Zong father take him in like become own family. Du Zong father wasn't look down on him, but didn't take seriously, until that man big like become a Mafia. Now important person, very hard to inviting him. Chinese way, came only to show respect, don't stay for dinner. Respect for making big celebration, he shows up. Mean gives lots of respect. Chinese custom. Chinese social life that way. If too important won't have to stay too long. He come to my wedding. I didn't see, I heard it. I gone to boy's side, they have YMCA dinner. Chinese age I was nineteen."

You should know that my mother's expressive command of English belies how much she actually understands. She reads the *Forbes* report, listens to *Wall Street Week*, converses daily with her stockbroker, reads all of Shirley MacLaine's books with ease—all kinds of things I can't begin to understand. But when I was growing up, my mother's "limited" English limited *my* perception of her. I was ashamed of her English. I believed that her English reflected the quality of what she had to say. That is, because she expressed them imperfectly, her thoughts were imperfect. And I had plenty of empirical evidence to support me: the fact that people in department stores, at banks, and at restaurants did not take her seriously, did not give her good service, pretended not to understand her, or even acted as if they did not hear her. Today, some of my friends tell me they understand fifty percent of what my mother says. Some say they understand eighty to ninety percent. Some say they understand none of it, as if she were speaking pure Chinese.

But to me, my mother's English is perfectly clear, perfectly natural. It's my mother tongue. Her language, as I hear it, is vivid, direct, full of observation and imagery. That was the language that helped shape the way I saw things, expressed things, made sense of the world. It captures my mother: her intent, her passion, her imagery, the rhythms of her speech, and the nature of her thoughts.

Writing Topic

What are the "different Englishes" Tan discusses, and how does she view them? What do you think of her view? To support your position, be sure to use specific evidence taken from your own experience, observations, or reading.

Vocabulary and Dictionary Practice

Part I.

Look up the following words used in "Mother Tongue." For each, write the two most common definitions on the lines provided, and include what part of speech each definition is (noun, verb, adjective, etc.). Then, under each of the two definitions, write a sentence that uses the word in a way that reflects that particular definition and part of speech.

1. evoke
2. wrought
3. nominalize
4. expressive
5. belie
6. empirical
7. vivid

1. **evoke**

   first definition: _____

   _____

   part of speech: _____

   sentence: _____

   _____

   second definition: _____

   _____

   part of speech: _____

   sentence: _____

   _____

2. **wrought**

   first definition: _____

   _____

part of speech: _____

sentence: _____

_____

second definition: _____

_____

part of speech: _____

sentence: _____

_____

3. **nominalize**

first definition: _____

_____

part of speech: _____

sentence: _____

_____

second definition: _____

_____

part of speech: _____

sentence: _____

_____

4. **expressive**

first definition: _____

_____

part of speech: _____

sentence: _____

_____

second definition: _____

_____

part of speech: _____

sentence: _____

_____

5. **belie**

first definition: _____

_____

part of speech: _____

sentence: _____

_____

second definition: _____

_____

part of speech: _____

sentence: _____

_____

6. **empirical**

first definition: _____

_____

part of speech: _____

sentence: _____

_____

second definition: _____

_____

part of speech: _____

sentence: _____

_____

7. **vivid**

first definition: _____

_____

part of speech: _____

sentence: _____

_____

second definition: _____

_____

part of speech: _____

sentence: _____

_____

Part II.

A. Write down each sentence from Tan's essay that contains the following words.

B. Tell which one of the word's various definitions best fits the sentence.

C. Paraphrase the sentence without using the vocabulary word; in other words, write the sentence using your own words.

1. **evoke**

A. _____

_____

B. _____

_____

C. _____

_____

2. **wrought**

    A. _____

    _____

    B. _____

    _____

    C. _____

    _____

3. **nominalize**

    A. _____

    _____

    B. _____

    _____

    C. _____

    _____

4. **expressive**

    A. _____

    _____

    B. _____

    _____

    C. _____

    _____

5. **belie**

    A. _____

    _____

B. _____

_____

C. _____

_____

6. **empirical**

A. _____

_____

B. _____

_____

C. _____

_____

7. **vivid**

A. _____

_____

B. _____

_____

C. _____

_____

Part III.

For each of these words from the essay, tell something new and interesting you learned about the word from the dictionary. For example, you might have found the correct way to pronounce a word you were already familiar with from reading but not from speaking, or you might have learned that a word you thought of as entirely English came from another language.

1. **evoke**

_____

_____

2. **wrought**

_____

_____

3. **nominalize**

_____

_____

4. **expressive**

_____

_____

5. **belie**

_____

_____

6. **empirical**

_____

_____

7. **vivid**

_____

_____

Follow-Up Activity

Write a five-sentence description of your bedroom, your pet, your car, or your good friend. Your description must include at least three of the vocabulary words above. Read your description aloud to the class.

Doing a Careful Reading of "Mother Tongue"

By now you should be aware of the importance of working systematically with a reading selection to make sure that you understand its purpose and ideas. In earlier assignments, you practiced some techniques to help you do a thoughtful reading of an essay; use them again now to better understand "Mother Tongue."

The steps are reproduced here, but your goal should be to memorize them so that they become a normal part of the writing process for you.

1. **Read the title.**
   - The title will tell you something about the reading's main topic.
   - It may also tell you something about Tan's opinion on the topic.
   - Think about what you already know about the topic and what more you want to know.

2. **Learn about the author.**
   - Read the biographical information about Tan at the top of the selection.
   - As you go through the remaining steps below, take note of how Tan's life or work might connect with her topic.

3. **Read through the selection once quickly.**
   - Read quickly through the reading so that you get a general impression of what it is about and what Tan's attitude is toward the topic.
   - Notice the things—people, places, experiences, concepts, for example—she brings up to develop and support her opinion about the topic.

4. **Read again to identify the thesis.**
   - Now read the selection a second time, but more slowly and carefully, and *with a pen or highlighter in your hand.*
   - Find the thesis and underline it or write it in the margin. Remember, the thesis states Tan's overall opinion on the topic of the reading. Often, the thesis is contained in a single sentence, but, in some cases, it takes several sentences to make the main argument of the reading selection clear. There are times, too, when the author does not state his or her thesis explicitly, but, if you read the selection carefully, you should be able to state it and then write it in the margin.
   - Ask yourself, "What does Tan seem to want readers to think about her topic?"

5. **Read slowly and methodically through the rest of the reading.**
   - Examine each body paragraph one at a time, and list or underline the kinds of evidence that Tan uses to support her thesis.
   - Look in each body paragraph for a *topic sentence*—a sentence that both presents an idea and tells how it gives support to the reading's overall opinion.
   - As you read and study the selection, *be sure to write down any thoughts you have* about Tan's opinion and supporting evidence.
   - It is your job to evaluate this evidence for its logic and validity, so be sure to *make notes in the margins* as you read.
   - *Mark the points* that you found interesting or convincing, and write a few words explaining your thoughts.
   - Note, too, any weaknesses you find.
   - When you look back at the notes you made in the margins, you should have a general idea of how convincing you found "Mother Tongue" and what you found to be its strengths and weaknesses.

6. **Read again for review.**
   - Once you have thought through the reading selection, read it once more, looking for places where you don't quite understand what is being said.
   - Underline any terms that you aren't familiar with, and look them up in a dictionary.
   - Mark any places in the reading that don't fit with your understanding of the reading as a whole. Decide whether this is something that Tan should have revised, or whether it is something that you need to read again because you don't understand it. You may find that you need to go back to Step 4 and begin working through the reading again.

• Once you are certain that you understand the entire reading, you are prepared to discuss, summarize, and/or respond to the reading with your own essay.

Follow-Up Activity

Close this book. Then, on a sheet of paper, try writing down the six steps for a careful reading, using your memory and your own words.

- Think back and remember the strategies you used to examine the arguments in earlier assignment units.
- When you are finished, open the book to this page and see how you did.
- Take careful note of any steps you omitted.
- Looking over your list, put a star next to the steps that are most helpful to you, and briefly explain why.
- Consider more carefully the steps that you did not star, and think about how you might alter them so that they would be more helpful.

Discuss the results of this activity with the class. Compare your results and conclusions.

Questions to Review Your Understanding of "Mother Tongue"

Answer the following questions to make sure that you have a clear understanding of Tan's argument as a whole. Be sure to respond to each as thoroughly as you can. "Don't get confused by the paragraph numbers for Tan's essay. "Mother Tongue" has six paragraphs.

Paragraph 1

Explain Amy Tan's use of and feelings about the English language.

Paragraph 2

Why did having her mother in the audience help Tan recognize that there are different forms of English? Explain the difference between standard English and these other forms.

Paragraph 3

In what situations and with what people would Tan use a nonstandard form of English? What meaning does the use of this nonstandard form have for her?

Paragraph 4

Rewrite Tan's mother's contribution to their conversation in standard English.

Paragraphs 5–6

Explain the difference between the way the young Amy felt about her mother's use of nonstandard English and the way she feels about it now.

Responding to the Writing Topic

You should now have a good understanding of the ideas and overall message of "Mother Tongue." You are ready to look again at the writing topic and begin thinking about how you will respond to it. Here it is again, this time with each of three requirements on its own line:

Writing Topic

What are the "different Englishes" Tan discusses, and how does she view them?

What do you think of her view?

To support your position, be sure to use specific evidence taken from your own experience, observations, or reading.

Here is a closer look at the writing topic's three parts:

- The first question asks you to summarize a specific aspect of "Mother Tongue." As you read it carefully, you will notice that it has two question words, **what** and **how**. Keep them in mind because they should shape your response to this question. In other words, your directed summary should tell both "what" and "how."

- The second question asks you to take a stand. You may not be ready to do so, but as you continue working through the activities and exercises here, you will clarify your thoughts and decide what argument you want to make.

- The last part of the writing topic is a directive that requires you to provide evidence in support of the stand you have taken.

Remember that you will have to respond carefully to all three parts of the writing topic.

Follow-Up Activity

How would you describe your day today if you were talking with a friend? How would you describe your day if you were talking with one of your professors? How would you describe your day to your mother, father, or grandfather? Explain any differences you noticed. Think about both the kind of information you would provide to each of the three and the language you would use.

Strategies to Help You Analyze a Reading Selection and Develop Your Ideas for Writing a Response

Now you are ready to build on the annotations you made earlier when you did a careful reading of "Mother Tongue." Remember the strategies of *questioning*, *freewriting*, and *listing* that you used in previous assignment units. By now, we hope you realize that these forms of prewriting are an important and productive part of the writing process. If you use them in a focused and sustained way, they lead you to a more systematic analysis of any reading selection. Use these strategies now on "Mother Tongue" as you begin to form your own opinions and ideas. They will guide and clarify your thinking about Tan's essay. They will also help you to put into words your own views on the topic she writes about—that standard and nonstandard forms of language have equally expressive power to foster understanding and connection.

Questioning

- questions about the highlighting you did:
  Why did I underline this part of the reading?

  How is this information important to Tan's point?

  What is the relationship between this information and the question I am being asked to write about?

- questions about Tan's ideas:
  What things in this essay do not make sense to me?

  Where do I think Tan should have explained further?

  How do the examples in the essay relate to her point?

- questions about "Mother Tongue" that seem important:
  What are some of the things that Tan says that I am happy to hear someone say?

  What things that she says seem true to me?

  What things that she says seem wrong to me?

What thing that she says is most important to me?

What idea in this essay is completely new to me?

Freewriting

Use freewriting now to explore your responses to the questions above:

- Pick one or more of your answers to the questions you have already answered, and just begin to write about them.
- While you are doing this writing, do not stop or censor yourself; just let the words come.
- Do this for about five or ten minutes without thinking about spelling, grammar, word choice, or even the sense of what you are saying.
- When you have completed this activity, you will want to take a break.
- After your brief break, come back and read what you have written. Most of what you now have down on paper will not end up in your essay, but, as you read through your freewriting, you will find one or more sentences or ideas that seem interesting, important, or even compelling to you. Highlight these points and ideas. Are you beginning to develop your thoughts in a way that will shape your essay?

Listing

With this strategy, you simply list all of the thoughts and reactions you have noted so far. By looking down your list, you may see a pattern of ideas develop, one that you can use to develop an essay of your own.

- List all of the annotations you made for "Mother Tongue."
- List the main ideas you can see in your answers to the questioning phase above.
- List any main ideas that developed from your responses to the follow-up activities above.
- Be sure to list all the items from your freewriting that you thought were interesting. As you make this list, other ideas may come into your head. Put them on your list as well.

Look over your list and group all the ideas that seem related to each other. See if you can find one related group of ideas that is longer than the others. These ideas may suggest what you want to say in response to Tan's essay.

Shaping Your Ideas into a Rough Draft

By now, you should feel prepared to begin planning your rough draft. If you aren't, go back through some of the activities above, and talk with classmates to see what they are thinking. Sometimes it takes a while before your ideas are formed enough; take as much time as you need to clarify your thoughts.

When you are ready to focus on your rough draft, you will have to think about each part of your essay and how you will compose it. Turn back to Part 2 and examine "A Suggested Structure for an Essay That Responds to Another Writer's Essay." Also, look again at the writing topic for "Mother Tongue." Remind yourself that it asks you to do three things:

1. **Write a summary** that identifies and explains the "different Englishes" that Tan discusses.

   Remember that you have already worked on this in earlier activities. Look back now to the work you did. You may be able to use some of it below, when you write your essay's *directed summary*.

2. **Take a position** on this idea; do you agree with Tan's view?

   This is your thesis statement, and it will unify your essay, so it's important that you write it out clearly. Turn back to the review questions you answered and the follow-up activities you did. What were your thoughts and ideas? You will use them below when you write a thesis statement. Remember that you can always revise it as you work on your rough draft.

3. **Support and develop your position using specific evidence** taken from your own experiences and readings. In other words, explain your thinking and why you have the view you present—and don't forget to include the specific "proof" that convinced you to take the position you take.

   The explanation of your thoughts and the evidence that led you to draw those conclusions will make up nearly your entire essay. Look back to earlier exercises in this unit to remind yourself of some of the thinking you did about the different forms of English you have used or experienced. You will be able to use some of this as evidence to support your thesis. Remember it when you begin working on body paragraphs.

Drafting Your Directed Summary

Here are some questions that will help you answer the first part of the writing topic. Answer each one as thoroughly and carefully as you can; then, use your answers and those you wrote in earlier activities to draft a directed summary that answers the first question:

What are the "different Englishes" Tan discusses, and **how** does she view them?

Notice that this question does *not* ask you to summarize the entire essay. Rather, it asks you to explain one aspect of Tan's essay. There are two important action words in this question, "what" and "how." You will have to identify the "different Englishes" Tan talks about in "Mother Tongue," and you will have to explain her point of view on them.

Here are some steps that will help you plan your directed summary in response to the first question.

1. List the "Englishes" that Tan identifies in her essay.

2. After each one, write down where she uses it.

3. Now find and list the descriptive words that she uses as she talks about each form of English.

4. Look over Tan's descriptions and see if you can identify the associations she makes for each form. What do you think she is trying to show readers?

Follow-Up Activity

1. On the board, write the lists you developed in the previous exercise. Compare your lists with your classmates' and discuss.

2. Draft your directed summary.

3. Working in small groups or with a partner, take turns reading your directed summary aloud. Discuss the strengths and weaknesses of each summary.

Developing Your Thesis Statement

The second question in the writing topic asks "What do you think of her view?" In other words, it asks you to *evaluate* Tan's point of view on nonstandard forms of English and *weigh the evidence* she uses to support her position. Do you agree with her view of nonstandard forms of English? Your answer to this will be your essay's thesis statement.

Think of your thesis as needing three parts:

- the subject being considered
- Tan's claim about the subject
- your opinion about the subject

To form your thesis statement, fill in your answer on the lines below.

The subject/Tan's idea about the subject AND your opinion about the subject

_____

_____

_____

_____

_____

After you have finished writing your sentence, review your statement to see that it contains the following elements:

- Tan's point of view on the subject
- your point of view on the subject

If either of these elements is missing, rewrite your thesis statement so that both are included.

Up to this point, you have been planning the draft of your introductory paragraph. Now that you have drafted your thesis statement, you can begin planning your body paragraphs. They will have to explain your ideas and give support to your thesis statement.

Developing Body Paragraphs for an Essay That Presents a Thesis

Reminders:

Body paragraphs make up the largest part of an essay.

- The job of each body paragraph is to develop one point that supports the thesis statement.
- Taken together, these points constitute the argument of the essay.
- Writing a good body paragraph can be easy once you understand the elements that the body paragraph must contain.

Here is a review of the three most important elements for paragraphs in an argumentative essay:

Parts of a Body Paragraph

an appropriate or suitable topic—one that supports the thesis statement

evidence—for instance, a concrete fact, example, or quotation—that demonstrates the point of the paragraph

a link to the thesis—sentences that show how and why the paragraph, including the evidence, relates to the thesis

A Basic Outline Form for an Essay That Presents a Thesis

Let's look back at all of the work you have done so far:

You have read and carefully annotated "Mother Tongue."

You have analyzed its ideas.

You have written a directed summary in response to the first question in the writing topic.

You have thought about your own experiences and decided on your thesis statement.

You have drafted your essay's introduction.

All of that work should be gathered together now into a shape that will become your essay, your response to the writing topic for "Mother Tongue."

- Remember that you should follow the basic structure of an academic essay.
- To refresh your memory, turn back to Part 2 and review the diagram of the academic essay format.
- As you begin filling in this diagram form, you should be able to turn back to material you have already drafted as you worked through the exercises in this unit.
- Fill in the diagram form as fully as you can. A good plan will help you draft an essay that is clear and coherent.

  I. Introductory Paragraph:

A. one or two opening sentences that give the reading selection's title, author, and main topic:

_____

_____

_____

B. the main points that will be included in the directed summary:

    1.

    2.

3.

4.

C. your thesis statement. Be sure that it presents a clear position in response to the writing topic. State your thesis in your own words.

_____

_____

_____

II. **Body Paragraphs: For each body paragraph you will include in your essay, plan the following parts:**

Write down the main point for the paragraph.

_____

_____

_____

List the evidence you will use to support your main point (fact, example, etc.).

_____

_____

_____

_____

_____

_____

Tell how the evidence and your ideas link to the thesis statement.

_____

_____

_____

_____

_____

_____

_____

(Repeat this part of the outline as often as necessary to plan all of your body paragraphs.)

III. **Conclusion: What are some general remarks you can make to close your essay? Perhaps you will remind your readers of the main argument of your paper, for example.**

_____

_____

_____

Drafting Your Essay

Now that you have a basic plan for the structure of your essay and a map of its various parts, you are ready to begin drafting.

- If your thinking changes as you write your draft, return to your outline and make necessary adjustments. Every time you decide to revise your outline and essay, remember that this is a good sign, a sign that your thinking is developing and becoming more thoughtful and convincing.

- As you draft your essay, keep turning back to all of the activities in this unit. Try to recall some of your reactions, thoughts, and ideas as you worked on these activities. This may help you to strengthen, expand on, or more fully develop your essay's argument.

Follow-Up Activity

Your draft will always benefit from careful rereadings, by you or someone else. Work with a classmate now to find areas in your draft that can be improved.

Use the following process to give and receive draft feedback.

1. Exchange essays with one of your classmates.
2. Using a pen and a highlighter, mark your classmate's draft in the following manner:
   - Using your pen, underline the subject of each sentence.
   - Use two lines to underline the verb in each sentence.
   - Identify the tense by writing it above the verb.
3. Using your highlighter:
   - If the subject and verb **do not agree**, highlight the sentence.
   - If the verb tense is **not correct**, highlight only the verb.
   - If the verb is irregular and **improperly** formed, highlight the verb.
4. Using your pen, underline the essay's thesis.
   - If the sentence is a **fragment**, enclose it in parentheses.
   - If the sentence is a **run-on**, draw two vertical lines between the independent clauses.
5. Using your pen, mark the following:
   - If it is clear, if it identifies a topic, and if it makes a claim about it, put a check in the margin.
   - If it needs more work or if you cannot find a thesis, put an X in the margin.
6. Return the drafts and discuss your marks and suggestions.

Supplemental Reading

The Hunger of Memory: The Education of Richard Rodriguez

Essay

RICHARD RODRIGUEZ

Richard Rodriguez received a BA from Stanford University and an MA from Columbia University. He is a writer, journalist, and speaker, and is widely known for his controversial first book, Hunger of Memory: The Education of Richard Rodriguez *(1982). It is an autobiographical account of his life, from childhood as part of an immigrant, Spanish-speaking family, to what he identifies as his full assimilation as an American, an assimilation that required a separation from his past, his family, and his culture. In spite of its controversial message, the book received wide critical acclaim. This selection is an excerpt taken from that book.*

In the early years of my boyhood, my parents coped very well in America. My father had steady work. My mother managed at home. They were nobody's victims. When we moved to a house many blocks from the Mexican-American section of town, they were not intimidated by those two or three neighbors who initially tried to make us unwelcome. ("Keep your brats away from my sidewalk!") But despite all they achieved, or perhaps because they had so much to achieve, they lacked any deep feeling of ease, of belonging in public. They regarded the people at work or in crowds as being very distant from us. Those were the others, *los gringos*. That term was interchangeable in their speech with another, even more telling: *los americanos*.

I grew up in a house where the only regular guests were my relations. On a certain day, enormous families of relatives would visit us, and there would be so many people that the noise and the bodies would spill out to the backyard and onto the front porch. Then for weeks no one would come. (If the doorbell rang, it was usually a salesman.) Our house stood apart—gaudy yellow in a row of white bungalows. We were the people with the noisy dog, the people who raised chickens. We were the foreigners on the block. A few neighbors would smile and wave at us. We waved back. But until I was seven years old, I did not know the name of the old couple living next door or the names of the kids living across the street.

(Continues)

In public, my father and mother spoke a hesitant, accented, and not always grammatical English. And then they would have to strain, their bodies tense, to catch the sense of what was rapidly said by *los gringos*. At home, they returned to Spanish. The language of their Mexican past sounded in counterpoint to the English spoken in public. The words would come quickly, with ease. Conveyed through those sounds was the pleasing, soothing, consoling reminder that one was at home.

During those years when I was first learning to speak, my mother and father addressed me only in Spanish; in Spanish I learned to reply. By contrast, English (*inglés*) was the language I came to associate with gringos, rarely heard in the house. I learned my first words of English overhearing my parents speaking to strangers. At six years of age, I knew just enough words for my mother to trust me on errands to stores one block away—but no more.

I was then a listening child, careful to hear the very different sounds of Spanish and English. Wide-eyed with hearing, I'd listen to sounds more than to words. First, there were English (*gringo*) sounds. So many words still were unknown to me that when the butcher or the lady at the drugstore said something, exotic polysyllabic sounds would bloom in the midst of their sentences. Often the speech of people in public seemed to me very loud, booming with confidence. The man behind the counter would literally ask, "What can I do for you?" But by being so firm and clear, the sound of his voice said that he was a gringo; he belonged in public society. There were also the high, nasal notes of middle-class American speech—which I rarely am conscious of hearing today because I hear them so often, but could not stop hearing when I was a boy. Crowds at Safeway or at bus stops were noisy with the birdlike sounds of *los gringos*. I'd move away from them all—all the chirping chatter above me.

My own sounds I was unable to hear, but I knew that I spoke English poorly. My words could not extend to form complete thoughts. And the words I did speak I didn't know well enough to make distinct sounds. (Listeners would usually lower their heads to hear better what I was trying to say.) But it was one thing for *me* to speak English with difficulty; it was more troubling to hear my parents speaking in public: their high-whining vowels and guttural consonants; their sentences that got stuck with "eh" and "ah" sounds; the confused syntax; the hesitant rhythm of sounds so different from the way gringos spoke. I'd notice, moreover, that my parents' voices were softer than those of gringos we would meet.

I am tempted to say now that none of this mattered. (In adulthood I am embarrassed by childhood fears.) And, in a way, it didn't matter very much that my parents could not speak English with ease. Their linguistic difficulties had no serious consequences. My mother and father made themselves understood at the county hospital clinic and at government offices. And yet, in another way, it mattered very much. It was unsettling to hear my parents struggle with English. Hearing them, I'd grow nervous, and my clutching trust in their protection and power would be weakened.

There were many times like the night at a brightly lit gasoline station (a blaring white memory) when I stood uneasily hearing my father talk to a teenage attendant. I do not recall what they were saying, but I cannot forget the sounds my father made as he spoke. At one point his words slid together to form one long word—sounds as confused as the threads of blue and green oil in the puddle next to my shoes. His voice rushed through what he had left to say. Toward the end, he reached falsetto notes, appealing to his listener's understanding. I looked away at the lights of passing automobiles. I tried not to hear any more. But I heard only too well the attendant's reply, his calm, easy tones. Shortly afterward, headed for home, I shivered when my father put his hand on my shoulder. The very first chance that I got. I evaded his grasp and ran on ahead into the dark, skipping with feigned boyish exuberance.

But then there was Spanish: *español*, the language rarely heard away from the house; *español*, the language which seemed to me therefore a private language, my family's language. To hear its sounds was to feel myself specially recognized as one of the family, apart from *los otros*. A simple remark, an inconsequential comment could convey that assurance. My parents would say something to me and I would feel embraced by the sounds of their words. Those sounds said: *I am speaking with ease in Spanish. I am addressing you in words I never use with los gringos. I recognize you as someone special, close, like no one outside. You belong with us. In the family, Ricardo.*

At the age of six, well past the time when most middle-class children no longer notice the difference between sounds uttered at home and words spoken in public, I had a different experience. I lived in a world compounded of sounds. I was a child longer than most. I lived in a magical world, surrounded by sounds both pleasing and fearful. I shared with my family a language enchantingly private —different from that used in the city around us.

Plainly it is not healthy to hear such sounds so often. It is not healthy to distinguish public from private sounds so easily. I remained cloistered by sounds, timid and shy in public, too dependent on the voices at home. And yet I was a very happy child when I was at home.

(Continues)

I remember many nights when my father would come back from work, and I'd hear him call out to my mother in Spanish, sounding relieved. In Spanish, his voice would sound the light and free notes that he never could manage in English. Some nights I'd jump up just hearing his voice. My brother and I would come running into the room where he was with our mother. Our laughing (so deep was the pleasure!) became screaming. Like others who feel the pain of public alienation, we transformed the knowledge of our public separateness into a consoling reminder of our intimacy. Excited, our voices joined in a celebration of sounds. *We are speaking now the way we never speak out in public—we are together*, the sounds told me. Some nights no one seemed willing to loosen the hold that sounds had on us.

Fortunately, my teachers were unsentimental about their responsibility. What they understood was that I needed to speak public English.

One Saturday morning, three nuns arrived at the house to talk to our parents. Stiffly they sat on the blue living-room sofa. From the doorway of another room, spying on the visitors, I noted the incongruity, the clash of two worlds, the faces and voices of school intruding upon the familiar setting of home.

With great tact, the visitors continued, "Is it possible for you and your husband to encourage your children to practice their English when they are home?" Of course my parents complied. What would they not do for their children's well-being? And how could they question the Church's authority which those women represented? In an instant they agreed to give up the language (the sounds) which had revealed and accentuated our family's closeness. The moment after the visitors left, the change was observed. "*Ahora*, speak to us only *en inglés*," my father and mother told us.

Again and again in the days following, as I grew increasingly angry, I was obliged to hear my mother and father encouraging me: "Speak to us *en inglés*." Only then did I determine to learn classroom English. Thus, sometime afterward it happened: One day in school, I raised my hand to volunteer an answer to a question. I spoke out in a loud voice and I did not think it remarkable when the entire class understood. That day I moved very far from being the disadvantaged child I had been only days earlier. Taken hold at last was the belief, the calming assurance, that I *belonged* in public.

There was a new silence at home. As we children learned more and more English, we shared fewer and fewer words with our parents. Sentences needed to be spoken slowly when one of us addressed our mother or father. Often the parent wouldn't understand. The child would need to repeat himself. Still the parent misunderstood. The young voice, frustrated, would end up saying, "Never mind"—the subject was closed. Dinners would be noisy with the clinking of knives and forks against dishes. My mother would smile softly between her remarks; my father, at the other end of the table, would chew and chew his food while he stared over the heads of his children.

Bilingual educators say today that children lose a degree of "individuality" by becoming assimilated into public society. (Bilingual schooling is a program popularized in the seventies, that decade when middle-class "ethnics" began to resist the process of assimilation—the "American melting pot.") But the bilingualists oversimplify when they scorn the value and necessity of assimilation. They do not seem to realize that a person is individualized in two ways. So they do not realize that, while one suffers a diminished sense of *private* individuality by being assimilated into public society, such assimilation makes possible the achievement of *public* individuality.

Simplistically again, the bilingualists insist that a student should be reminded of his difference from others in mass society, of his "heritage." But they equate mere separateness with individuality. The fact is that only in private—with intimates—is separateness from the crowd a prerequisite for individuality; an intimate "tells" me that I am unique, unlike all others, apart from the crowd. In public, by contrast, full individuality is achieved, paradoxically, by those who are able to consider themselves members of the crowd. Thus it happened for me. Only when I was able to think of myself as an American, no longer an alien in gringo society, could I seek the rights and opportunities necessary for full public individuality.

Discussion Questions

1. For the young Richard Rodriquez, how did private speech differ from public speech in terms of language, tone, and emotion?

2. In what ways did Rodriquez's parents' way of speaking English both matter and not matter? Discuss any similarities and differences between his boyhood experiences and feelings about the English of his parents, and those of the young Amy Tan's experiences and feelings about her mother's English.

3. What caused Rodriquez to learn to speak English well? Do you think the actions of his teachers (the nuns) and his parents were in young Richard's best interest? Why or why not?

(Continues)

4. In the end, what conclusion does Rodriquez come to about the role speaking English well plays in terms of functioning as an American? What stand on bilingual education results from this conclusion? Do you think Amy Tan would support his arguments about English in American culture and bilingual education? Explain.

Why and When We Speak Spanish in Public

Essay

Myriam Marquez

> *Myriam Marquez is a journalist and the executive editor of* El Nuevo Herald, *the largest Spanish-language newspaper in the US. She is well known for her editorials advocating for the rights of all citizens, and for her anecdotal pieces about the experiences of being a bilingual and bicultural American.*

When I'm shopping with my mother or standing in line with my step-dad to order fast food or anywhere else we might be together, we're going to speak to one another in Spanish. That may appear rude to those who don't understand Spanish and overhear us in public places. Those around us may get the impression that we're talking about them. They may wonder why we would insist on speaking in a foreign tongue, especially if they knew that my family has lived in the United States for forty years and that my parents do understand English and speak it, albeit with difficulty and a heavy accent.

Let me explain why we haven't adopted English as our official family language. For me and most of the bilingual people I know, it's a matter of respect for our parents and comfort in our cultural roots. It's not meant to be rude to others. It's not meant to alienate anyone or to Balkanize America. It's certainly not meant to be un-American—what constitutes an "American" being defined by English speakers from North America.

Being an American has very little to do with what language we use during our free time in a free country. From its inception, this country was careful not to promote a government-mandated official language. We understand that English is the common language of this country and the one most often heard in international business circles from Peru to Norway. We know that, to get ahead here, one must learn English.

But that ought not mean that somehow we must stop speaking in our native tongue whenever we're in a public area, as if we are ashamed of who we are, where we're from. As if talking in Spanish—or any other language, for that matter—is some sort of litmus test used to gauge American patriotism.

(Continues)

Throughout this nation's history, most immigrants—whether from Poland or Finland or Italy or wherever else—kept their language through the first generation and, often, the second. I suspect that they spoke among themselves in their native tongue—in public. Pennsylvania even provided voting ballots written in German during much of the 1800s for those who weren't fluent in English.

In this century, Latin American immigrants and others have fought for this country in US-led wars. They have participated fully in this nation's democracy by voting, holding political office, and paying taxes. And they have watched their children and grandchildren become so "American" that they resist speaking in Spanish.

You know what's rude? When there are two or more people who are bilingual and another person who speaks only English and the bilingual folks all of a sudden start speaking Spanish, which effectively leaves out the English-only speaker. I don't tolerate that.

One thing's for sure. If I'm ever in a public place with my mom or dad and bump into an acquaintance who doesn't speak Spanish, I will switch to English and introduce that person to my parents. They will respond in English, and do so with respect.

Discussion Questions

1. Why does Myriam Marquez believe that bilingual people speak their native language in public? What do you think might be some other reasons for them to speak a language other than English in public settings?

2. What are some of the criticisms Marquez has heard about people who speak Spanish in public? How does she counter these criticisms? Explain why you do or do not find her counterarguments convincing.

3. Tell about a time in public when you overheard a conversation in a language you did not understand. How did that make you feel?

Follow-Up Activity

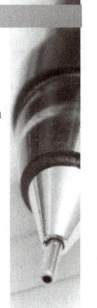

1. Read the following student essay. Then, using a pen or pencil, do the following:

   a. underline the thesis statement. If you cannot find it, or if you think it needs more work, say so and make any revisions you can to improve it;

   b. mark two places in the essay that aren't clear or that need more development, and explain why you marked them;

   c. mark two places in the essay that are good, and tell why you marked them.

2. Now, working with a partner,

   a. compare your ideas about the essay;

   b. use the scoring rubric on pages 51–53 and decide together what score you think the essay deserves.

Student Essay 1

In the essay "Mother Tongue," Amy Tan discusses the "different English" she uses to communicate with her family. "Different English" is a kind of English that relates to family talk that family members use to communicate with each other. Besides, the other trait of "different English" is that outsiders may have a hard time to understand it. Therefore, "different English" is a kind of language to show intimacy. Tan feels comfortable with "different English." The author believes her mother's "different English" is perfect and clear, and this is the natural way her mother expresses herself. In the essay, the author correctly explains the advantages of speaking a language at home that is different from standard English.

Speaking a family language that differs from standard English can be valuable for family members. For example, it is a source of calmness when there is so much stress. For example, one of my friend's grandfather was very sick at home in another country. She cannot do anything to help but wait to hear news. In that period of waiting for a call about her grandfather's condition, she told me that she was so worried about her grandfather because she grew up with him. In that time, I thought she felt so stressed and worried. She was crying a lot and eating less. About three days later, she talked to her mother who spoke in the dialect of her village. To be honest, I did not understand. However, one thing I can be sure of was she told me those words made her feel calmer. She felt comforted when she heard her mother's tongue. I think this is the power of family language; my friend and her mother can share and understand each other's worries that someone outside of the family cannot. The way family language expresses things gives people a feeling of intimacy. The feeling of intimacy can be a source of comfort in times of stress. Therefore, family language is valuable.

Another advantage of family language is that it makes communication vivid and lively. For instance, my family language is a kind of dialect. My mother uses it a lot because she believes it is the best language to describe things. Some of the things she says cannot even be written down as real words, but they make sense clearly to those who can speak the dialect. According to the author, although most of the people think her mother's "different English" is a poor in expression, Tan still believes that her family language, or "different English," is perfect and natural. When she hears it, it is vivid and full of observation and imagery. Family languages have their unique charms, and they cannot be replaced by other official languages. Therefore, the valuable part of family language is this language is vivid for those who understand it.

All in all, family languages make people feel comfortable in time of stress by showing intimacy between family members. Also, they are clear, natural, and vivid for family members. Therefore, we should always keep our family language.

Follow-Up Activity

Working with a partner, read the following essay aloud. Mark three grammar or sentence changes you would make. Rewrite or correct the sentences you marked.

Then, compare the directed summaries in Essay 1 and Essay 2. Determine which one does the best job, finding at least two reasons for your decision. Identify what could be added or revised to make it even stronger.

Student Essay 2

In the essay "Mother Tongue," Amy Tan is aware of two different Englishes she uses. The first one is standard English that Tan learned in school. She uses it to write books and to give lectures in a club. She uses complex sentences to clarify things for people. The second one is the family talk, the language she grew up with. Tan uses this kind of English with her family all the time. Even though there are not even complete sentences in this English sometimes, Tan and her mother can clearly understand each other. I really agree with Tan's idea of this kind of "family talk" or "Mother Tongue." It always has meaning deep inside; it contains the love from family. It is lovely English.

The family talk connects the members by special memories they shared. It can be anything from a New Year's Eve to someone's birthday party, or even a hike in spring. These memories prove families had fun; it's totally different from the other things of people in society. They have no pressure here, and they don't really need to care about every single word they say. So when families talk about the things in the past, they can always remember the people with them. They will always be there for them at the important times. Tan was walking down the street with her mother and husband. They used family talk and had a great time. They didn't care about the proper way of saying English; they cared about shared memories and the happiness they shared. I thin family talk signals the connection which binds them together.

Family talk is really not about the words themselves; its about the meaning behind those words. I remember a boy from a rich family. His dream was becoming a professional game player, making money by playing games. This was such a bad idea for him and for his family, but his mother only told him these words, "you be live you dream." Those simple words not only showed her trust in her son, but also the love from parents to their kids. This is why family talk is so clear. Members know the meaning and feeling behind the words. They know each other well; they understand the family talk.

Family talk can also reflect a person's nature and thought. Look at the speech of her mother Tan gave in the essay; we can see Tan's mother is such a brave woman. Even though she knew her English is not very good, she would still speak out the thought inside. And the speech also shows her intent, her nature as Tan found out. Personality is reflected through the family, actions, and by words. The speech is simple, but it shows respect and family love. It makes families love each other more for the words they use.

For the families, they don't need so many words to make sure the others in the family understand. They just need to get the feeling that the family always is there for them, and that love explains the advantage of speaking a home language different from standard English.

Assignment 8

Read the following essay and the writing topic that follows it. Then, use the exercises and activities that follow to move through the writing process and develop your own essay in response to the argument Richard Crasta presents in "What's in a Name?"

What's in a Name?

RICHARD CRASTA

Essay

> *Richard Crasta was born in Mangalore, India, and has lived in the United States since 1980. He earned an MFA degree from Columbia University, and he is a freelance writer and author. His has published several novels. His early one,* The Revised Kama Sutra *(1993), was published under the name* Avatar Prabhu *in the United States and Germany, and has since been published in twelve editions and in ten countries.*

No wonder a newborn baby cries. It is hungry, naked, and—if it is an American—already owes the government $12,010.57, its approximate share of the US national debt. But if that baby happens to be, like mine, the American-born child of recent immigrant parents from Asia or Africa, it has all the more reason to cry because its parents must face the genuine problem of whether to give the child a name from their old country or their new. And until an adventurer named James M. Fail came along, the burden weighed even more heavily on me, a three-time father who had always regarded with utmost seriousness, with almost somber awe, the responsibility of naming a child.

Let me clarify. Though my name is Richard, I am, from my history to my abject dependence on regular injections of red pepper, a real Indian from the real India. Living in a part-Catholic, innocent corner of South India—the multiethnic town of Mangalore—I had always been proud of my name (Richard the Lionheart was big in my childhood storybooks).

Of course, when I went to work in North India, I did encounter chauvinistic people ignorant of the fact that Christianity, dating from the first century, was India's third most populous religion, and who implied, with exaggerated smiles and pseudo-British accents, that my name was not quite Indian. It was also at the time that Richard "Tricky Dick" Nixon was spreading his notoriety, and there were moments when my name was called out in public and I wanted to duck. But when I came to the United States, I decided I would, despite my history, give my child a name that was more recognizably "Indian."

And then, five years later, my first child, a son, was born. Give him an American name, advised many of my friends (meaning, of course, give him an Anglo-European name), passionately. He'll have enough problems in school with his looks without an extra oral reminder to bring attention to them, without having to battle teasers and mispronouncers, without being scarred by it all for life—so said (among others) a white American father who had named his two adopted Korean girls Jacqueline and Susan. I know what it is like to have a foreign face and an "American" name. Americans will often ask, when I introduce myself, "But what is your *real*, your *Indian* name?" Sometimes, peeved, I will answer with "Abdul the Bull Bull Abbasid"—something tongue-twisting—and I am amazed at how credulously most people will accept my Abdul bull.

On the other hand, I thought, any child born here is going to be an outright American no matter what name I give him. America is so addicting. Now, at age eight, my son is already a perfect consumer of American television and its commercial offerings, parroting with an innocently straight face their sales pitches as infallible fact. Unless we move back to India before he reaches the age of unreason (between seven and seventeen)—that is, well beyond the age of sweet unreason—he is unlikely ever to choose to adopt his parents' country. So why not leave him some little stamp of his heritage—a little memory aid—an Indian name? So long as one doesn't go overboard with tongue-twisting ethnicity, calling one's children Mbongo Bow-Wow or Mu Mu Zwbingli or Venkatagiri Pillaiswamy, isn't an ethnic name your vote (and your child's) for the principle and future of cultural diversity and well-exercised tongues in the America of the twentieth century? But then, what is permanent about a name that my son could easily change when he grows up—as indeed adult immigrant Indians (and others) under the assault of massacred and mispronounced names are constantly doing in America—from Balwinder to Billy, from Subramanian to Sam, from Saraswati to Sarah, from Krishna to Chris?

(Continues)

I have often, woolly-headedly, wished for a world where names and national origins didn't matter. Until then, however, we finally decided out of concern for our child's well-being and happiness to choose an "American" name. At the time, I was under the spell of James Joyce's *Ulysses*, and Bertrand Russell had always been my kind of philosopher, passionate and caring, not cold and academic. And, moved by novelist Ralph Ellison's admission that his being named after Ralph Waldo Emerson had been the formative influence in his life, we named our son James Russell. But by the time of his christening party, a month later, his name was expanded, like the federal budget, to accommodate a variety of special and parochial interests, such as in-laws, Indian pride, and my sense of humorous resignation. The name on the cake read: James Russell Charles Ashok Prabhu Crasta.

Then we read about a man named James M. Fail who, despite his failure-prone last name, had *succeeded* wildly—having, with an absurd thousand-dollar personal investment (and the right connections), raked in a dizzying $1.8 billion in American government subsidies to build up a savings and loan empire. Wow! For a miserable fraction of that amount, a measly half-million, I'd be willing to change my name to Genghis H. Hoolamoola and still be so ecstatic that I'd spend half my remaining days lying on my back, wiggling my arms and legs in the air, and gurgling with pleasure like a baby just stuffed with infant formula. Hadn't I put myself through a lot of unnecessary agony?

And if the whole internal brouhaha was a personal sorting out of a personal identity crisis, its result is a small squeak of protest against those Indians who pretend that their name encapsulates the exclusive, inalienable essence of Indianness, who spit out your name at you, who preach internationalism, then practice cultural chauvinism, who say on the one hand that Hinduism is a way of life, an inclusive, absorptive, and tolerant religion, and on the other hand, dressed in tight pants and pointy shoes with Pantene heads, Mc Fast Foods burger in hand, speak with mild scorn amongst themselves of Indians with names different from their own. Once, I had seriously considered changing to a more "Indian" name, but had been stopped by the bureaucratic work. Now I ask, "What's in a name? A Narayana Nambudiri by any other name is often as ridiculous."

Writing Topic

What does Crasta observe about the relation of a person's name to that individual's personal identity and identity within a culture? To what extent does your own experience support these observations? To support your position, be sure to use specific evidence. This evidence may be taken from your own experience, observations, or reading, including the reading that is part of this unit.

Vocabulary and Dictionary Practice
Part I.

Look up the following words used in "What's in a Name." For each, write the two most common definitions on the lines provided, and include what part of speech each definition is (noun, verb, adjective, etc.). Then, under each of the two definitions, write a sentence that uses the word in a way that reflects that particular definition and part of speech.

1. genuine
2. somber
3. clarify
4. chauvinistic
5. ignorant
6. notoriety
7. peeved
8. credulous
9. infallible
10. tongue-twisting
11. massacre
12. woolly-headed
13. formative
14. christening
15. parochial
16. measly
17. gurgle
18. brouhaha
19. encapsulate
20. pseudo

1. word: **genuine**

   first definition: _____

   _____

part of speech: _____

sentence: _____

_____

second definition: _____

_____

part of speech: _____

sentence: _____

_____

2. word: **somber**

first definition: _____

_____

part of speech: _____

sentence: _____

_____

second definition: _____

_____

part of speech: _____

sentence: _____

_____

3. word: **clarify**

first definition: _____

_____

part of speech: _____

sentence: _____

_____

second definition: _____

_____

part of speech: _____

sentence: _____

_____

4. word: **chauvinistic**

first definition: _____

_____

part of speech: _____

sentence: _____

_____

second definition: _____

_____

part of speech: _____

sentence: _____

_____

5. word: **ignorant**

first definition: _____

_____

part of speech: _____

sentence: _____

_____

second definition: _____

_____

part of speech: _____

sentence: _____

_____

6. word: **notoriety**

   first definition: _____

   _____

   part of speech: _____

   sentence: _____

   _____

   second definition: _____

   _____

   part of speech: _____

   sentence: _____

   _____

7. word: **peeved**

   first definition: _____

   _____

   part of speech: _____

   sentence: _____

   _____

   second definition: _____

   _____

   part of speech: _____

sentence: _____

_____

8. word: **credulous**

first definition: _____

_____

part of speech: _____

sentence: _____

_____

second definition: _____

_____

part of speech: _____

sentence: _____

_____

9. word: **infallible**

first definition: _____

_____

part of speech: _____

sentence: _____

_____

second definition: _____

_____

part of speech: _____

sentence: _____

_____

10. word: **tongue-twisting**

    first definition: _____

    _____

    part of speech: _____

    sentence: _____

    _____

    second definition: _____

    _____

    part of speech: _____

    sentence: _____

    _____

11. word: **massacre**

    first definition: _____

    _____

    part of speech: _____

    sentence: _____

    _____

    second definition: _____

    _____

    part of speech: _____

    sentence: _____

    _____

12. word: **woolly-headed**

first definition: _____

_____

part of speech: _____

sentence: _____

_____

second definition: _____

_____

part of speech: _____

sentence: _____

_____

13. word: **formative**

first definition: _____

_____

part of speech: _____

sentence: _____

_____

second definition: _____

_____

part of speech: _____

sentence: _____

_____

14. word: **christening**

   first definition: _____

   _____

   part of speech: _____

   sentence: _____

   _____

   second definition: _____

   _____

   part of speech: _____

   sentence: _____

   _____

15. word: **parochial**

   first definition: _____

   _____

   part of speech: _____

   sentence: _____

   _____

   second definition: _____

   _____

   part of speech: _____

   sentence: _____

   _____

16. word: **measly**

first definition: _____

_____

part of speech: _____

sentence: _____

_____

second definition: _____

_____

part of speech: _____

sentence: _____

_____

17. word: **gurgle**

first definition: _____

_____

part of speech: _____

sentence: _____

_____

second definition: _____

_____

part of speech: _____

sentence: _____

_____

18. word: **brouhaha**

first definition: _____

_____

part of speech: _____

sentence: _____

_____

second definition: _____

_____

part of speech: _____

sentence: _____

_____

19. word: **encapsulate**

first definition: _____

_____

part of speech: _____

sentence: _____

_____

second definition: _____

_____

part of speech: _____

sentence: _____

_____

20. word: **pseudo**

first definition: _____

_____

part of speech: _____

sentence: _____

_____

second definition: _____

_____

part of speech: _____

sentence: _____

_____

Part II.

Write down the sentence from the reading selection that contains the following words. Tell which one of the word's various definitions best fits the sentence. Paraphrase the sentence without using the vocabulary word; in other words, write the sentence using your own words.

1. word: **genuine**

   sentence:_____

   _____

   definition: _____

   _____

   paraphrase: _____

   _____

2. word: **somber**

   sentence: _____

   _____

   definition: _____

   _____

paraphrase:_____

_____

3. word: **clarify**

sentence:_____

definition: _____

_____

paraphrase: _____

_____

4. word: **chauvinistic**

sentence: _____

_____

definition: _____

_____

paraphrase: _____

_____

5. word: **ignorant**

sentence:_____

_____

definition: _____

_____

paraphrase: _____

_____

6. word: **notoriety**

   sentence: _____

   _____

   definition: _____

   _____

   paraphrase: _____

   _____

7. word: **peeved**

   sentence: _____

   _____

   definition: _____

   _____

   paraphrase: _____

   _____

8. word: **credulous**

   sentence: _____

   _____

   definition: _____

   _____

   paraphrase: _____

   _____

9. word: **infallible**

   sentence: _____

   _____

definition: _____

_____

paraphrase: _____

_____

10. word: **tongue-twisting**

sentence: _____

_____

definition: _____

_____

paraphrase: _____

_____

11. word: **massacre**

sentence: _____

_____

definition: _____

_____

paraphrase: _____

_____

12. word: **woolly-headed**

sentence: _____

_____

definition: _____

_____

paraphrase: _____

_____

13. word: **formative**

   sentence: _____

   _____

   definition: _____

   _____

   paraphrase: _____

   _____

14. word: **christening**

   sentence: _____

   _____

   definition: _____

   _____

   paraphrase: _____

   _____

15. word: **parochial**

   sentence: _____

   _____

   definition: _____

   _____

   paraphrase: _____

   _____

16. word: **measly**

    sentence: _____

    _____

    definition: _____

    _____

    paraphrase: _____

    _____

17. word: **gurgle**

    sentence: _____

    _____

    definition: _____

    _____

    paraphrase: _____

    _____

18. word: **brouhaha**

    sentence: _____

    _____

    definition: _____

    _____

    paraphrase: _____

    _____

19. word: **encapsulate**

    sentence: _____

    _____

definition: _____

_____

paraphrase: _____

_____

20. word: **pseudo**

sentence: _____

_____

definition: _____

_____

paraphrase: _____

_____

Part III.

Choose ten of these words from the essay and tell something new and interesting you learned about the word from the dictionary. For example, you might have found the correct way to pronounce a word you were already familiar with from reading but not from speaking, or you might have learned that a word you thought of as entirely English came from another language.

1. eord: **genuine**

_____

_____

2. word: **somber**

_____

_____

3. word: **clarify**

_____

_____

4. word: **chauvinistic**

_____

_____

5. word: **ignorant**

_____

_____

6. word: **notoriety**

_____

_____

7. word: **peeved**

_____

_____

8. word: **credulous**

_____

_____

9. word: **infallible**

_____

_____

10. word: **tongue-twisting**

_____

_____

11. word: **massacre**

_____

_____

12. word: **woolly-headed**

_____

_____

13. word: **formative**

_____

_____

14. word: **christening**

_____

_____

15. word: **parochial**

_____

_____

16. word: **measly**

_____

_____

17. word: **gurgle**

_____

_____

18. word: **brouhaha**

_____

_____

19. word: **encapsulate**

_____

_____

20. word: **pseudo**

_____

_____

Follow-Up Activity

Write a five-sentence description of your day so far. Your description must include at least three of the vocabulary words above. Read your description aloud to the class.

Doing a Careful Reading of "What's in a Name?"

By now, you should be aware of the importance of working systematically with a reading selection to make sure that you understand its purpose and ideas. If you've completed any of the previous assignment units, you have had practice using the following helpful techniques for doing a thoughtful reading of an essay. Use them again now to better understand Crasta's essay.

The steps are reproduced here, but your goal should be to memorize them so that they become a normal part of the writing process for you.

1. **Read the title.**
   - The title will tell you something about the reading's main subject.
   - It may also tell you something about Crasta's opinion on the subject.
   - Think about what you already know about the subject and what more you want to know.

2. **Learn about the author.**
   - Read the biographical information about Crasta at the top of the selection.
   - As you go through the remaining steps below, take note of how Crasta's life or work might connect with his subject.

3. **Read through the selection once quickly.**
   - Read quickly through the reading again so that you get a general impression of what it is about and what Crasta's attitude is toward the subject.
   - Notice the things—people, places, experiences, concepts, for example—he brings up to develop and support his opinion about the subject.

4. **Read again to identify the thesis.**
   - Now read the selection a second time, but more slowly and carefully, and *with a pen or highlighter in your hand.*
   - Find the thesis and underline it or write it in the margin. Remember, the thesis states Crasta's overall opinion on the subject of the reading. Often, the thesis is contained in a single sentence, but, in some cases, it takes several sentences to make the main argument of the reading selection clear. There are times, too, when the author does not state his or her thesis explicitly, but, if you read the selection carefully, you should be able to state it and then write it in the margin.
   - To help, ask yourself, "What does Crasta seem to want readers to think about his subject?"

5. Read slowly and methodically through the rest of the reading.

- Examine each body paragraph one at a time, and list or underline the kinds of evidence that Crasta uses to support his thesis.

- Look in each body paragraph for a *topic sentence*—a sentence that both presents an idea and tells how it gives support to the reading's overall opinion.

- As you read and study the selection, *be sure to write down any thoughts you have* about Crasta's opinion and supporting evidence.

- It is your job to evaluate this evidence for its logic and validity, so be sure to *make notes in the margins* as you read.

- *Mark the points* that you found interesting or convincing, and write a few words explaining your thoughts.

- Note, too, any weaknesses you find.

- When you look back at the notes you made in the margins, you should have a general idea of how convincing you found "What's in a Name?" and what you found to be its strengths and weaknesses.

6. Read again for review.

- Once you have thought through the reading selection, read it once more, looking for places where you don't quite understand what is being said.

- Underline any terms that you aren't familiar with, and look them up in a dictionary.

- Mark any places in the reading that don't fit with your understanding of the reading as a whole. Decide whether this is something that Crasta should have revised, or whether it is something that you need to read again because you don't understand it. You may find that you need to go back to Step 4 and begin working through the reading again.

- Once you are certain that you understand the entire reading, you are prepared to discuss, summarize, and/or respond to the reading with your own essay.

Follow-Up Activity

Close this book. Then, on a sheet of paper, try writing down the six steps for a careful reading, using your memory and your own words.

- To help yourself, think back and remember the strategies you used to help you carefully examine some of the previous essays in Part 3.

- When you are finished, open the book to this page and see how you did.

- Take careful note of any steps you left out.

- Looking over your list, put a star next to the steps that are most helpful to you, and briefly explain why.

- Consider more carefully the steps that you did not star and think about how you might alter them so that they would be more helpful.

Discuss the results of this activity with the class. Compare your results and conclusions.

Questions to Review Your Understanding of "What's in a Name?"

Answer the following questions to make sure that you have a clear understanding of Crasta's argument as a whole. Be sure to respond to each as thoroughly as you can.

Paragraph 1

What explanation does Richard Crasta have for the cry of newborn American babies? For what reason, according to him, do immigrant babies cry? What is the author's tone when he makes these statements? What is the real concern of the author?

Paragraph 2

Where did the author grow up? What was the religion of the southern region where he was born?

Paragraph 3

Why did his name become a problem when he relocated to a different region? After moving to America, what decision did the author make about the name of his child?

Paragraph 4

What advice on this matter did his friends give him? Here in America, what question was the author continually asked about his own name? How did the author respond emotionally and sometimes orally to that question?

Paragraph 5

What happens, according to Crasta, to the ethnic identity of children who grow up in America? When immigrant parents give children foreign-sounding names, what result might occur when the child grows up?

Paragraph 6

Why did the author decide to give his son an American or Anglo-European name? How did the author come to name his son James Russell? What name appeared on the cake at baby James's christening?

Paragraph 7

What anecdotal evidence does the author provide to show that a child's name does not have to shape his future?

Paragraph 8

Why does he believe that the attitude toward names held by other Indians can often be hypocritical? What decision does the author finally reach regarding the importance of a name? If you do not already recognize the quotation Crasta uses to make his own attitude clear, research the origin of the quotation. How does concluding with this particular quotation strengthen Crasta's point?

Follow-Up Activity

Share with your classmates the most unusual name you ever heard. Explain any preconceptions you may have had about that person when you first heard the name. After you learned about or got to know the person, how did your feelings about that individual's name change?

Responding to the Writing Topic

You should now have a good understanding of the ideas and overall message of "What's in a Name?" You are ready to look again at the writing topic and begin thinking about how you will respond to it. Here it is again, this time with each of three requirements on its own line:

Writing Topic

Here, again, is the writing topic for "What's in a Name?"

What does Crasta observe about the relation of a person's name to that individual's personal identity and identity within a culture? To what extent does your own experience support these observations? To support your position, be sure to use specific evidence. This evidence may be taken from your own experience, observations, or reading, including the reading that is part of this unit.

Always pay careful attention to any writing topic. In this one, it is important to notice the writing topic's three parts:

- You are first asked a question about an observation the author makes in "What's in a Name?" This question asks you to identify the relationship the author sees between a person's name and his or her personal identity, as well as his or her identity within a culture. You will have to locate within Crasta's essay the answer to both aspects of this question—the connection between 1) a person's name and his or her *personal identity*, and 2) a person's name and his or her *identity within his or her culture*. Your directed summary should respond to both of these aspects. When you examine a writing topic, you should always notice all of the important aspects of the question asked.

- The second question in the writing topic asks you to specify the extent to which your own experiences confirm those of the author. Do you see the role of names in determining identity the same way he does? Your answer to this question will become the thesis of your essay.

- The third part of this writing topic reminds you that in building your essay, you must support your claim—your thesis statement—with examples; these examples can be taken from your own personal experience with names, your observation of others' names, or any reading you may have done about the topic. The following activities will help you to begin to find these examples. Be sure to keep notes on your ideas, your classmates' experiences shared in the discussions, and the background readings you are assigned so that you can review and use this material to help you plan your essay.

Follow-Up Activity

1. Make a list of five names you think you might choose for your own child. Compare your list with those of your classmates. What name or names appeared on more than one person's list? Discuss the reason(s) the name or names might be popular now.

2. Make a list of five people you have met or heard about with unusual names. In a small group, share or try to guess the reasons the parents might have had for selecting each name. How often are the names significant in terms of ethnic identity? Have you observed or read about any traits or behaviors that might be related to the name?

3. Write a paragraph about your own name. What do you like and/or dislike about it? Why do you think that you were given this name?

4. Write a paragraph about the name you would now choose for yourself. Why would you choose it? What does it say about your personal identity and/or cultural identity?

5. Compare and discuss your paragraphs with your classmates. Does the information in the paragraphs seem to support or refute connections between names and personal and cultural identity?

Strategies to Help You Analyze a Reading Selection and Develop Your Ideas for Writing a Response

Now you are ready to build on the annotations you made earlier when you did a careful reading of "What's in a Name?" Remember the strategies of *questioning*, *freewriting*, and *listing* that you used in previous assignments in Part 3? By now, we hope you realize that these forms of prewriting are an important and productive part of the writing process. If you use them in a focused and sustained way, they lead you to a more systematic analysis of any reading selection. Use these strategies now on "What's in a Name?" as you begin to form your own opinions and ideas. They will help to guide and clarify your thinking about Crasta's essay. They will also help you to put into words your own views on the topic he writes about.

Questioning

- Questions about the highlighting you did:

  Why did I underline this part of the reading?

  How is this information important to Crasta's point?

  What is the relationship between this information and the question I am being asked to write about?

- Questions about Crasta's ideas:

  What things in this essay do not make sense to me?

  Where do I think Crasta should have explained further?

  How do the examples in the essay relate to his point?

- Questions about "What's in a Name?" that seem important:

  What are some of the things that Crasta says that I am happy to hear someone say?

What things that he says seem true to me?

What things that he says seem wrong to me?

What thing that he says is most important to me?

What idea in this essay is completely new to me?

Freewriting

Use freewriting now to explore your responses to the questions above:

- Pick one or more of your answers to the questions you have already answered, and just begin to write about it.
- While you are doing this writing, do not stop or censor yourself; just let the words come.
- Do this for about five or ten minutes without thinking about spelling, grammar, word choice, or even the sense of what you are saying.
- When you have completed this activity, you will want to take a break.
- After your brief break, come back and read what you have written. Most of what you now have down on paper will not end up in your essay, but, as you read through your freewriting, you will find one or more sentences or ideas that seem interesting, important, or even compelling to you. Highlight these points and ideas. Are you beginning to develop your thoughts in a way that will shape your essay?

Listing

With this strategy, you simply list all of the thoughts and reactions you have noted so far. By looking down your list, you may see a pattern of ideas develop, one that you can use to develop an essay of your own.

- List all of the annotations you made for "What's in a Name?"
- List the main ideas you can see in your answers to the questioning phase above.

- List any main ideas that developed from your responses to the follow-up activities above.
- Be sure to list all the items from your freewriting that you thought were interesting. As you make this list, other ideas may come to you. Put them on your list as well.

Look over your list and group all the ideas that seem related to each other. See if you can find one related group of ideas that is longer than the others. These ideas may suggest what you want to say in response to Crasta's essay.

Shaping Your Ideas into a Rough Draft

By now, you should feel prepared to begin planning your rough draft. If you aren't, go back through some of the activities above and talk with classmates to see what they are thinking. Sometimes it takes a while before your ideas are formed enough; take as much time as you need to clarify your thoughts.

When you are ready to focus on your rough draft, you will have to think about each part of your essay and how you will compose it. Turn back to Part 2 and examine "A Suggested Structure for an Essay That Responds to Another Writer's Essay." Also, look again at the writing topic for "What's in a Name?" Remind yourself that it asks you to do three things:

1. Write a summary that identifies Crasta's view of the way in which our names define us both personally and socially. Explain his ideas as well as you can.

   Remember that you have already worked on this in earlier activities. Look back now to the work you did. You may be able to use some of it below, when you write your essay's *directed summary*.

2. Take a position on this idea; do you agree with Crasta's view?

   This is your thesis statement, and it will unify your essay, so it's important that you write it out clearly. Turn back to the review questions you answered and the follow-up activities you did. What were your thoughts and ideas? You will use them below when you write a thesis statement. Remember that you can always revise it as you work on your rough draft.

3. Support and develop your position using specific evidence taken from your own experiences and readings. In other words, explain your thinking and why you have the view you present—and don't forget to include the specific evidence from your experience or your reading that convinced you to take the position you take.

The explanation of your thoughts and the evidence that led you to draw those conclusions will make up nearly your entire essay. Look back to earlier exercises in this unit to remind yourself of some of the thinking you did about the different forms of English you have used or experienced. You will be able to use some of this as evidence to support your thesis. Remember it when you begin working on body paragraphs.

Drafting Your Directed Summary

Here are some questions that will help you answer the first part of the writing topic. Answer each one as thoroughly and carefully as you can; then, use your answers and those you wrote in earlier activities to draft a directed summary. Begin drafting the directed summary by reviewing the writing topic for "What's in a Name?," paying particular attention to the first question asked.

What does Crasta observe about the relation of a person's name to that individual's personal identity and identity within a culture?

- The answer you give to this question is called a *directed summary* because it summarizes only the parts of Crasta's essay that answer this first question.

- As you learned in Part 2, the question that calls for a directed summary often opens with a question word such as *what*, *why*, or *how*. In Crasta's essay, the first question asks, "*What* does Crasta observe about the relation of a person's name to that individual's personal identity and identity within a culture?" You will have to go back to the essay to find information about identity formation and names. It will not be enough just to discuss the fact that some names are typically considered "American" while other names are uncommon in this country and suggest a connection to another cultures. You will have to summarize the arguments the author has heard about the name an individual is given and who he or she is or is perceived to be; then, you must explain the author's reaction to these arguments.

- Be sure to turn back to the essay itself and mark the sentences that answer this first writing topic question. Don't rely on your memory alone. Also, review your own responses and classroom discussion notes to "Questions to Review Your Understanding." You will most likely discover that you have already found important information that you can use in your directed summary.

You should avoid including any of the following in a directed summary:

1. minor details or points that are irrelevant to the question,
2. your own opinion or ideas, and
3. examples of your own, and, unless particularly helpful, those of the author.

Follow-Up Activity

1. Working as a class, draw a triangle on the board. At the tips of each of the triangle's three points, write the arguments Crasta has encountered both for and against giving ethnic names to American-born immigrant children, and his own response to these arguments. Label the points E (for ethnic name), A (for American name), and C (for Crasta's reaction). From a piece of paper, cut out three angles and label them E, A, and C.

2. Place your three angles on the places in your summary that correspond to the information each represents. Make a note to yourself about any of the angles you could not place on your summary.

3. Form small groups and read your summary aloud to your group. Share with the group your conclusion about the completeness of your summary. Ask for feedback about your conclusion.

Developing Your Thesis Statement

The second question in the writing topic asks you to *evaluate* Crasta's point of view on the importance we place on names and *weigh the evidence* he uses to support his position. Do you agree with him? Your answer to this will be your essay's thesis statement.

Think of your thesis as needing three parts:

- the subject being considered
- Crasta's claim about the subject
- your opinion about the subject

Fill in your answer on the line below to form your thesis statement.

_____

_____

After you have finished writing your sentence, review your statement to see that it contains the following elements:

- identifies Crasta's argument
- makes clear your opinion about what he says

If either of these elements is missing, rewrite your thesis statement so that both are included.

Up to this point, you have been planning the draft of your introductory paragraph. Now that you have drafted your thesis statement, you can begin planning your body paragraphs. They will have to explain your ideas and give support to your thesis statement.

Developing Body Paragraphs for an Essay That Presents a Thesis

Reminders:

Body paragraphs make up the largest part of an essay.

- The job of each body paragraph is to develop one point that supports the thesis statement.
- Taken together, these points constitute the argument of the essay.
- Writing a good body paragraph can be easy once you understand the criteria that the body paragraph must fulfill.

Here is a review of the three most important requirements for paragraphs in an argumentative essay:

Parts of a Body Paragraph

An appropriate or suitable topic—one that supports the thesis statement

Evidence—for instance, a concrete fact, example or quotation—that demonstrates the point of the paragraph

A link to the thesis—sentences that show how and why the paragraph, including the evidence, relates to the thesis

A Basic Outline Form for an Essay That Presents a Thesis

Let's look back at all of the work you have done so far:

You have read and carefully annotated "What's in a Name?"

You have analyzed its ideas.

You have written a directed summary in response to the first question in the writing topic.

You have thought about your own experiences and decided on your thesis statement.

You have drafted your essay's introduction.

All of that work should be gathered together now into a shape that will become your essay, your response to the writing topic for Crasta's essay.

- Remember that you should follow the basic structure of an academic essay.
- To refresh your memory, turn back to Part 2 and review the diagram of the academic essay format.
- As you begin filling in this diagram, you should be able to turn back to material you have already drafted as you worked through the exercises in this unit.
- Fill in the outline form below as fully as you can. A good plan will help you draft an essay that is clear and coherent.

I. Introductory Paragraph:

A. One or two opening sentences that give the reading selection's title, author, and main topic:

_____

_____

_____

B. The main points that will be included in the directed summary:

1.

2.

3.

4.

C. Your thesis statement. Be sure that it presents a clear position in response to the writing topic. State your thesis in your own words.

_____

_____

_____

II. **Body Paragraphs: For each body paragraph you will include in your essay, plan the following parts:**
Write down the main point for the paragraph.

_____

_____

_____

List the evidence you will use to support your main point (fact, example, etc.).

_____

_____

_____

_____

_____

_____

Tell how the evidence and your ideas link to the thesis statement.

_____

_____

_____

_____

_____

_____

_____

_____

_____

_____

(Repeat this part of the outline as often as necessary to plan all of your body paragraphs.)

III. Conclusion: What are some general remarks you can make to close your essay? Perhaps you will remind your readers of the main argument of your paper, for example.

_____

_____

_____

Drafting Your Essay

Now that you have a basic plan for the structure of your essay and a map of its various parts, you are ready to begin drafting.

- If your thinking changes as you write your draft, return to your outline and make necessary adjustments. Every time you decide to revise your outline and essay, remember that this is a good sign, a sign that your thinking is developing and becoming more thoughtful and convincing.

- Keep turning back to all of the activities in this unit as you draft your essay. Try to recall some of your reactions, thoughts, and ideas as you worked on these activities. This may help you to strengthen, expand on, or more fully develop your essay's argument.

Follow-Up Activity

Your draft will always benefit from careful rereadings, by you or someone else. Work with a classmate now to find areas in your draft that can be improved.

Use the following process to give and receive draft feedback.

1. Exchange a typed copy of your essay with one of your classmate's.

2. Using a pen and a highlighter, mark your classmate's draft in the following manner:
    - Using your pen, underline the subject of each sentence.
    - Use two lines to underline the verb in each sentence.
    - Identify the tense by writing it above the verb.

3. Using your highlighter:
    - If the subject and verb **do not agree**, highlight the sentence.
    - If the verb tense **is not correct**, highlight only the verb.
    - If an irregular verb is **improperly formed**, highlight the verb.
    - If the sentence is a **fragment**, enclose it in parentheses.
    - If the sentence is a **run-on**, draw two vertical lines between the independent clauses.

4. Using your pen, underline the essay's thesis.
    - If it is clear, if it identifies a subject, and if it makes a claim about it, put a check in the margin.
    - If it needs more work or if you cannot find a thesis, put an X in the margin.

5. Return the drafts and discuss your marks and suggestions.

Supplemental Reading

'Blaxicans' and Other Reinvented Americans

Essay

RICHARD RODRIGUEZ

Richard Rodriguez received a BA from Stanford University and an MA from Columbia University. He is a writer, journalist, and speaker, and is widely known for his controversial first book, Hunger of Memory: The Education of Richard Rodriguez *(1982). It is an autobiographical account of his life, from childhood as part of an immigrant, Spanish-speaking family, to what he identifies as his full assimilation as an American, an assimilation that required a separation from his past, his family, and his culture. In spite of its controversial message, the book received wide critical acclaim.*

There is something unsettling about immigrants because. . . well, because they chatter incomprehensibly, and they get in everyone's way. Immigrants seem to be bent on undoing America. Just when Americans think we know who we are—we are Protestants, culled from Western Europe, are we not?—then new immigrants appear from Southern Europe or from Eastern Europe. We—we who are already here—we don't know exactly what the latest comers will mean to our community. How will they fit in with us? Thus, we—we who were here first—we begin to question our own identity.

After a generation or two, the grandchildren or the great-grandchildren of immigrants to the United States and the grandchildren of those who tried to keep immigrants out of the United States will romanticize the immigrant, will begin to see the immigrant as the figure who teaches us most about what it means to be an American. The immigrant, in mythic terms, travels from the outermost rind of America to the very center of American mythology. None of this, of course, can we admit to the Vietnamese immigrant who served us our breakfast at the hotel this morning. In another forty years, we will be prepared to say to the Vietnamese immigrant that he, with his breakfast tray, with his intuition for travel, with his memory of tragedy, with his recognition of peerless freedoms, he fulfills the meaning of America.

In 1997, Gallup conducted a survey on race relations in America, but the poll was concerned only with white and black Americans. No question was put to the aforementioned Vietnamese man. There was certainly no question for the Chinese grocer, none for the Guatemalan barber, none for the tribe of Mexican Indians who reroofed your neighbor's house. The American conversation about race has always been a black-and-white conversation, but the conversation has become as bloodless as badminton. I have listened to the black-and-white conversation for most of my life. I was supposed to attach myself to one side or the other, without asking the obvious questions: What is this perpetual dialectic between Europe and Africa? Why does it admit so little reference to anyone else?

I am speaking to you in American English that was taught me by Irish nuns—immigrant women. I wear an Indian face; I answer to a Spanish surname as well as this California first name, Richard. You might wonder about the complexity of historical factors, the collision of centuries, that creates Richard Rodriguez. My brownness is the illustration of that collision, or the bland memorial of it. I stand before you as an Impure-American, an Ambiguous-American.

In the nineteenth century, Texans used to say that the reason Mexicans were so easily defeated in battle was because we were so dilute, being neither pure Indian nor pure Spaniard. Yet, at the same time, Mexicans used to say that Mexico, the country of my ancestry, joined two worlds, two competing armies. José Vasconcelos, the Mexican educator and philosopher, famously described Mexicans as *la raza cósmica*, the cosmic race. In Mexico, what one finds as early as the eighteenth century is a predominant population of mixed-race people. Also, once the slave had been freed in Mexico, the incidence of marriage between Indian and African people there was greater than in any other country in the Americas and has not been equaled since.

Race mixture has not been a point of pride in America. Americans speak more easily about "diversity" than we do about the fact that I might marry your daughter; you might become we; we might become us. America has so readily adopted the Canadian notion of multiculturalism because it preserves our preference for thinking ourselves separate—our elbows need not touch, thank you. I would prefer that table. I can remain Mexican, whatever that means, in the United States of America.

I would propose that instead of adopting the Canadian model of multiculturalism, America might begin to imagine the Mexican alternative—that of a *mestizaje* society. Because of colonial Mexico, I am *mestizo*. But I was reinvented by President Richard Nixon. In the early 1970s, Nixon instructed the Office of Management and Budget to identify the major racial and ethnic groups in the United States. OMB

(Continues)

came up with five major ethnic or racial groups. The groups are white, black, Asian/Pacific Islander, American Indian/Eskimo, and Hispanic. It's what I learned to do when I was in college: to call myself a Hispanic. At my university, we even had separate cafeteria tables and "theme houses," where the children of Nixon could gather—of a feather: Native Americans united, African Americans, Casa Hispanic.

The interesting thing about Hispanics is that you will never meet us in Latin America. You may meet Chileans and Peruvians and Mexicans. You will not meet Hispanics. If you inquire in Lima or Bogotá about Hispanics, you will be referred to Dallas. For "Hispanic" is a gringo contrivance, a definition of the world according to European patterns of colonization. Such a definition suggests I have more in common with Argentine Italians than with American Indians, that there is an ineffable union between the white Cuban and the mulatto Puerto Rican because of Spain. Nixon's conclusion has become the basis for the way we now organize and understand American society.

The Census Bureau foretold that by the year 2003, Hispanics would outnumber blacks to become the largest minority in the United States. And, indeed, the year 2003 has arrived, and the proclamation of Hispanic ascendancy has been published far and wide. While I admit a competition has existed—does exist—in America between Hispanic and black people, I insist that the comparison of Hispanics with blacks will lead, ultimately, to complete nonsense. For there is no such thing as a Hispanic race. In Latin America, one sees every race of the world. One sees white Hispanics, one sees black Hispanics, one sees brown Hispanics who are Indians, many of whom do not speak Spanish because they resist Spain. One sees Asian Hispanics. To compare blacks and Hispanics, therefore, is to construct a fallacious equation. Some Hispanics have accepted the fiction. Some Hispanics have too easily accustomed themselves to impersonating a third race, a great new third race in America. But Hispanic is an ethnic term. It is a term denoting culture. So when the Census Bureau says by the year 2060 one-third of all Americans will identify themselves as Hispanic, the Census Bureau is not speculating in pigment or quantifying according to actual historical narratives, but rather is predicting how by the year 2060 one-third of all Americans will identify themselves culturally. For a country that traditionally has taken its understandings of community from blood and color, the new circumstance of so large a group of Americans identifying themselves by virtue of language or fashion or cuisine or literature is an extraordinary change, and a revolutionary one.

People ask me all the time if I envision another Québec forming in the United States because of the large immigrant movement from the south. Do I see a Québec forming in the Southwest, for example? No, I don't see that at all. But I do notice the Latin American immigrant population is as much as ten years younger than the US national population. I notice the Latin American immigrant population is more fertile than the US national population. I see the movement of the immigrants from south to north as a movement of youth—like approaching spring!—into a country that is growing middle-aged. I notice immigrants are the archetypal Americans at a time when we—US citizens—have become post-Americans, most concerned with subsidized medications.

I was at a small Apostolic Assembly in East Palo Alto a few years ago—a mainly Spanish-speaking congregation in an area along the freeway, near the heart of the Silicon Valley. This area used to be black East Palo Alto, but it is quickly becoming an Asian and Hispanic Palo Alto neighborhood. There was a moment in the service when newcomers to the congregation were introduced. Newcomers brought letters of introduction from sister evangelical churches in Latin America. The minister read out the various letters and pronounced the names and places of origin to the community. The congregation applauded. And I thought to myself: It's over. The border is over. These people were not being asked whether they had green cards. They were not being asked whether they had arrived here legally or illegally. They were being welcomed within a new community for reasons of culture. There is now a north-south line that is theological, a line that cannot be circumvented by the US Border Patrol.

I was on a British Broadcasting Corporation interview show, and a woman introduced me as being "in favor" of assimilation. I am not in favor of assimilation any more than I am in favor of the Pacific Ocean or clement weather. If I had a bumper sticker on the subject, it might read something like ASSIMILATION HAPPENS. One doesn't get up in the morning, as an immigrant child in America, and think to oneself, "How much of an American shall I become today?" One doesn't walk down the street and decide to be forty percent Mexican and sixty percent American. Culture is fluid. Culture is smoke. You breathe it. You eat it. You can't help hearing it—Elvis Presley goes in your ear, and you cannot get Elvis Presley out of your mind. I am in favor of assimilation. I am not in favor of assimilation. I recognize assimilation.

(Continues)

A few years ago, I was in Merced, California—a town of about 75,000 people in the Central Valley where the two largest immigrant groups at that time (California is so fluid, I believe this is no longer the case) were Laotian Hmong and Mexicans. Laotians have never in the history of the world, as far as I know, lived next to Mexicans. But there they were in Merced, and living next to Mexicans. They don't like each other. I was talking to the Laotian kids about why they don't like the Mexican kids. They were telling me that the Mexicans do this and the Mexicans don't do that, when I suddenly realized that they were speaking English with a Spanish accent.

On his interview show, Bill Moyers once asked me how I thought of myself. As an American? Or Hispanic? I answered that I am Chinese, and that is because I live in a Chinese city and because I want to be Chinese. Well, why not? Some Chinese American people in the Richmond and Sunset districts of San Francisco sometimes paint their houses (so many qualifiers!) in colors I would once have described as garish: lime greens, rose reds, pumpkin. But I have lived in a Chinese city for so long that my eye has taken on that palette, has come to prefer lime greens and rose reds and all the inventions of this Chinese Mediterranean. I see photographs in magazines or documentary footage of China, especially rural China, and I see what I recognize as home. Isn't that odd?

I do think distinctions exist. I'm not talking about an America tomorrow in which we're going to find that black and white are no longer the distinguishing marks of separateness. But many young people I meet tell me they feel like Victorians when they identify themselves as black or white. They don't think of themselves in those terms. And they're already moving into a world in which tattoo or ornament or movement or commune or sexuality or drug or rave or electronic bombast are the organizing principles of their identity. The notion that they are white or black simply doesn't occur. And increasingly, of course, one meets children who really don't know how to say what they are. They simply are too many things. I met a young girl in San Diego at a convention of mixed race children, among whom the common habit is to define one parent over the other—black over white, for example. But this girl said that her mother was Mexican and her father was African. The girl said "Blaxican." By reinventing language, she is reinventing America.

America does not have a vocabulary like the vocabulary the Spanish empire evolved to describe the multiplicity of racial possibilities in the New World. The conversation, the interior monologue of America, cannot rely on the old vocabulary—black, white. We are no longer a black-white nation. So, what myth do we tell ourselves? The person who got closest to it was Karl Marx. Marx predicted that the discovery of gold in California would be a more central event to the Americas than the discovery of the Americas by Columbus—which was only the meeting of two tribes, essentially, the European and the Indian. But when gold was discovered in California in the 1840s, the entire world met. For the first time in human history, all of the known world gathered. The Malaysian stood in the gold fields alongside the African, alongside the Chinese, alongside the Australian, alongside the Yankee. That was an event without parallel in world history and the beginning of modern California—why California today provides the mythological structure for understanding how we might talk about the American experience: not as biracial, but as the re-creation of the known world in the New World.

Sometimes truly revolutionary things happen without regard. I mean, we may wake up one morning and there is no black race. There is no white race either. There are mythologies, and—as I am in the business, insofar as I am in any business at all, of demythologizing such identities as black and white—I come to you as a man of many cultures. I come to you as Chinese. Unless you understand that I am Chinese, then you have not understood anything I have said.

Discussion Questions

1. Discuss the five major categories of race and ethnicity defined by Nixon's Office of Management and Budget. Why do you think they are or are not descriptive, adequate, and necessary?

2. Identify Richard Rodriquez's thesis, and explain the difference between a multicultural society and a *mestizaje* society. Which term do you think best describes the America of today? Explain the reasons and give examples to support your answer.

3. Describe the revolutionary power of such things as language, food, and style in determining identity.

4. Why does Richard Rodriquez self-identify as Chinese? What about his claim surprises you? If you do not see that his claim is true, what is the point, according to him, that have you failed to understand?

Two Ways to Belong in America

Essay

BHARATI MUKHERJEE

Bharati Mukherjee received her BA from the University of Calcutta and her PhD from the University of Iowa. At the time of her death in 2017, she was professor emerita in the department of English at the University of California, Berkeley. She has written novels, short stories, and essays, including The Tiger's Daughter *(1971),* The Holder of the World *(1993), and* The Tree Bride *(2004). The following essay appeared for the first time in the* New York Times *in 2013.*

This is a tale of two sisters from Calcutta, Mira and Bharati, who have lived in the United States for some thirty-five years, but who find themselves on different sides in the current debate over the status of immigrants. I am an American citizen and she is not. I am moved that thousands of long-term residents are finally taking the oath of citizenship. She is not. Mira arrived in Detroit in 1960 to study child psychology and preschool education. I followed her a year later to study creative writing at the University of Iowa. When we left India, we were almost identical in appearance and attitude. We dressed alike, in saris; we expressed identical views on politics, social issues, love, and marriage in the same Calcutta convent-school accent. We would endure our two years in America, secure our degrees, then return to India to marry the grooms of our father's choosing.

Instead, Mira married an Indian student in 1962 who was getting his business administration degree at Wayne State University. They soon acquired the labor certifications necessary for the green card of hassle-free residence and employment. Mira still lives in Detroit, works in the Southfield, Michigan, school system, and has become nationally recognized for her contributions in the fields of preschool education and parent-teacher relationships. After thirty-six years as a legal immigrant in this country, she clings passionately to her Indian citizenship and hopes to go home to India when she retires. In Iowa City in 1963, I married a fellow student, an American of Canadian parentage. Because of the accident of his North Dakota birth, I bypassed labor-certification requirements and the race-related "quota" system that favored the applicant's country of origin over his or her merit. I was prepared for (and even welcomed) the emotional strain that came with marrying outside my ethnic community. In thirty-three years of marriage, we have lived in every part of North America. By choosing a husband who was not my father's selection, I was opting for fluidity, self-invention, blue jeans and T-shirts, and renouncing three thousand years (at least) of caste-observant, "pure culture" marriage in the Mukherjee family. My books have often been read as unapologetic (and in some quarters overenthusiastic) texts for cultural and psychological "mongrelization." It's a word I celebrate.

Mira and I have stayed sisterly close by phone. In our regular Sunday morning conversations, we are unguardedly affectionate. I am her only blood relative on this continent. We expect to see each other through the looming crises of aging and ill health without being asked. Long before Vice President Gore's "Citizenship USA" drive, we'd had our polite arguments over the ethics of retaining an overseas citizenship while expecting the permanent protection and economic benefits that come with living and working in America.

Like well-raised sisters, we never said what was really on our minds, but we probably pitied one another, she, for the lack of structure in my life, the erasure of Indianness, the absence of an unvarying daily core, and I, for the narrowness of her perspective, her uninvolvement with the mythic depths or the superficial pop culture of this society. But, now, with the scapegoating of "aliens" (documented or illegal) on the increase, and the targeting of long-term legal immigrants like Mira for new scrutiny and new self-consciousness, she and I find ourselves unable to maintain the same polite discretion. We were always unacknowledged adversaries, and we are now, more than ever, sisters.

"I feel used," Mira raged on the phone the other night. "I feel manipulated and discarded. This is such an unfair way to treat a person who was invited to stay and work here because of her talent. My employer went to the INS and petitioned for the labor certification. For over thirty years, I've invested my creativity and professional skills into the improvement of *this* country's preschool system. I've obeyed all the rules, I've paid my taxes, I love my work, I love my students, and I love the friends I've made. How dare America now change its rules in midstream? If America wants to make new rules curtailing benefits of legal immigrants, they should apply only to immigrants who arrive after those rules are already in place." To my ears, it sounded like the description of a long-enduring, comfortable, yet loveless marriage, without risk or recklessness. Have we the right to demand, and to expect, that we be loved? (That, to me, is the

(Continues)

subtext of the arguments by immigration advocates.) My sister is an expatriate, professionally generous and creative, socially courteous and gracious, and that's as far as her Americanization can go. She is here to maintain an identity, not to transform it.

I asked her if she would follow the example of others who have decided to become citizens because of the anti-immigration bills in Congress. And here, she surprised me. "If America wants to play the manipulative game, I'll play it too," she snapped "I'll become a US citizen for now, then change back to Indian when I'm ready to go home. I feel some kind of irrational attachment to India that I don't to America. Until all this hysteria against legal immigrants, I was totally happy. Having my green card meant I could visit any place in the world I wanted to and then come back to a job that's satisfying and that I do very well."

In one family, from two sisters alike as peas in a pod, there could not be a wider divergence of immigrant experience. America spoke to me—I married it—I embraced the demotion from expatriate aristocrat to immigrant nobody, surrendering those thousands of years of "pure culture," the saris, the delightfully accented English. She retained them all. Which of us is the freak? Mira's voice, I realize, is the voice not just of the immigrant South Asian community but of an immigrant community of the millions who have stayed rooted in one job, one city, one house, one ancestral culture, one cuisine, for the entirety of their productive years. She speaks for greater numbers than I possibly can. Only the fluency of her English and the anger, rather than fear, born of confidence from her education, differentiate her from the seamstresses, the domestics, the technicians, the shop owners, the millions of hard-working but effectively silenced documented immigrants as well as their less fortunate "illegal" brothers and sisters.

Nearly twenty years ago, when I was living in my husband's ancestral homeland of Canada, I was always well-employed but never allowed to feel part of the local Québec or larger Canadian society. Then, through a Green Paper that invited a national referendum on the unwanted side effects of "nontraditional" immigration, the Government officially turned against its immigrant communities, particularly those from South Asia. I felt then the same sense of betrayal that Mira feels now. I will never forget the pain of that sudden turning, and the casual racist outbursts the Green Paper elicited. That sense of betrayal had its desired effect and drove me, and thousands like me, from the country.

Mira and I differ, however, in the ways in which we hope to inter-act with the country that we have chosen to live in. She is happier to live in America as an expatriate Indian than as an immigrant Ameri-can. I need to feel like a part of the community I have adopted (as I tried to feel in Canada as well). I need to put roots down, to vote and make the difference that I can. The price that the immigrant willingly pays, and that the exile avoids, is the trauma of self-transformation.

Discussion Questions

1. In what ways were the author of "Two Ways to Belong in America" and her sister alike when they came to college in The United States? What goals did they share? They came here to study in the 1960s; discuss ways you think their goals are similar to and differ-ent from those of recent international students attending college in America today.

2. Explain the fundamental difference in the sisters' relationships with the United States. What is meant by the term "mongrelization"? Why does one of the sisters embrace and "celebrate" that identity? What examples and effects of "mongrelization" have you observed in America today?

3. Explain the immigration status change one sister experienced in Canada and the other sister experienced here. What particular event was responsible for the change? How did the change make the sis-ters feel? Do you think their feelings were justified? Explain.

4. How do you think Richard Crasta would respond to Mukherjee's argument? What do you think he would say to her sister? Explain.

Student Essay 1

According to the passage "What's in a Name" by Richard Crasta A person's identity relates to his or her name. Crasta observes that every immigrant parent struggles with the thought of whether or not to give their children American names or traditional names because they fear what their children are going to face while growing up. Even though the parents choose the name of their children for the children's well-being and happiness. Crasta realizes that it did not matter what people called him as long as he could live life the way he dreamed of. Anyway, a name should be a code of a person that does not define the person's identity and reflects which culture they engage with and live with.

Even though a name can create some unpleasant expectations, it does not define a person's outcome in society. I remember that I would always dread the first day of school or when we had to get a substitute teacher. This was because the first thing they would do is take attendance. When teachers tried to call my name, I would say, "You can call me Lena," like an automatic response to a trigger. I would notice the awkward pause as the teacher held the list of names a bit closer to his/her squirming face with an expression saying "Great, this is going to be hard to pronounce." Having an American name made me feel like I was inside the American circle. But no matter whether people calls my Chinese name of my American name, it won't change who I really am and my personal identity. Crasta uses the name of James M. Fail as an example. He states, "despite his failure, had successful wildly having an absurd thousand dollar personal investment. . . ." Perhaps it was the very nature of his last name that gave him the motivation to prove to everyone what he was not going to end up a failure. Crasta even goies further saying that he would give up his own name and change it to Erenglish Hoolmoola if it means he could trade it for money. This made sense to me because even though I had friends with similar names, we all had different personalities. This point is, I learned to accept my name was just given to me by parents, and it did not define who I was and it won't change my person's identity.

However, a person's name has connections with the culture he or she engages with. No matter where I was, I could not please everyone. If my Chinese parents and relations heard me called Lena, I would be ridiculed for the unfamiliar sound of my American name. They said I could be proud of my heritage and uphold traditions. Crasta had a similar reaction as he recounts his meeting with some "Indians who pretend their names encapsulates the exclusive inaliable essence of Indian-ness." On the other hand, if I was around my American friends at school, I could be made to be an outcast because of my foreign name, my Chinese name. When they call me that name, they know where I come from, and they will know that my family live with Chinese culture. No matter whether my name is Chinese or American the names both reflect the culture I engage with and live in.

In conclusion, name should be a beautiful code , a name given by parents and not chosen by the person themselves. Name does not define who he or she was, and the freedom of identification was left to the person. No matter where people live, which culture people engage, name always shows your culture and is accepted by people.

Use the following steps to evaluate the essay. For help, turn back to Part 2 in this book to review the parts of an academic essay.

1. Check to see if the introduction gives the title of Crasta's essay and his name as the author.

2. Underline the sentences that make up the directed summary portion of the introduction. Check to see if the directed summary answers the first question of the writing topic.

3. Look for the thesis statement in the introduction (it should be the last sentence) and underline it twice. Does it give the subject of Crasta's essay, Crasta's point of view on the subject, and the student's point of view? If not, what is missing?

4. Look carefully at each body paragraph. For each paragraph, underline the topic sentence. Then, put boxes around the evidence (a specific example or fact). Finally, underline twice the sentence or sentences that link the paragraph to the thesis statement.

5. Which body paragraph is the best of the essay? What makes it the best?

6. Which body paragraph is the weakest? What does it need to be better?

7. Make a list of the three most important things you think need to be done to make this student's essay more successful.

Student Essay 2

In the passage, "What's In a Name?" by Richard Crasta, naming a child is a difficulty. Especially for Mr. Crasta, since he is of Indian descent, having his child be born and raised in the United States became a challenge once a name was needed for his son. For Mr. Crastra, a name doesn't interface with someone's identity, but within a culture people usually chose names to conform to common names in the area to fit into the society they live in. Throughout my adolescence, I have been called a portion of my whole name. Though it doesn't bother me any more, growing up it was a nuisance that I faced every day.

A name is given to a child once he/she is born, and the parents are faced with the dilemma to figure out a name that best suits the child. Mr. Crasta mentions a man named James M. Fail, just by reading his name one can imagine that he might just be a failure in life, but surprisingly he is a billionaire. I'm faced with the last name "Moran." It is a common name, but one that closely resembles the word "moron." My childhood wasn't that bad, but because of something I couldn't change I began to deal with the fact that a name doesn't mean anything. It's something everyone is born with, and if it's not appealing to some they can later change their name to whatever. A name has no connection to one's identity because it is just something our parents gave us before the age where we could speak and have a say about it.

Culture brings out tradition, heritage, values, and even the use of a name to signify meaning. Mr. Crasta explains how immigrants from India change their names that seemed tongue-twisting to a more easy and recognizable name after coming to the United States in order to fit in. In my English class I've had peers who actually use a different name than the one given to them by their parents. It's easier for many of them to use an American name rather than the one fiven to them by their parents. It's easier for many of them to give an American name more than a Chinese name, which most people here at UCR can't even pronounce. When people leave a society and move into a completely different environment, they succumb to change to fit in and leave their culture behind. They seem different to us, in fact if people from the United States were to move to China, they'll find that they too will change and embrace that culture. Though our identity within culture can only be distinguished if the person is not from the same area. Uf they are, their parents will likely have given their son/daughter a more native name just as Mr. Crasta gave his son an American name first but his last name still reflects his Indian heritage. Our identity is developed by the person we become though our environment, the people we come across, and most importantly culture. A name can only do so much to represent an individual but not as an identity. Being picked on for having a funny name does have a consequence in self-esteem, but sooner or later it won't matter because it's just a name. Aname doesn't define us; we define it.

Use the following steps to evaluate the essay. For help, turn back to Part 2 in this book to review the parts of an academic essay.

1. Check to see if the introduction gives the title of Crasta's essay and his name as the author.

2. Underline the sentences that make up the directed summary portion of the introduction. Check to see if the directed summary answers the first question of the writing topic.

3. Look for the thesis statement in the introduction (it should be the last sentence) and underline it twice. Does it give the subject of Crasta's essay, Crasta's point of view on the subject, and the student's point of view? If not, what is missing?

4. Look carefully at each body paragraph. For each paragraph, underline the topic sentence. Then, put boxes around the evidence (a specific example or fact). Finally, underline twice the sentence or sentences that link the paragraph to the thesis statement.

5. Which body paragraph is the best of the essay? What makes it the best?

6. Which body paragraph is the weakest? What does it need to be better?

7. Make a list of the three most important things you think need to be done to make this student's essay more successful.

Student Essay 3

Essay

In the essay "What's in a name", Richard Crasta from Columbia University observes that the relation of a person's name to that individual's personal identity and identity within a culture isn't so much related to each other. From Richard's essay, it is known that his name is Richard. It is a pretty common name in America, but determining from his foreign

(Continues)

face, people always like to ask what the author's real name is. Instead of arguing with them, the author makes up some acceptable awkward names. Names are really irrelevant to our individual personalities and our identity within a culture. In the end, people always will remember a person by his value while living. Name is just an empty title.

For instance, China has the largest population in the world. Repeating names happen a lot in China, but it never becomes a trouble for people. Another example is from a book, the main character living in an immigrant family keeps his motherland's name. At the same moment, his family celebrates another land's festival. In summary, a person's name has little effect onone's individual identity and identity within a culture.

Despite that a person's name is a part of his or her culture, it really seems effortless for us to name some of new born babies. For instance, China happens to be the largest population in the world. It is unavoidable to not have one's name repeated by others. Sometimes people have exactly the same name as some else at work or at school. Those names show no difference in pronunciation, and it is easy for people to mix up those names. Although it is such trick for people to confuse between the same names, sharing names never became a major cultural problem. It's true a name might mean a lot of things; people in the community like to believe personal abilities will separate out the individuals with the same sounding names. This proves that changing a name is not necessary, not in real life, but also in the article. As the author mentioned, "Once I had seriously considered changing to a more "Indian" name, but had been stopped by bureaucratic work. A Naryayana Nambudiri by any other name is often as ridiculous." All in all, it's never about what mane we have because a person's name is just an addition to a person, and it never changes an individual's personal identity within a culture. As the previous example shows, personal identity is never changed by our name; on the other hand, it never increases or decreases our personal value in a culture. For example, as first generation Chinese immigrants, our family usually respected our Chinese culture before we immigrated to America, so they gave me a full Chinese name when I was born. Since my family moved to a new totally different culture, America, they decided to give me an English nickname to make my life easier in western culture. But the problem is that having a nickname doesn't change my individual life a lot. I still have to go to school every day. My family still easts their favorite Chinese dishes three meals a day. And we celebrate our Chinese New Year festival every year. Even though the nickname might help make my school life easier, it never changes myself and my identity as a Chinese. Similarly in the essay the author tried tomane his son an American name, but in the end, his son was named a very long and complicated name. I know he wanted his son to become part of both cultures, his son's identity with Indian culture would never change. Therefore, no matter how fancy named we are, the relationship to culture never changes.

In the essay "What's in a Name," Richard Crasta tried to demonstrate that the relation of a person's name to that individual's personal identity with a culture is not as meaningful as always. Even culture in the Chinese community shows this.

Use the following steps to evaluate the essay. For help, turn back to Part 2 in this book to review the parts of an academic essay.

1. Check to see if the introduction gives the title of Crasta's essay and his name as the author.

2. Underline the sentences that make up the directed summary portion of the introduction. Check to see if the directed summary answers the first question of the writing topic.

3. Look for the thesis statement in the introduction (it should be the last sentence) and underline it twice. Does it give the subject of Crasta's essay, Crasta's point of view on the subject, and the student's point of view? If not, what is missing?

4. Look carefully at each body paragraph. For each paragraph, underline the topic sentence. Then, put boxes around the evidence (a specific example or fact). Finally, underline twice the sentence or sentences that link the paragraph to the thesis statement.

5. Which body paragraph is the best of the essay? What makes it the best?

6. Which body paragraph is the weakest? What does it need to be better?

7. Make a list of the three most important things you think need to be done to make this student's essay more successful.

Assignment 9

Read the following essay and the writing topic that follows it. Then, use the exercises and activities that follow to move through the writing process and develop your own essay in response to the argument Maxine Hong Kingston presents in "No Name Woman."

No Name Woman

Essay

MAXINE HONG KINGSTON

> *Maxine Hong Kingston, a Chinese American, earned a BA at the University of California, Berkeley, and is a bestselling author and Professor Emerita at UC Berkeley. Much of her writing has contributed to the feminist movement, especially the autobiographical and award-winning book* The Woman Warrior: Memoirs of a Girlhood among Ghosts *(1976). Her book* China Men *(1980) won the National Book Award for Nonfiction (1981), and in July, 2014, President Barack Obama awarded Kingston the National Medal of Arts for 2013. Much of her work presents a reinterpretation of traditional Chinese stories and myths. Her most recent book,* I Love a Broad Margin to My Life *(2011), is a memoir written in free verse.*

"You must not tell anyone," my mother said, "what I am about to tell you. In China, your father had a sister who killed herself. She jumped into the family well. We say that your father has all brothers because it is as if she had never been born.

"In 1924, just a few days after our village celebrated seventeen hurry-up weddings—to make sure that every young man who went 'out on the road' would responsibly come home—your father and his brothers and your grandfather and his brothers and your aunt's new husband sailed for America, the Gold Mountain. It was your grandfather's last trip. Those lucky enough to get contracts waved goodbye from the decks. They fed and guarded the stowaways and helped them off in Cuba, New York, Bali, Hawaii. 'We'll meet in California next year,' they said. All of them sent money home.

"I remember looking at your aunt one day when she and I were dressing; I had not noticed before that she had such a protruding melon of a stomach. But I did not think, 'She's pregnant,' until she began to look like other pregnant women, her shirt pulling and the white tops of her black pants showing. She could not have been pregnant, you see, because her husband had been gone for years. No one said anything. We did not discuss it. In early summer she was ready to have the child, long after the time when it could have been possible.

"The village had also been counting. On the night the baby was to be born, the villagers raided our house. Some were crying. Like a great saw, teeth strung with lights, files of people walked zigzag across our land, tearing the rice. Their lanterns doubled in the disturbed black water, which drained away through the broken bunds. As the villagers closed in, we could see that some of them, probably men and women we knew well, wore white masks. The people with long hair hung it over their faces. Women with short hair made it stand up on end. Some had tied white bands around their foreheads, arms, and legs.

"At first they threw mud and rocks at the house. Then they threw eggs and began slaughtering our stock. We could hear the animals scream their deaths—the roosters, the pigs, a last great roar from the ox. Familiar wild heads flared in our night windows; the villagers encircled us. Some of the faces stopped to peer at us, their eyes rushing like searchlights. The hands flattened against the panes, framed heads, and left red prints.

"The villagers broke in the front and the back doors at the same time, even though we had not locked the doors against them. Their knives dripped with the blood of our animals. They smeared blood on the doors and walls. One woman swung a chicken, whose throat she had slit, splattering blood in red arcs about her. We stood together in the middle of our house, in the family hall with the pictures and tables of the ancestors around us, and looked straight ahead.

"At that time, the house had only two wings. When the men came back, we would build two more to enclose our courtyard and a third one to begin a second courtyard. The villagers pushed through both wings, even your grandparents' rooms, to find your aunt's, which was also mine until the men returned. From this room a new wing for one of the younger families would grow. They ripped up her clothes and shoes and broke her combs, grinding them underfoot. They tore her work from the loom. They scattered the cooking fire and rolled the new weaving in it. We could hear them in the kitchen breaking our bowls

(Continues)

and banging the pots. They overturned the great waist-high earthenware jugs; duck eggs, pickled fruits, vegetables burst out and mixed in acrid torrents. The old woman from the next field swept a broom through the air and loosed the spirits-of-the broom over our heads. 'Pig.' 'Ghost.' 'Pig,' they sobbed and scolded while they ruined our house.

"When they left, they took sugar and oranges to bless themselves. They cut pieces from the dead animals. Some of them took bowls that were not broken and clothes that were not torn. Afterward, we swept up the rice and sewed it back up into sacks. But the smells from the spilled preserves lasted. Your aunt gave birth in the pigsty that night. The next morning when I went for the water, I found her and the baby plugging up the family well.

"Don't let your father know that I told you. He denies her. Now that you have started to menstruate, what happened to her could happen to you. Don't humiliate us. You wouldn't like to be forgotten as if you had never been born. The villagers are watchful."

Whenever she had to warn us about life, my mother told stories that ran like this one, a story to grow up on. She tested our strength to establish realities. Those in the emigrant generations who could not reassert brute survival died young and far from home. Those of us in the first American generations have had to figure out how the invisible world the emigrants built around our childhoods fits in solid America.

The emigrants confused the gods by diverting their curses, misleading them with crooked streets and false names. They must try to confuse their offspring as well, who, I suppose, threaten them in similar ways—always trying to get things straight, always trying to name the unspeakable. The Chinese I know hide their names; sojourners take new names when their lives change and guard their real names with silence.

Chinese Americans, when you try to understand what things in you are Chinese, how do you separate what is peculiar to childhood, to poverty, insanities, one family, your mother who marked your growing with stories, from what is Chinese? What is Chinese tradition, and what is the movies?

If I want to learn what clothes my aunt wore, whether flashy or ordinary, I would have to begin, "Remember Father's drowned-in-the-well sister?" I cannot ask that. My mother has told me once and for all the useful parts. She will add nothing unless powered by Necessity, a riverbank that guides her life. She plants vegetable gardens rather than lawns; she carries the odd-shaped tomatoes home from the fields and eats food left for the gods.

Whenever we did frivolous things, we used up energy; we flew high kites. We children came up off the ground over the melting cones our parents brought home from work and the American movie on New Year's Day—*Oh, You Beautiful Doll* with Betty Grable one year, and *She Wore a Yellow Ribbon* with John Wayne another year. After the one carnival ride each, we paid in guilt; our tired father counted his change on the dark walk home.

Adultery is extravagance. Could people who hatch their own chicks and eat the embryos and the heads for delicacies and boil the feet in vinegar for party food, leaving only the gravel, eating even the gizzard lining—could such people engender a prodigal aunt? To be a woman, to have a daughter in starvation time, was a waste enough. My aunt could not have been the lone romantic who gave up everything for sex. Women in the old China did not choose. Some man had commanded her to lie with him and be his secret evil. I wonder whether he masked himself when he joined the raid on her family.

Perhaps she had encountered him in the fields or on the mountain where the daughters-in-law collected fuel. Or perhaps he first noticed her in the marketplace. He was not a stranger because the village housed no strangers. She had to have dealings with him other than sex. Perhaps he worked an adjoining field, or he sold her the cloth for the dress she sewed and wore. His demand must have surprised, then terrified her. She obeyed him; she always did as she was told.

When the family found a young man in the next village to be her husband, she had stood tractably beside the best rooster, his proxy, and promised before they met that she would be his forever. She was lucky that he was her age and she would be the first wife, an advantage secure now. The night she first saw him, he had sex with her. Then he left for America. She had almost forgotten what he looked like. When she tried to envision him, she only saw the black and white face in the group photograph the men had had taken before leaving.

The other man was not, after all, much different from her husband. They both gave orders: She followed. "If you tell your family, I'll beat you. I'll kill you. Be here again next week." No one talked sex, ever. And she might have separated the rapes from the rest of living if only she did not have to buy her oil from him or gather wood in the same forest. I want her fear to have lasted just as long as rape lasted so that the fear could have been contained. No drawn-out fear. But women at

(Continues)

sex hazarded birth and hence lifetimes. The fear did not stop but permeated everywhere. She told the man, "I think I'm pregnant!" He organized the raid against her.

On nights when my mother and father talked about their life back home, sometimes they mentioned an "outcast table" whose business they still seemed to be settling, their voices tight. In a commensal tradition, where food is precious, the powerful older people made wrongdoers eat alone. Instead of letting them start separate new lives like the Japanese, who could become samurais and geishas, the Chinese family, faces averted but eyes glowering sideways, hung on to the offenders and fed them leftovers. My aunt must have lived in the same house as my parents and eaten at an outcast table. My mother spoke about the raid as if she had seen it, when she and my aunt, a daughter-in-law to a different household, should not have been living together at all. Daughters-in-law lived with their husbands' parents, not their own; a synonym for marriage in Chinese is "taking a daughter-in-law." Her husband's parents could have sold her, mortgaged her, stoned her. But they had sent her back to her own mother and father, a mysterious act hinting at disgraces not told me. Perhaps they had thrown her out to deflect the avengers.

She was the only daughter; her four brothers went with her father, husband, and uncles "out on the road" and for some years became western men. When the goods were divided among the family, three of the brothers took land, and the youngest, my father, chose an education. After my grandparents gave their daughter away to her husband's family, they had dispensed all the adventure and all the property. They expected her alone to keep the traditional ways, which her brothers, now among the barbarians, could fumble without detection. The heavy, deep-rooted women were to maintain the past against the flood, safe for returning. But the rare urge west had fixed upon our family, and so my aunt crossed boundaries not delineated in space.

The work of preservation demands that the feelings playing about in one's guts not be turned into action. Just watch their passing like cherry blossoms. But perhaps my aunt, my forerunner, caught in a slow life, let dreams grow and fade and after some months or years went toward what persisted. Fear at the enormities of the forbidden kept her desires delicate, wire and bone. She looked at a man because she liked the way the hair was tucked behind his ears, or she liked the question-mark line of a long torso curving at the shoulder and straight at the hip. For warm eyes or a soft voice or a slow walk—that's all—a few hairs, a line, a brightness, a sound, a pace, she gave up family. She offered us up for a charm that vanished with tiredness, a pigtail that didn't toss when the wind died. Why, the wrong lighting could erase the dearest thing about him.

It could very well have been, however, that my aunt did not take subtle enjoyment of her friend, but, a wild woman, kept rollicking company. Imagining her free with sex doesn't fit, though. I don't know any women like that, or men either. Unless I see her life branching into mine, she gives me no ancestral help.

To sustain her being in love, she often worked at herself in the mirror, guessing at the colors and shapes that would interest him, changing them frequently in order to hit on the right combination. She wanted him to look back.

On a farm near the sea, a woman who tended her appearance reaped a reputation for eccentricity. All the married women blunt-cut their hair in flaps about their ears or pulled it back in tight buns. No nonsense. Neither style blew easily into heart-catching tangles. And at their weddings, they displayed themselves in their long hair for the last time. "It brushed the backs of my knees," my mother tells me. "It was braided, and even so, it brushed the backs of my knees!"

At the mirror, my aunt combed individuality into her bob. A bun could have been contrived to escape into black streamers blowing in the wind or in quiet wisps about her face, but only the older women in our picture album wear buns. She brushed her hair back from her forehead, tucking the flaps behind her ears. She looped a piece of thread, knotted into a circle between her index fingers and thumbs, and ran the double strand across her forehead. When she closed her fingers as if she were making a pair of shadow geese bite, the string twisted together, catching the little hairs. Then she pulled the thread away from her skin, ripping the hairs out neatly, her eyes watering from the needles of pain. Opening her fingers, she cleaned the thread, then rolled it along her hairline and the tops of her eyebrows. My mother did the same to me and my sisters and herself. I used to believe that the expression "caught by the short hairs" meant a captive held with a depilatory string. It especially hurt at the temples, but my mother said we were lucky we didn't have to have our feet bound when we were seven. Sisters used to sit on their beds and cry together, she said, as their mothers or their slaves removed the bandages for a few minutes each night and let the blood gush back into their veins. I hope that the man my aunt loved appreciated a smooth brow, that he wasn't just a tits-and-ass man.

(Continues)

Once my aunt found a freckle on her chin, at a spot that the alma-nac said predestined her for unhappiness. She dug it out with a hot needle and washed the wound with peroxide.

More attention to her looks than these pullings of hairs and pick-ings at spots would have caused gossip among the villagers. They owned work clothes and good clothes, and they wore good clothes for feasting the new seasons. But since a woman combing her hair hexes beginnings, my aunt rarely found an occasion to look her best. Women looked like great sea snails—the corded wood, babies, and laundry they carried were the whorls on their backs. The Chinese did not admire a bent back; goddesses and warriors stood straight. Still, there must have been a marvelous freeing of beauty when a worker laid down her bur-den and stretched and arched.

Such commonplace loveliness, however, was not enough for my aunt. She dreamed of a lover for the fifteen days of New Year's, the time for families to exchange visits, money, and food. She plied her secret comb. And sure enough, she cursed the year, the family, the vil-lage, and herself.

Even as her hair lured her imminent lover, many other men looked at her. Uncles, cousins, nephews, brothers would have looked, too, had they been home between journeys. Perhaps they had already been restraining their curiosity, and they left, fearful that their glances, like a field of nesting birds, might be startled and caught. Poverty hurt, and that was their first reason for leaving. But another, final reason for leav-ing the crowded house was the never-said.

She may have been unusually beloved, the precious only daughter, spoiled and mirror-gazing because of the affection the family lavished on her. When her husband left, they welcomed the chance to take her back from the in-laws; she could live like the little daughter for just a while longer. There are stories that my grandfather was different from other people, "crazy ever since the little Jap bayoneted him in the head." He used to put his naked penis on the dinner table, laugh-ing. And one day he brought home a baby girl, wrapped up inside his brown western-style greatcoat. He had traded one of his sons, prob-ably my father, the youngest, for her. My grandmother made him trade back. When he finally got a daughter of his own, he doted on her. They must have all loved her, except perhaps my father, the only brother who never went back to China, having once been traded for a girl.

Brothers and sisters, newly men and women, had to efface their sexual color and present plain miens. Disturbing hair and eyes, a smile like no other, threatened the ideal of five generations living under one roof. To focus blurs, people shouted face to face and yelled from room to room. The immigrants I know have loud voices, unmodulated to American tones even after years away from the village where they called their friendships out across the fields. I have not been able to stop my mother's screams in public libraries or over telephones. Walking erect (knees straight, toes pointed forward, not pigeon-toed, which is Chinese-feminine) and speaking in an inaudible voice, I have tried to turn myself American-feminine. Chinese communication was loud, public. Only sick people had to whisper. But at the dinner table, where the family members came nearest one another, no one could talk, not the outcasts nor any eaters. Every word that falls from the mouth is a coin lost. Silently they gave and accepted food with both hands. A preoccupied child who took his bowl with one hand got a sideways glare. A complete moment of total attention is due everyone alike. Children and lovers have no singularity here, but my aunt used a secret voice, a separate attentiveness.

She kept the man's name to herself throughout her labor and dying; she did not accuse him that he be punished with her. To save her inseminator's name, she gave silent birth.

He may have been somebody in her own household, but intercourse with a man outside the family would have been no less abhorrent. All the village were kinsmen, and the titles shouted in loud country voices never let kinship be forgotten. Any man within visiting distance would have been neutralized as a lover—"brother," "younger brother," "older brother"—one hundred and fifteen relationship titles. Parents researched birth charts probably not so much to assure good fortune as to circumvent incest in a population that has but one hundred surnames. Everybody has eight million relatives. How useless then sexual mannerisms, how dangerous.

As if it came from an atavism deeper than fear, I used to add "brother" silently to boys' names. It hexed the boys, who would or would not ask me to dance, and made them less scary and as familiar and deserving of benevolence as girls.

But, of course, I hexed myself also—no dates. I should have stood up, both arms waving, and shouted out across libraries, "Hey, you! Love me back." I had no idea, though, how to make attraction selective, how to control its direction and magnitude. If I made myself American-pretty so that the five or six Chinese boys in the class fell in love with me,

(Continues)

everyone else—the Caucasian, Negro, and Japanese boys—would too. Sisterliness, dignified and honorable, made much more sense.

Attraction eludes control so stubbornly that whole societies designed to organize relationships among people cannot keep order, not even when they bind people to one another from childhood and raise them together. Among the very poor and the wealthy, brothers married their adopted sisters, like doves. Our family allowed some romance, paying adult brides' prices and providing dowries so that their sons and daughters could marry strangers. Marriage promises to turn strangers into friendly relatives—a nation of siblings.

In the village structure, spirits shimmered among the live creatures, balanced and held in equilibrium by time and land. But one human being flaring up into violence could open up a black hole, a maelstrom that pulled in the sky. The frightened villagers, who depended on one another to maintain the real, went to my aunt to show her a personal, physical representation of the break she had made in the "roundness." Misallying couples snapped off the future, which was to be embodied in true offspring. The villagers punished her for acting as if she could have a private life, secret and apart from them.

If my aunt had betrayed the family at a time of large grain yields and peace, when many boys were born, and wings were being built on many houses, perhaps she might have escaped such severe punishment. But the men—hungry, greedy, tired of planting in dry soil—had been forced to leave the village in order to send food-money home. There were ghost plagues, bandit plagues, wars with the Japanese, floods. My Chinese brother and sister had died of an unknown sickness. Adultery, perhaps only a mistake during good times, became a crime when the village needed food.

The round moon cakes and round doorways, the round tables of graduated sizes that fit one roundness inside another, round windows and rice bowls—these talismans had lost their power to warn this family of the law: A family must be whole, faithfully keeping the descent line by having sons to feed the old and the dead, who in turn look after the family. The villagers came to show my aunt and her lover-in-hiding a broken house. The villagers were speeding up the circling of events because she was too shortsighted to see that her infidelity had already harmed the village, that waves of consequences would return unpredictably, sometimes in disguise, as now, to hurt her. This roundness had to be made coin-sized so that she would see its circumference: punish her at the birth of her baby. Awaken her to the inexorable.

People who refused fatalism because they could invent small resources insisted on culpability. Deny accidents and wrest fault from the stars.

After the villagers left, their lanterns now scattering in various directions toward home, the family broke their silence and cursed her. "*Aiaa*, we're going to die. Death is coming. Death is coming. Look what you've done. You've killed us. Ghost! Dead ghost! Ghost! You've never been born." She ran out into the fields, far enough from the house so that she could no longer hear their voices, and pressed herself against the earth, her own land no more. When she felt the birth coming, she thought that she had been hurt. Her body seized together. "They've hurt me too much," she thought. "This is gall, and it will kill me." With forehead and knees against the earth, her body convulsed and then relaxed. She turned on her back, lay on the ground. The black well of sky and stars went out and out and out forever; her body and her complexity seemed to disappear. She was one of the stars, a bright dot in blackness, without home, without a companion, in eternal cold and silence. An agoraphobia rose in her, speeding higher and higher, bigger and bigger; she would not be able to contain it; there would be no end to fear.

Flayed, unprotected against space, she felt pain return, focusing her body. This pain chilled her—a cold, steady kind of surface pain. Inside, spasmodically, the other pain, the pain of the child, heated her. For hours she lay on the ground, alternately body and space. Sometimes a vision of normal comfort obliterated reality: She saw the family in the evening gambling at the dinner table, the young people massaging their elders' backs. She saw them congratulating one another, high joy on the mornings the rice shoots came up. When these pictures burst, the stars drew yet further apart. Black space opened.

She got to her feet to fight better and remembered that old-fashioned women gave birth in their pigsties to fool the jealous, pain-dealing gods, who do not snatch piglets. Before the next spasms could stop her, she ran to the pigsty, each step a rushing out into emptiness. She climbed over the fence and knelt in the dirt. It was good to have a fence enclosing her, a tribal person alone.

Laboring, this woman who had carried her child as a foreign growth that sickened her every day, expelled it at last. She reached down to touch the hot, wet, moving mass, surely smaller than anything human, and could feel that it was human after all—fingers, toes, nails, nose. She pulled it up on to her belly, and it lay curled there, butt in the air, feet precisely tucked one under the other. She opened her loose shirt and

(Continues)

buttoned the child inside. After resting, it squirmed and thrashed and she pushed it up to her breast. It turned its head this way and that until it found her nipple. There, it made little snuffling noises. She clenched her teeth at its preciousness, lovely as a young calf, a piglet, a little dog.

She may have gone to the pigsty as a last act of responsibility: She would protect this child as she had protected its father. It would look after her soul, leaving supplies on her grave. But how would this tiny child without family find her grave when there would be no marker for her anywhere, neither in the earth nor the family hall? No one would give her a family hall name. She had taken the child with her into the wastes. At its birth, the two of them had felt the same raw pain of separation, a wound that only the family pressing tight could close. A child with no descent line would not soften her life but only trail after her, ghostlike, begging her to give it purpose. At dawn, the villagers on their way to the fields would stand around the fence and look.

Full of milk, the little ghost slept. When it awoke, she hardened her breasts against the milk that crying loosens. Toward morning, she picked up the baby and walked to the well.

Carrying the baby to the well shows loving. Otherwise, abandon it. Turn its face into the mud. Mothers who love their children take them along. It was probably a girl; there is some hope of forgiveness for boys.

"Don't tell anyone you had an aunt. Your father does not want to hear her name. She has never been born." I have believed that sex was unspeakable and words so strong and fathers so frail that "aunt" would do my father mysterious harm. I have thought that my family, having settled among immigrants who had also been their neighbors in the ancestral land, needed to clean their name, and a wrong word would incite the kinspeople even here. But there is more to this silence: they want me to participate in her punishment. And I have.

In the twenty years since I heard this story, I have not asked for details nor said my aunt's name; I do not know it. People who can comfort the dead can also chase after them to hurt them further—a reverse ancestor worship. The real punishment was not the raid swiftly inflicted by the villagers, but the family's deliberately forgetting her. Her betrayal so maddened them, they saw to it that she would suffer forever, even after death. Always hungry, always needing, she would have to beg food from other ghosts, snatch and steal it from those whose living descendants give them gifts. She would have to fight the ghosts massed at crossroads for the buns a few thoughtful citizens leave to decoy her away from village and home so that the ancestral spirits could feast unharassed. At peace, they could act like gods, not ghosts, their descent lines providing them with paper suits and dresses, spirit money, paper houses, paper automobiles, chicken, meat, and rice into eternity—essences delivered up in smoke and flames, steam and incense rising from each rice bowl. In an attempt to make the Chinese care for people outside the family, Chairman Mao encourages us now to give our paper replicas to the spirits of outstanding soldiers and workers, no matter whose ancestors they may be. My aunt remains forever hungry. Goods are not distributed evenly among the dead.

My aunt haunts me—her ghost drawn to me because now, after fifty years of neglect, I alone devote pages of paper to her, though not origamied into houses and clothes. I do not think she always means me well. I am telling on her, and she was a spite suicide, drowning herself in the drinking water. The Chinese are always very frightened of the drowned one, whose weeping ghost, wet hair hanging and skin bloated, waits silently by the water to pull down a substitute.

Writing Topic

In Kingston's story, what events lead her aunt to commit suicide with her infant child, and why does she choose that way to die? If the story that Kingston tells us is accurate, who bears responsibility for her aunt's death? Leave the last line, Support your answer with details from the story, historical facts, or your own social or cultural experience.

Vocabulary and Dictionary Practice

Part I.

Look up the meaning of each of the following words used in "No Name Woman" and write its definition on the lines provided.

1. word: **stowaway**

   definition: _____

   _____

   _____

2. word: **protruding**

   definition: _____

   _____

   _____

3. word: **slaughter**

   definition: _____

   _____

   _____

4. word: **loom**

   definition: _____

   _____

   _____

5. word: **acrid**

   definition: _____

   _____

   _____

6. word: **humiliate**

   definition:_____

   _____

   _____

7. word: **sojourner**

   definition: _____

   _____

   _____

8. word: **flashy**

   definition:_____

   _____

   _____

9. word: **frivolous**
   definition:_____

   _____

   _____

10. word: **extravagance**

    definition: _____

    _____

    _____

11. word: **prodigal**

    definition: _____

    _____

    _____

12. word: **tractable**

    definition: _____

    _____

    _____

13. word: **hazard** (verb)

    definition: _____

    _____

    _____

14. word: **commensal**

    definition: _____

    _____

    _____

15. word: **deflect**

    definition: _____

    _____

    _____

16. word: **avenger**

    definition: _____

    _____

    _____

17. word: **rollicking**

    definition: _____

    _____

    _____

18. word: **eccentricity**

    definition: _____

    _____

    _____

19. word: **hex** (verb)

    definition: _____

    _____

    _____

20. word: **dote**

    definition: _____

    _____

    _____

21. word: **abhorrent**

    definition: _____

    _____

    _____

22. word: **atavism**

    definition: _____

    _____

    _____

23. word: **maelstrom**

    definition: _____

    _____

    _____

24. word: **inexorable**

    definition: _____

    _____

    _____

25. word: **agoraphobia**

    definition: _____

    _____

    _____

26. word: **flay**

    definition: _____

    _____

    _____

27. word: **obliterate**

    definition: _____

    _____

    _____

28. word: **origami**

    definition: _____

    _____

    _____

Part II.

Find the sentence in which each of the following words is used in the story. Paraphrase that sentence; in other words, rephrase the sentence in your own words without using the word from this vocabulary list.

1. word: **stowaway**

   original sentence: _____

   _____

   paraphrase: _____

   _____

2. word: **protruding**

   original sentence: _____

   _____

   paraphrase: _____

   _____

3. word: **slaughter**

   original sentence: _____

   _____

   paraphrase: _____

   _____

4. word: **loom**

   original sentence: _____

   _____

   paraphrase: _____

   _____

5. word: **acrid**

   original sentence: _____

   _____

   paraphrase: _____

   _____

6. word: **humiliate**

   original sentence: _____

   _____

   paraphrase: _____

   _____

7. word: **sojourner**

   original sentence: _____

   _____

   paraphrase: _____

   _____

8. word: **flashy**

   original sentence: _____

   _____

   paraphrase: _____

   _____

9. word: **frivolous**

original sentence: _____

_____

paraphrase: _____

_____

10. word: **extravagance**

original sentence: _____

_____

paraphrase: _____

_____

11. word: **prodigal**

original sentence: _____

_____

paraphrase: _____

_____

12. word: **tractable**

original sentence: _____

_____

paraphrase: _____

_____

13. word: **hazard**

original sentence: _____

_____

paraphrase: _____

_____

14. word: **commensal**

original sentence: _____

_____

paraphrase: _____

_____

15. word: **deflect**

original sentence: _____

_____

paraphrase: _____

_____

16. word: **avenger**

original sentence: _____

_____

paraphrase: _____

_____

17. word: **rollicking**

original sentence: _____

_____

paraphrase: _____

_____

18. word: **eccentricity**

  original sentence: _____

  _____

  paraphrase: _____

  _____

19. word: **hex**

  original sentence: _____

  _____

  paraphrase: _____

  _____

20. word: **dote**

  original sentence: _____

  _____

  paraphrase: _____

  _____

21. word: **abhorrent**

  original sentence: _____

  _____

  paraphrase: _____

  _____

22. word: **atavism**

   original sentence: _____

   _____

   paraphrase: _____

   _____

23. word: **maelstrom**

   original sentence: _____

   _____

   paraphrase: _____

   _____

24. word: **inexorable**

   original sentence: _____

   _____

   paraphrase: _____

   _____

25. word: **agoraphobia**

   original sentence: _____

   _____

   paraphrase: _____

   _____

26. word: **flay**

   original sentence: _____

   _____

paraphrase: _____

_____

27. word: **obliterate**

original sentence: _____

_____

paraphrase: _____

_____

28. word: **origami**

original sentence: _____

_____

paraphrase: _____

_____

Follow-Up Activity

Write a short paragraph identifying your favorite pastime. Your paragraph must include at least five of the vocabulary words above. Read your paragraph aloud to the class.

Doing a Careful Reading of "No Name Woman"

By now, you should be aware of the importance of working systematically with a reading selection to make sure that you understand its purpose and ideas. As in previous assignment units, use the following guides so that you better understand Kingston's story. You are working with a work of literature in this unit, so the writing process steps will use a few terms that are different from those you used when working with a reading. Use each of the steps systematically and thoroughly.

1. **Read the title.**
   - The title will tell you something about the story's main theme.
   - It may also tell you something about Kingston's opinion on the theme.
   - Think about what more you want to know now that you've considered the story's title and tried to identify the story's theme.

2. **Learn about the author.**
   - Read the biographical information about Kingston at the top of the selection.
   - As you go through the remaining steps below, take note of how Kingston's life or work might connect with her theme.

3. **Read through the selection once quickly.**
   - Read quickly through the reading so that you get a general impression of what it is about and what Kingston's attitude is toward the theme.
   - Notice the things—people, places, experiences, concepts, for example—she brings up to develop and support her opinion about the theme.

4. **Read again to identify the thesis—the author's message about the theme.**
   - Now read the selection a second time, but more slowly and carefully, and *with a pen or highlighter in your hand*.
   - In works of literature, the author does not always state his or her thesis explicitly, but, if you read the selection carefully, you should be able to state it and then write it in the margin. As you read the story again, identify what meaning you can draw from the story's events.
   - To help, ask yourself, "What does Kingston seem to want readers to think about her theme?"

5. **Look over the story again, this time looking more carefully at the way it is written.**
   - Examine each body paragraph one at a time, and list or underline the kinds of evidence that Kingston uses to support her thesis.

- Look in each body paragraph for any important ideas that contribute to the story's meaning.
- As you read and study the selection, *be sure to write down any thoughts you have* about Kingston's opinion and supporting evidence.
- It is your job to interpret the story's argument or message, so be sure to *make notes in the margins* as you read.
- Mark the points that you found interesting or convincing, and write a few words explaining your thoughts.
- Note, too, any weaknesses you find.
- When you look back at the notes you made in the margins, you should have a general idea of how the story's parts led you to your interpretation of the story's meaning.

6. **Read again for review.**
   - Once you have thought through the reading selection, read it once more, looking for places in the story that you found to be especially important. For each, make a note about why you think that particular part of the story is important to your interpretation.
   - Underline any terms that you aren't familiar with, and look them up in a dictionary.
   - Mark any places in the reading that don't fit with your understanding of the reading as a whole. Decide whether this is something that Kingston should have revised, or whether it is something that you need to read again to be sure that it doesn't lead you to change your interpretation. You may find that you need to go back to Step 4 and begin working through the reading again.
   - Once you are certain that you understand the entire reading, you are prepared to discuss, summarize, and/or respond to the reading with your own essay.

Follow-Up Activity

Put a star in the margin beside three places in the story you found to be especially important. Explain why you think these specific parts of the story are important. For example, do they show the story's theme? Do they reveal something important about a character? Do they encourage you to have certain feelings about what is occurring? Compare your choices and explanations with others in the class.

Some Questions to Deepen Your Understanding of "No Name Woman"

Answer the following questions. Be sure to respond to each as thoroughly as you can.

1. Why does the narrator's family claim that her father has only brothers?

2. Could one of the narrator's uncles commit a crime or take an action that would cause the family to erase his existence in a similar manner?

3. What actions do the villagers take against the narrator's aunt, and what circumstances motivate their violent actions?

4. Why does the narrator's mother tell her this story at this particular time? Would the mother have told this story to a son? Explain.

5. Why does the narrator say that "imagining her free with sex doesn't fit"? How does the narrator think this has happened? Is there anything in the story that might suggest the narrator is wrong in how she imagines that her aunt's predicament has come about?

6. What parts of the story might suggest that the Chinese women are conflicted about being attractive to men?

7. What emotions lead No Name Woman to commit suicide in the way that she does? How can her death be viewed as an act of female empowerment? How can it be viewed as a selfish, destructive, and spiteful act?

Follow-Up Activity

1. List the social groups or clubs that existed at your high school. Then, list words or phrases used by you or others to describe peers who were not part of any group.
2. Now list words or phrases that might describe the way the individuals outside of any groups felt about the way their peers identified them.
3. Discuss some actions you personally observed or heard about, possibly through the media, taken by teenagers who felt they did not fit into the high school social culture.
4. Share one of these stories with the class.

Responding to the Writing Topic

You should now have a good understanding of the ideas and overall message of "No Name Woman." You are ready to look again at the writing topic and begin thinking about how you will respond to it. Here it is again, this time with some guides to help you respond fully to all of its parts.

Writing Topic

In Kingston's story, what events lead her aunt to commit suicide with her infant child, and why does she choose that way to die? If the story that Kingston tells us is accurate, who bears responsibility for her aunt's death? Support your answer with details from the story, historical facts, or your own social or cultural experience.

- You are first asked a question about specific aspects of "No Name Woman"—a question that uses both **what** and **why**. You are asked to tell **what** happens to make No Name Woman end her life, and to explain **why** she chooses the specific method she uses to die. Your directed summary will have to provide answers to those two questions.

- The second question in the writing topic asks you to evaluate her choice and decide if what she did was justified. If you read and annotated the story carefully, you will be able to go back and find her other options. Did these options offer her real and better choices? How is the method of her death a comment on these other options? Your answers to these questions will help you decide if her final act was justified. Your statement of your opinion about her death will become the thesis of your essay on "No Name Woman."

- The third part of the writing topic asks you to support your thesis with details from the story, facts about history and culture, and examples from your own experiences. You may not have experiences exactly similar to the story of No Name Woman, but you may have heard such stories being told about events from the past, or you may have observed or had experience with individuals who had reason to feel rejected by their society, culture, or peer group. The follow-up activity below should help you begin to find some examples.

Follow-Up Activity

As a class, make two lists on the board, one listing reasons why No Name Woman's final act is justifiable, and the other listings reasons why it isn't. Write all ideas on the lists, without debate. The, break into partners and discuss which of the two lists seems most convincing. You and your partner may not agree. Discuss the thinking behind your choice.

Strategies to Help You Analyze a Reading Selection and Develop Your Ideas for Writing a Response

Now you are ready to build on the annotations you made earlier when you did a careful reading of "No Name Woman." Remember the strategies of *questioning*, *freewriting*, and *listing* that you used in writing about the earlier units in this book? Use them again in a focused and sustained way so that they lead you to a more systematic analysis of this story.

Questioning

- Questions about the highlighting you did:
  Why did I underline this part of the reading?

  How is this information important to the story's meaning?

  What is the relationship between this information and the question I am being asked to write about?

- Questions about the story's ideas:
  What things in this story seem strange to me?

  Why do I find them strange?

  How do these parts of the story lead me to find meaning in the story?

- Questions about "No Name Woman" that seem important:
  What parts of the story make me happy?

What parts in the story are sad?

What event in the story seems most important?

What makes it so important?

Freewriting

Use freewriting now to explore your responses to the questions above:

- Pick one or more of your answers to the questions you have already answered, and just begin to write about them.
- While you are doing this writing, do not stop or censor yourself; just let the words come.
- Do this for about five or ten minutes without thinking about spelling, grammar, word choice, or even the sense of what you are saying.
- When you have completed this activity, you will want to take a break.
- After your brief break, come back and read what you have written. Most of what you now have down on paper will not end up in your essay, but, as you read through your freewriting, you will find one or more sentences or ideas that seem interesting, important, or even compelling to you. Highlight these points and ideas. Are you beginning to develop your thoughts in a way that will shape your essay?

Listing

With this strategy, you simply list all of the thoughts and reactions you have noted so far. By looking down your list, you may see a pattern of ideas develop, one that you can use to develop an essay of your own.

- List all of the annotations you made for "No Name Woman."
- List the main ideas you can see in your answers to "Questioning," above.
- List any main ideas that developed from your responses to the follow-up activity above.

- Be sure to list all the items from your freewriting that you thought were interesting. As you make this list, other ideas may come to you. Put them on your list as well.

Look over your list, and group all the ideas that seem related to each other. See if you can find one related group of ideas that is longer than the others. These ideas may suggest what you want to say as you respond to the writing topic.

Shaping Your Ideas into a Rough Draft

By now, you should feel prepared to begin planning your rough draft. If you aren't, go back through some of the activities above, and talk with classmates to see what they are thinking. Sometimes it takes a while before your ideas are formed enough; take as much time as you need to clarify your thoughts.

When you are ready to focus on your rough draft, you will have to think about each part of your essay and how you will compose it. Turn back to Part 2 and examine "A Suggested Structure for an Essay That Responds to Another Writer's Essay." Also, look again at the writing topic for "No Name Woman." Remind yourself that it asks you to do three things:

1) Write a summary that identifies the events that lead to No Name Woman's decision to commit suicide and why she decides to kill herself in the way she does.

   Remember that you have already worked on this in earlier activities. Look back now to the work you did. You may be able to use some of it below, when you write your essay's *directed summary*.

2) Take a position on this idea; do you think that No Name Woman's act, as Kingston represents it in the story, is justifiable? Who bears responsibility for her death?

   This is your thesis statement, and it will unify your essay, so it's important that you write it out clearly. Turn back to the review questions you answered and the follow-up activities you did. What were your thoughts and ideas? You will use them below when you write a thesis statement. Remember that you can always revise it as you work on your rough draft.

3) Support and develop your position using specific evidence taken from your own experiences and readings. In other words, explain your thinking and why you have the view you present—and don't forget to include the specific evidence from your experience or your reading that convinced you to take the position you take.

The explanation of your thoughts and the evidence that led you to draw those conclusions will make up nearly your entire essay. Look back to earlier exercises in this unit to remind yourself of some of the thinking you did as you consider who bears responsibility for the death of No Name Woman. You will be able to use some of this as evidence to support your thesis. Remember it when you begin working on body paragraphs.

Drafting Your Directed Summary

Here are some questions that will help you answer the first part of the writing topic. Answer each bullet point as thoroughly and carefully as you can; then, use your answers and those you wrote in earlier activities to draft a directed summary. Begin your draft by reviewing the writing topic for "No Name Woman," paying particular attention to the first question asked.

In Kingston's story, what events lead her aunt to commit suicide with her infant child, and why does she choose that way to die?

- The answer you give to this question is called a *directed summary* because it summarizes only the parts of Kingston's essay that answer this first question.

- As you learned in Part 2, the question that calls for a directed summary often opens with a question word such as *what, how,* or *why*. In the writing topic for Kingston's story, the first question asks, *"What* events lead her aunt to commit suicide, and *why* does she choose that way to die?" You will have to go back to the essay to find the information that tells *what* these events are. You will also have to consider *"why* No Name Woman chooses that particular way to die." In other words, what, *for her*, is the significance of the way she chooses to die? Go back to the story and see if you can find sentences or passages that reveal reasons behind her choice of death in this way.

- Be sure to turn back to the essay itself and mark the sentences that answer this first writing topic question. Don't rely on your memory alone. Also, review your own responses and classroom discussion notes to "Some Questions to Deepen Your Understanding of No Name Woman." You will most likely discover that you have already found important information that you can use in your directed summary.

You should avoid including any of the following in a directed summary:

1. minor details or points that are irrelevant to the question,
2. your own opinion or ideas, and
3. examples of your own, and, unless particularly helpful, those of the author.

Follow-Up Activity

Working alone or with a partner, compose a list of elements from the story that show No Name Woman as a heroine. Now, construct another list, this time of elements that show her as antiheroic. Compare the two lists and discuss your findings.

Developing Your Thesis Statement

The second question in the writing topic asks you to interpret the story by stating who you think is responsible for No Name Woman's death. Support your answer with details from the story, historical facts, or your own social or cultural experience.

Think of your thesis as needing these parts:

- the subject being considered,
- the story's point of view about the subject, as you interpret it,

Draft a working thesis by identifying the subject that the first question asks you to think about, AND your opinion about the subject.

_____

_____

After you have finished writing your sentence, review your statement to see that it contains the following elements:

- identifies the subject of the story you are interpreting
- makes clear your interpretation about that subject

If either of these elements is missing, rewrite your thesis statement so that both are included.

Up to this point, you have been planning the draft of your introductory paragraph. Now that you have drafted your thesis statement, you can begin planning your body paragraphs. They will have to explain your ideas and give support to your thesis statement.

Developing Body Paragraphs for an Essay That Presents a Thesis

Reminders:

Body paragraphs make up the largest part of an essay.

- The job of each body paragraph is to develop **one** point that supports the thesis statement.
- Taken together, these points constitute the argument of the essay.
- Writing a good body paragraph can be easy once you understand the criteria that the body paragraph must fulfill.

Here is a review of the three most important requirements for paragraphs in an argumentative essay:

> **Parts of a Body Paragraph**
>
> **An appropriate or suitable point**—one that supports the thesis statement
>
> **Evidence**—for instance, a concrete fact, example, or quotation—that demonstrates the point of the paragraph
>
> **A link to the thesis**—sentences that show how and why the paragraph, including the evidence, relates to the thesis

A Basic Outline Form for an Essay That Presents a Thesis

Let's look back at all of the work you have done so far:

You have read and carefully annotated "No Name Woman."

You have analyzed its ideas.

You have written a directed summary in response to the first question in the writing topic.

You have thought about and decided on your thesis statement.

You have drafted your essay's introduction.

All of that work should be gathered together now into a shape that will become your essay, your response to the writing topic for Kingston's story.

- Remember that you should follow the basic structure of an academic essay.

- To refresh your memory, turn back to Part 2 and review the diagram of the academic essay format.

- As you begin filling in this diagram, you should be able to turn back to material you have already drafted as you worked through the exercises in this unit.

- Fill in the outline form below as fully as you can. A good plan will help you draft an essay that is clear and coherent.

I. Introductory Paragraph:

A. One or two opening sentences that give the reading selection's title, author, and main topic:

_____

_____

_____

B. The main points that will be included in the directed summary:

1.

2.

3.

4.

C. Your thesis statement. Be sure that it presents a clear position in response to the writing topic. State your thesis in your own words.

_____

_____

_____

II. Body Paragraphs: For each body paragraph you will include in your essay, plan the following parts:

Write down the main point for the paragraph.

_____

_____

_____

List the evidence you will use to support the main point (fact, example, etc.).

_____

_____

_____

_____

_____

_____

Tell how the evidence and your ideas link to the thesis statement.

_____

_____

_____

_____

_____

_____

(Repeat this part of the outline as often as necessary to plan all of your body paragraphs.)

III. Conclusion: What are some general remarks you can make to close your essay? Perhaps, for example, you will briefly remind readers of No Name Woman's tragic life and why her final decision can, or cannot, be justified.

_____

_____

_____

_____

_____

Drafting Your Essay

Now that you have a basic plan for the structure of your essay and a map of its various parts, you are ready to begin drafting.

- If your thinking changes as you write your draft, return to your outline and make necessary adjustments. Every time you decide to revise your outline and essay, remember that this is a good sign, a sign that your thinking is developing and becoming more thoughtful and convincing.

- Keep turning back to all of the activities in this unit as you draft your essay. Try to recall some of your reactions, thoughts, and ideas as you worked on these activities. Doing this may help you to strengthen, expand on, or more fully develop your essay's argument.

Follow-Up Activity

Your draft will always benefit from careful rereadings, by you or some-one else. Work with a classmate now to find areas in your draft that can be improved.

Use the following process to give and receive draft feedback.

1. Exchange a typed copy of your essay with one of your classmate's.
2. Using a pen and a highlighter, mark your classmate's draft in the fol-lowing manner:
    - Using your pen, underline the subject of each sentence.
    - Use two lines to underline the verb in each sentence.
    - Identify the tense by writing it above the verb.
3. Using your highlighter:
    - If the subject and verb **do not agree**, highlight the sentence.
    - If the verb tense **is not correct**, highlight only the verb.
    - If an irregular verb is **improperly** formed, highlight the verb.
    - If the sentence is a **fragment**, enclose it in parentheses.
    - If the sentence is a **run-on**, draw two vertical lines between the independent clauses.
4. Using your pen, underline the essay's thesis.
    - If it is clear, if it identifies a subject, and if it states an opinion about it, put a check in the margin.
    - If it needs more work or if you cannot find a thesis, put an X in the margin.
5. Return the drafts and discuss your marks and suggestions.

A Glossary of Key Terms

annotation
a comment, underline, or other marking that a reader makes on a reading or in its margins to understand and critically evaluate the text

argument
in a paragraph's topic sentence or an essay's thesis statement, a declaration of the point of view that the author wants to persuade readers is true or valid; also, the act of trying to persuade others of a particular opinion

argument essay
a type of writing that tries to persuade readers that a certain opinion is valid or correct

body
the main section of an essay, often consisting of several paragraphs, that develops and supports the author's thesis and that appears between the introduction and conclusion

conclusion
the closing section of an essay that may restate the thesis and its supporting points, offer the reader an emotional appeal, or relate an interesting anecdote that gracefully signals the end of an essay

copyright
the legal ownership of published material

directed summary
a type of focused writing that summarizes a particular aspect of a reading selection in response to an essay topic

drafting
a stage of the writing process in which a writer develops and organizes the ideas in a paper in an effort to present the essay's points with clarity and effectiveness

editing
the stage in the writing process in which work is checked for grammatical and mechanical errors

evidence
specific details that support an argument and that usually appear in the form of anecdotes (personal stories), examples, statistics, facts, or authorities (quoted experts)

freewriting
a prewriting activity in which the writer quickly puts down on paper random thoughts and ideas on a topic as a method of discovery

handbook
a text that guides the writer through the various stages of writing and provides complete information on the grammar, mechanics, and conventions of written English

homophones
two words that sound the same and may be spelled the same but that have different meanings

idiom
a phrase or expression whose meaning differs from the obvious, literal meaning and whose significance is expected to be automatically understood when used by people from a particular district, community, class, city, region, or nation

index
an alphabetical list of all subjects mentioned in the text, followed by the page numbers on which those subjects appear

introduction
the opening paragraph or paragraphs of an essay that provide a context for the material that follows

listing
a prewriting activity in which a writer lists his or her ideas about a topic as a way of generating useful material for an essay

literacy
a well-developed ability to read and write

outline
a brief list of an essay's thesis statement, main points, main supporting ideas, and specific details

paragraph
related sentences grouped around a central idea or thought

paraphrase
a restatement of an author's piece of writing, expressed with different wording and sentence structure but conveying the same meaning in about the same number of words

part of speech
the idea and function that a word has in a sentence

plagiarism
the act of using another author's ideas or words as one's own without crediting the source

post-grade evaluation
a process in which a writer, after receiving instructor feedback on a paper, determines patterns of weakness and strength in his or her writing and formulates a plan for improvement

prewriting
invention techniques or strategies—such as clustering, questioning, freewriting, or listing—for exploring ideas about a topic

questioning
a prewriting activity in which the writer asks and answers questions about the topic as a way to generate useful material for an essay

quotation
a restatement of an author's *exact* words, enclosed in quotation marks

revising
the process of rethinking and rewriting the initial draft

scoring rubric
a guide for evaluating the strengths and weaknesses of an essay

summary
a short presentation in the writer's own words of the argument and main point of a reading

syllable
the smallest unit of pronunciation in a word

syllabus
a plan or summary outline of a course of study

table of contents
a topical list at the beginning of a text that shows at a glance the text's chapters and subjects and the pages on which they are located

theme
a topic or issue of focus and concern

thesis statement
a sentence or sentences found in an essay's introduction that give the essay's central argument, the perspective or idea that locks the other components of the essay together

timed essay
usually a response to a question or topic written in a supervised setting in a designated amount of time

topic
the subject of a piece of writing or speech

topic sentence
the sentence in a paragraph that states the paragraph's main point

transition
a word, phrase, or device used to provide a connection between sentences or paragraphs

vocabulary
a collection or stock of words used in a language to express thoughts and ideas

writing process
the stages of writing that include prewriting, drafting, revising, and editing

Index

531

CPSIA information can be obtained
at www.ICGtesting.com
Printed in the USA
LVHW012120040619

R14860500001B/R148605PG619313LVX1B/1/P